BARBED

BARBED

A Memoir

Julie Morrison

books with *soul* • Flagstaff, AZ

For Mom, Ellen, Lucy, Jane, Linda,
Nikki, Jen, Kim, Pam, and Katie,
who helped disentangle me from the barbs

And for Lisa, who insisted that I write about them

AUTHOR'S NOTE

Because none of the heroes in this book ever requested recognition,
to respect their humility and privacy
all names have been changed except the first name of the author.

Barbed: A Memoir

© 2021 by Julie Morrison

All rights reserved. Published 2021. Except for use in a review, the reproduction or utilization of this work in any form or by any electronic, mechanical, or other means, now known or here-after invented, including xerography, photocopying, and recording, and in any information storage and retrieval system, is forbidden without the written permission of the publisher. The author has changed names, places, and recognizable details to protect the privacy of friends and family members mentioned in the book.

ISBN: 978-1-7349899-0-8 (paperback)
ISBN: 978-1-7349899-1-5 (ebook)
Library of Congress Control Number: 2021910228

Cover designed by Lindy Martin
Interior designed by Erica Smith and Tamara Dever for TLC Book Design,
TLCBookDesign.com
Editorial services by Julie Hammonds and Claudine Taillac
Printing by Sheridan Books, Chelsea, Michigan, USA

Soulstice Publishing
PO Box 791
Flagstaff, AZ 86002
(928) 814-8943
connect@soulsticepublishing.com
www.soulsticepublishing.com

9 8 7 6 5 4 3 2 1

CONTENTS

BEGINNINGS

When two adults start down the back side of life toward burnout, a casual remark can sound like the harmonic bridge toward rhapsody.

Dad spoke the buoyant notes into a scene for a dirge. My husband and I were slumped into chairs in my mother's kitchen, our presence in Flagstaff, Arizona, planned as what we thought would be a routine quarterly visit from our equally woodsy but much wetter home outside Seattle. It had been a day: of travel by too many hours and conveyances for us, of too many hassles on the family ranch for Dad, of too much preparation with nobody's help for Mom. The mood was glum despite the soaring summer evening, fatigue devolving our pre-dinner chat into a litany of grievances, when Dad joked, "Anytime you want a change, you guys could just move down here and help me out."

Sorry, Dad, can't hear you for the hallelujahs. Honey, can you turn down the choirs of angels there over your head? Mom's saying dinner's ready . . .

Our mythologies, individual and shared, had let us down: adulthood had not been a leveling off; marriage was not the ultimate in romance; and hard work was paying, but our debts were long from paid off. In all the classic stories I'd heard and subscribed to, the demons, once defeated, are done. None of my favorite tales had clued me in to self-doubts that do not depart at any age; power-and-laurel-hungry superiors that feed unto thriving on typical workplace hierarchy; or the daily gremlins of weight and obligation—all far too easy to take on, all but impossible to work off. I kept expecting my showdowns with daily challenges to reward me with the plateau of "making it." All the components were there—advanced college degrees, marriage, home, health—but try as I might to plot them into a hero's journey, I woke up each day feeling more like a fool with errands.

"Really?" Brent asked, eyes already alight with boyhood fantasy.

For my Colorado-born husband, who had summered with his granddad in Oklahoma haying cattle by the clunk and rumble of a farm truck, the title of "rancher" was the ultimate in workplace daydreams.

"Well, yeah," Dad said, the simplicity of the words lost to the glory of a paradise found—the family's atrophied ranch holdings suddenly a gateway for Brent to the land of Theodore Roosevelt's daring, Lewis and Clark's backbone, the Marlboro Man's making. That any of those examples is also deeply flawed unto impossible on closer examination was but a trifling argument I did not make. I hadn't lived in Arizona for more than ten years, each one seeming to take me further from my roots or any sense of familiarity. I wanted nothing more than to feel at home: within my marriage, my life, and myself.

HOW TO GET SADDLED
IN UNCERTAIN FOOTING

Bitter coffee aftertaste bites back at my tongue as I step out of the truck into crisp, pine-scented air, my eyes immediately drawn toward the line of horses with sleepy eyes and cocked feet, tied to rough-weld hitching posts.

Happy anniversary, Jules. Let's celebrate by riding for hours across rocky terrain in the hopes that we'll gather the ranch's cattle along with everything else that's wayward in our lives, jobs and marriage.

No pressure for a first roundup.

Trying not to feel like a visitor to a place that was owned by relatives for decades, I push myself into the rousing day. It's Labor Day weekend, but mountain elevations invite an early fall. I shove my hands into my lined canvas vest pockets, hoping for warmth—something I won't expect from the group of cowboys near the tack room, eyeing me like a scale just shy of balance. They are not the company I would have picked for an anniversary, but Brent and I have opted to spend the occasion fostering a beginning rather than celebrating a completion. Dad has seriously offered us the ranch's management, suggesting we come get a firsthand look at what a day in the life is like at that job before we accept.

Looking at my husband's luminous expression, I'm guessing even if he got the calf's day instead of the cowboy's, being headlocked, branded, and castrated would still look better to him than going back to a corporate job.

Belayed aggravation is something everyone in the cinder-sand yard seems to share, the grit underfoot only slightly less rocky than the start we've made: we're late, which is an annoyance at any workplace and an actual barrier to entry here, as no one can get started until the trucks and trailers are loaded with everyone who will be riding the forest across the freeway from our headquarters to first locate our grazing herd, then move it south into the next fenced pasture.

I humbly crunch my way through the cinders to the end of the horse line where a cowboy just finished tying a horse, ready to offer apologies.

"This is Shorty," says the cowboy before I can speak, tossing a saddle onto the back of a large, sturdy bay gelding. I assume he's speaking of the horse and am glad of the introduction as, even with an asphalt stare, Shorty looks more welcoming than the cowboy, whose calloused hands are tacking the horse up at a payday pace. I'm struck by his hat, the only uniform element among the waiting crew: faded black, creased by sweat and rain. We might both be in our mid-thirties, but it's difficult to tell: miles wear harder than years. We're both tall, with long legs that seem to fit better in a saddle than anywhere else, but where he is trail-worn lean, I am decidedly curvy, even under all my layers: long-sleeve T-shirt, fleece, vest. He wears only snap-front, long-sleeve cotton, its plaid irregular from the stains of work. Now, he wraps a hand through Shorty's tail, pulling for reasons I can't fathom, reminding me of my own long, brown ponytail fed through the back of my ball cap. The cowboy's hair is cut short, in hard and harsh angles around his red ears and neck—the only sign that he might be feeling the cold.

"Done," he says, releasing his hand to intentionally fall, catching himself in a stumble toward the tack room.

Is that what amounts to fun here? Blink-length weightlessness? A catch and release between tasks?

"Hi, Pal," I say, stepping toward Shorty's shoulder, extending my hand toward his nose so he can smell me. My horses at home tend to welcome this kind of gesture, as they have learned from experience that a carrot or some other treat is about to follow. "I'm Julie."

I freeze when Shorty stiffens, raising his head.

"Don't do that," the cowboy says, striding back from the tack room with a bridle. "He don't like anything near his face—he has a thing about his ears. I'll bridle him."

I hasten out of the cowboy's way. "Oh, thanks—"

"He don't know about petting," the cowboy cuts me off. "We don't do that much here."

I drop my hand lamely into a vest pocket. I don't know if I've just been coached, or mocked. I also still don't know the cowboy's name and feel too awkward to ask for it.

The cowboy pushes a rawhide stuff headstall over the reportedly sensitive ears without incident. "Now he's kinda dull."

Shorty twitches, but doesn't move his feet.

"Do ya got spurs?" the cowboy asks, looking pointedly at my boots.

"Just small ones . . ." I pivot an ankle, relieved, thinking something about me might pass muster, a hope which passes like a shadow to cloud.

"But they have a rowel?" he asks, stepping to check.

I cock my foot to show him, feeling the visual will be more acceptable than any explanation I might offer.

"Well." He steps away, dismissing me for the other horses awaiting saddles. "You'll be OK. Just ride him like you stole 'im."

I nod my understanding, but he's already striding away in great, lanky steps.

The last time I heard that expression, I was about to enter an event at a horse show, proud to exhibit my mount, recently purchased from my trainer's wife. Seeing my nerves, she'd offered the same advice: "Ride him like you stole him." It struck me as odd at the time that she would choose those words, since she knew better than anyone that his purchase price had been far from free. I learned later that she meant I should ride hard and fast and not spare my spurs. Instead, I flubbed the pattern and zeroed my score. As a consequence, I'm not particularly fond of the expression, which seems a haunting fit, as I am about to spend the better part of the day with people and livestock who don't seem particularly fond of me.

Shorty's dozing.

Untasked for the moment, I glance idly around the ranch. Oldham Park is a postcard-perfect clearing between ponderosas on three sides;

the fourth side is interstate. The log cabin curling chimney smoke into the air and the stock tank beside it combine to make up the park's most rustic, but functional, infrastructure. The tack room behind us is crumbling cinderblock requiring mousetraps in every corner. The holding pens surrounding us were welded from a retired, repurposed oil rig. My great-uncle's legacy on the ranch is everywhere: the cheap side of resourceful, eroding to spare. In construction as well as family, he considered the initial investment more than enough care to last.

My father attempts to practice very different management, but what he views as a business has been a lifestyle for the foreman and ranch hands, and what seems intuitive to either, vastly different backgrounds present as a mystery to the other. It doesn't help that no one in my immediate family grew up here: the ranch acreage was solely a project of relatives until estate plans directed that it be divided between my great-uncle's and grandfather's widows. Functionally, that meant my octogenarian grandmother's half became my father's to worry about from day to day. Dad hired Woods, until then one of the cowboys, as his foreman, plus another couple local ranch hands, but so far, the experience has not included lessons in how to play well with others. Not that cooperation is often a requirement of the job; scale and distance dictate that most of the work on this ranch is conducted alone.

Per the estate plan, my grandmother owns four parcels totaling two hundred acres of land on and off the Coconino Plateau, which are only occasionally adjacent to the thousands of acres our cattle graze in pastures assigned by the U.S. Forest Service. The term "pastures" is as generous a description as calling today's anniversary a "celebration." Nature has seeded the volcanic hillocks where our cattle roam with scrub oak, conifers, and the odd tuft of meadow grass, where just one pasture is a fenced square mile.

I think of the lyrics to "Home on the Range" and imagine the cattle might have only discouraging words to offer about the landscape.

"What's funny?" Brent asks as he crunches through the cinders from my parents' trailer, where he'd gone with Dad to zip on a pair of chaps. He's tall, with a runner's build, though, since knowing me, he has become equally comfortable in boots as running shoes. His short, curly brown hair is hidden under a ball cap, suggesting he's decided not to try signaling premature belonging among the cowboy crew by wearing the requisite black hat. It's also very possible that the ball cap is the only one he packed.

"Evidently not much around here," I answer in a low voice. "I don't know that we're so welcome."

"Too bad," he says. "We're here."

He says this with the same optimistic practicality he used to exhibit during the predawn miles we'd run while training for marathons together. "Just sixteen miles today, right? Quick little jog before breakfast?"

I miss those days, early in our courtship, when we both looked forward to a wee-hour wake-up just to be running together, never mind that we'd be sweating through summer swamp temperatures over more miles than we had fingers. We haven't run together lately. I've gotten into dance aerobics and yoga, partly to be out with people, as our home in Washington is lovely, but life on a hill near an often-flooded river valley means seeing another person during my day is about as likely as my pampered show mare signing up for ranch-horse duty.

That Brent stopped running when I did had been a surprise. That the river flooded had been a surprise. That working a ranch where grass grows as an afterthought would look welcome compared to the isolated care of livestock in a near-rainforest is also a surprise. I suspect that, as with so many other decisions I've made, the choices I'm considering are not as they may appear at first. I also know that opportunities wait only so long for investigation.

"You might want to go help your dad with getting saddled," he says in the tone he used a few times in our early days to suggest maybe I didn't want to go home yet. I simultaneously flutter and ache to hear it, because it's been absent for so long. "He seems to be struggling."

I smile my understanding and hurry over to my parents' horse trailer, where Sage, my folks' tricolor paint gelding, is tied while Dad rustles and slams around the trailer's tack compartment. Mom has opted not to ride today, as there's no telling how long we'll be out, and too many hours in the saddle are not good for her back. She told me privately she wishes Dad wouldn't go either, for the same reason, but he's determined to introduce Brent and me to the ranch himself.

"Dad?" I call out. "Can I help with anything?"

"Saddle Sage, will you, Jules?" he calls back. "I'm just having a devil of a time with these spurs."

My parents stage out of their trailer rather than the tack room because the foreman told them there's not enough room for their saddles—the tack room's too small. I bristle a bit at Dad's having to struggle. Owner, or any, inconvenience is of no consequence, it seems, to the cowboys. Hardship is a rite of passage: those who would work around rather than through its risks and discomforts cheat themselves and the brotherhood of its sanctity.

Sage doesn't need to be ridden with spurs, and trying to put them on after zipping his chaps makes everything much harder, but I don't want to upset Dad any further with either of these points, so I do as I'm asked. Dad twists and shoves his stiff, six-foot frame into the awkward, one-legged pose necessary to reach his heel. His spurs are child-size compared to the hooks the cowboys wear, and I hide a grin, knowing my mother has had some hand in rightsizing them to match my Dad's novice riding ability and uncannily bad saddle luck. He's had reins break, bridles come unbuckled, and stirrups fall off just in the few months he's been going along on roundups. Knowing this, I check all the saddle rigging a few more times than is probably necessary.

"Oh, geez," he says, frustrated. "Have you seen my glasses?"

He lifts brushes, pads, bridles, and assorted other gear Mom had carefully stacked and sorted.

"Here," I say, finding them by the brush box.

"Oh, good, thanks," he says, polishing the lenses with a shirttail he has to untuck first. "You should put on your mother's chaps."

I look to where he's nodded. "I usually don't wear any."

"No, you'll need them," he insists. "It gets rough out there. And do you and Brent have your cell phones?"

I blink for a minute, the question seeming so misplaced as to make me question Dad's wellness.

"I have mine," I say. "I don't know if Brent has his."

Nor do I think there's much we can do about it if he doesn't. The question would have been better about forty-five minutes ago, before we left the Flagstaff house in stocking feet, trying to not wake my mother. It's not far from the house to the ranch—only about twenty minutes from town to here—but a round trip to collect anything we'd forgotten would crush any hopes of being done by midday.

Dad explained on our way out that Woods's custom is to trailer out at first light and ride until the cows are gathered and moved, without packing food or stopping for breaks. "Lunch" and any other human needs would simply wait for our return, whether that was at eleven a.m. or after dark.

"Well," he says uncertainly, reaching for a bridle. "Maybe we should ride separately so that each group has a phone with them."

Also on the drive out this morning, Dad had suggested that Brent ride with the cowboys. If we come to work on the ranch, Brent will be given the title of manager along with the leadership and decision-making responsibilities for the cattle, the range, and the employees. I will be an assistant, my work being to develop and sell any horses not suited for ranch life. As such, it's important to Dad that Brent get acquainted with the cowboys today, and I guess his agitation about cell phones has more to do with Brent's ability to connect with his team than with actual physical hazards he might encounter.

I've just finished bridling Sage when Woods takes the lead rope from my hands to lead Sage none too graciously toward one of the ranch's stock trailers. He's a thin man with black hair, mustache, and eyebrows, but an even darker manner—human foreshadowing, without the villainous cloak or theme music, accompanied by dogs who resemble vultures, hungry eyes tracking Sage as Woods walks him by the truck bed where they perch, awaiting next orders.

Woods leads Sage to the empty trailer door, drops the lead rope, and nudges at his rump. Sage stands for a moment before choosing a tentative step toward the foreman instead of the trailer.

"Nah," Woods growls. "Git up in there." He waves his back arm toward Sage's hindquarters. Two other cowboys close in.

"I've got it," I announce, jogging past Woods to where Sage has spun off to wander toward anything more inviting than the dank inside of a metal box. Cinders crunch beneath my feet as I struggle for footing.

"Damn cinders," Woods comments.

I ignore both his comment and impatient look as I recover Sage's lead rope to stroke his neck for a minute. The cinders and Sage are both new to the ranch—recent imports my parents brought in to be helpful. The summer monsoon had been a gully-washer, leaving the ranch soaked, slick, and churned up by spinning wheels and sloshing boots. The cinders were Mom's investment against falls, strains, or other damage to all species. Choosing Sage, a mustang, was similarly strategic: Mom and Dad needed horses who could keep their minds on their riders while traversing the relentlessly steep, alternately silty and stony ground that is our ranch. Sage and his companion Cheyenne were adopted out of an eastern Oregon herd managed by the Bureau of Land Management, trained, then originally homed to amateurs who couldn't keep them busy. Although they, like the cinders now on the ranch, are perfectly suited to their work and a demonstrable improvement on what was formerly available, they have not earned the cowboys' approval.

Sage sighs, dropping his head back into his usual nonchalant posture, which I take as willingness to be led back to task. I push at the lead rope toward the empty space where Sage will ride, encouraging a step up. This is hardly Sage's first trailer ride: he's loaded into conveyances of all kinds since the day he left the range. His hesitation isn't about fear—it's about honor. In this way, he and our foreman have more in common than they know. They'll do as they're asked, if and only if you ask them in a certain way.

Sage extends his neck but doesn't move his feet.

One of the cowboys gets a rope out and beats it against his leg, then starts to wave it above his head, intending to scare Sage into forward motion.

"Don't, please," I say as Sage's ears swivel back and his jaw locks. "I've got it. Go ahead if you want to. We can follow."

This is against all cowboy code. The hands take care of the boss, even waiting to eat until he takes his first bite. That I have now taken a horse away from not only the hands but the foreman is likely such a departure from custom as to indemnify anyone from its usual standard, but I can't help this. I know Sage: I was there when my parents were introduced to him, I've spent considerable time with his trainers, and I am confident that trying to scare or threaten him into compliance will be a losing battle. I'm only dimly aware that I must have a code of my own—as deeply ingrained and inviolable as the cowboy one I've just trampled.

Mumbling and motion behind me tell me the waiting cowboys are only too eager to get on with the day. I try to ignore the feeling that they're also ready to be done with me as I again square Sage to the trailer and pet him, telling him what a good boy he is. I pick up his front foot and place it in the trailer.

He holds it there for a minute. Again I tell him he's a good boy.

He pulls his foot out.

I sigh, battling a sense of both frustration and betrayal. No animal knows or cares what sacrifice we've made on their behalf. The central issue to them, always, is the relative safety of further interaction.

A truck guns its engine behind me, but I can't afford to heed its message. Sage is the key to my father's safety, and keeping his good will is much more important to me at the moment than the sun breaking over the ridge.

Again, I place Sage's foot in the trailer and push at his lead rope.

Sage considers for a moment, then with the cautious holds of a rock climber, propels himself up one foot at a time.

"Good boy!" I cheer as I close the gates behind him, my victory cut short by having to fumble with the unfamiliar gate latches. Why are these things never standard?

The cowboy who'd saddled Shorty for me steps over to flip, slide, jiggle, and pound the bars and locks home.

"Thanks," I say, but he's already gone around to the driver's side of the truck. It only occurs to me then that he would have to wait for us because he, not Dad, would know where to begin gathering the cattle. Dad is still new enough to management that he doesn't know all the pullouts, trailheads, and tanks that are as second nature to the cowboys as pulling on their boots.

"Do you have your cell phone?" I whisper to Brent as we gather our saddlebags and take our seats in the truck.

"Yeah," he says, lifting his fleece to show it's on his belt holster. "Why?"

"No idea," I whisper. "Dad just asked."

"OK," Brent laughs. I wonder at his immunity to the tension. Maybe the morning's events, like so many things in our lives, were actually simpler, even better, than they seemed, and the problem was just with my perception. It's a matter of both convenience and efficacy rather than masochism that I go faultfinding with myself: if I created the problem, I'm the one who can solve it.

The cowboy starts the truck as soon as we close the doors behind us, the vehicle jouncing and jostling as it rolls forward.

"Cinders are too deep," the cowboy comments as he shifts gears. "Makes it harder on the trucks."

"Yeah," I say, tired of the comments. "Mom just thought the mud was worse."

"Well," Dad says from the front seat, holding his hat in his hands to dust its crown. "We probably need to spread 'em around a little more. Even things out."

The cowboy nods.

"They'll pack down," Brent says from beside me.

We bounce along, silence strained by the four points of the ranch's future compass: family loyalty, cultural deference, tradition, and optimism for change.

WHY CELL PHONES ARE
MORE USEFUL THAN LARIATS

The truck isn't just dusty, it's dirty. Assorted wrappers, CD cases, crumbs, cinders, and grit litter the seats, floor mats and door pockets. I reposition my feet, and a plastic water bottle croaks as I wedge it into a different place with my boot.

"Sorry," the cowboy says. Then, with uncharacteristic loquacity, he continues, "This is the truck Jake took up to Montana. Guess he hasn't had a chance to clean it up yet."

Mom and Dad already told Brent and me the story about Jake, the former ranch hand whose ranch horse business line idea required a shopping trip to Billings' annual horse auction. Jake proposed that his training, along with daily ranch work, could develop horses of decent breeding to be valuable and ultimately profitable investments for resale. Unfortunately, a week after returning from the buying trip, Jake and Woods had fallen out with each other. Dad received scant information, besides terse calls from both reporting Jake had quit.

Brent braves the name mystery that's been evading me all morning.

"So, you're not Jake. What's your name?"

The cowboy actually smiles. "I'm Chris."

Time passes a little easier as Brent asks Chris about the ranches where he's worked before—most of which are in or outside towns in Arizona I've never heard of, a fact I keep to myself. My self-talk has been convincing me that anyplace in Arizona is more home than where I've been living, and there's no room in the dialogue for exception.

The road widens a bit. We've been winding deeper into the Forest Service holding between the freeway to Flagstaff and Oak Creek Canyon, which puts us back into country where dirt is brown, rather than the red of the Sedona rocks to the south. Darker brown than usual, I know, due to its still being saturated by the late-summer storms. When it's dry, it's saddle brown, rather than today's coffee color.

Ponderosas flank us like curious teenagers as we pull off onto a shoulder and stop.

"We'll pick this up on the way out," Chris says as he tucks the keys behind the truck's front left tire.

"Do we need to call to let the others know where the keys are?" I ask, wondering if this is the reason for the cell phones.

Chris glances at me but doesn't stop as he makes his way toward the trailer gates. "You obviously haven't ridden out with cowboys before."

I might bristle at that, except that he's kept the fitting remark to a tactful minimum.

Dad laughs awkwardly.

Sage steps carefully down from the trailer. I note that offloading only takes one request, and that he's already eyeing the pale green meadow grasses growing in sparse clumps outside the roadbed.

I help Dad get mounted before I take Shorty from Chris and step up into my own saddle, carefully avoiding the coiled lariat tied just beneath my saddle horn.

"We have a lot of ground to cover, so Chris and Brent are going to ride off down the hill and push whatever they find there back up toward us. We'll go this way, Jules," Dad says, motioning to his right. "We'll meet up with the others later at the tank."

I'm guessing "the tank" is as known to the cowboys as "the lake" is to Minnesotans. They always know which one they mean, even if no one else does.

"OK." I look at my husband, heart fluttering again to see him so genuinely excited. "Have fun, darlin'."

He's already grinning widely as he touches his hat. "You too."

I giggle as I turn Shorty to follow Dad into the forest.

In northern Arizona, grass doesn't grow on plains; it grows between rocks and ridges and fallen logs in anemic stands of yucca green to cactus-rib brown. There are no paths or trails to ride. There are just rocks, making steering a horse an exercise in testing equine annoyance. Navigation is by instinct and landmark—cows like shade, water, and hollows, all of which change by season and time of day. The point of a roundup is the count, as much as it's the move. This is a business banking on the growth of its investment spread across thousands of acres of hide-and-seek. It's also a matter of husbandry; cows will absolutely die of thirst, predators, or exposure if they're allowed to remain lost.

Sage, being a mustang built for this kind of ground, outpaces my quarter horse, so where it's at all feasible, and even in some places where it's not, I urge Shorty into a trot, trying to keep up with Dad.

"We'll ride this fence line back toward White Tank," Dad says. "Woods said he thought there were a couple dozen cows left on this side. Most of the rest have already gone down there looking for water."

I am disoriented enough to have no earthly idea what any of this means, but I'm horseback on a beautiful, early-fall day, and rough terrain and bristly cowboys aside, I'm enjoying myself.

Less so after an hour: we've seen no cows, and I'm starting to get stiff.

"Walk break," I announce, swinging off Shorty to drop gratefully to the ground. The area between my shoulder blades feels tight and hot with pain from the bracing I've been doing in anticipation of Shorty's tripping. I roll my shoulders front and back as I lift the reins over the horse's head to lead him.

Shorty pricks his ears in his first genuinely curious look of the day. I have no doubt this is the first break he's heard of that doesn't involve parts of a saddle falling off or an animal going immovably lame.

Dad and Sage clamber through the brush to intercept me.

"Are you all right?" Dad asks.

"Sure. Just need a little walk. I guess I'm not used to riding this long."

"Oh, dear," Dad says, tension in his voice. I know he's thinking about falling too far behind the rest of the group. "Well maybe—"

"It's OK," I smile. "I just need a minute, and then I'll get back on."

"Oh, good," Dad says, relieved, "because we have quite a bit more ground to cover."

Riding up beside me, Dad further observes, "You know, you really can't imagine how hard this work is until you do it."

I don't feel much need to imagine anything at the moment, but I take his point.

"This is one of the easiest pastures to ride that we have," Dad goes on.

As onboarding speeches go, I feel this one excels in realism but is perhaps a bit short on buoyancy.

"You know, for the cowboys it's just work—all day, every day. You have to go out every day until you find the cows to get them from place to place, and you don't have any way of knowing where they'll be. You can ride all day, day after day until you find them, and then it all starts again when you move them to the different pastures. And in between times there are gates to fix, fences to repair, and the cowboys insist on doing all their own horseshoeing. Then, on top of everything, you just don't get paid much. So you'd better love it because it's just that hard."

Mentally, I write the job posting:

> *Wanted: relentless riders of the range, content with*
> *barely better than beer money and bragging rights.*

"The thing is that in some ways, the cowboys have the most valuable work, because they know the ranch is going to pay them. The owners don't have that guarantee," Dad says balefully. We haven't talked extensively about this new venture in his life, but I've inferred it's come with more than a few disappointments and unwelcome surprises. It's not as though Dad's a cupcake: he grew up farming and became a Navy pilot after college, a lawyer after his military service, a priest after kids, and a professor in between times. He's run marathons, been sued by vengeful swindlers, and defended political asylum seekers with stories more gruesome than their bodily scars. Yet becoming ranch manager sounds as though it's been his hardest job. True, he's wedged between his mother's estate, his father's memory, and his own expectations for not only himself but the ranch as a living piece of heritage and a family-owned concern. He inhabits more a precipice than peak from day to day. A failure of any kind is a dangerous erosion of the trembling foothold he's scrambled to maintain.

"Then, why do it?" I ask.

"Well . . . oh, a couple reasons, I guess." Dad pulls Sage to a stop before dismounting. "Hold him for me, will you? I'll be right back."

I walk the horses a few more steps, looking off into the distance opposite from where Dad has gone. Stops like these are a regular part of his life—thankfully the only remnant of his successful battle with prostate cancer ten years ago. My mind balks at trying to envision my father as a victim to anything, but I remind myself that in more recent years, there have been stress-induced mini-strokes too. Most men carrying his age and anyone aged by his experience would be retired and watching ballgames with their buddies, but it's not Dad's way.

We find a stump for Dad to climb on to help him up into the saddle—his legs may be strong as tree trunks, but Dad's not the most flexible guy—and we're off again.

"You asked, why do this," Dad says, right as I'm starting to rein away to our agreed-upon span to maximize our search space.

I still my hand.

"First, because it's a family-held asset and I think, and your grandmother thinks, that it's better to make use of things we own than to just let them sit," he explains. "And, you know, we've been doing a lot of work to see if we can do things in a way that could make the ranch profitable. With all the research we've been doing into breeding programs and vaccination programs, we're starting to get better money for our calves. And with all the ideas you and Brent have, maybe we could really turn a corner and make some money. I hope we can."

"We do too," I reply, trying for a neutral tone. When Mom and Dad issued the invitation to ride roundup, it began conversations suggesting our anniversary weekend could also be something of an orientation, a try-before-you-buy exploration into the ranch as a project for us all.

I suppose most prospects have their extremes—shuddering downsides compared to upsides that exceed dreams. In our case, the move would mean more physical work than either of us has ever known, for less pay than either of us has made, individually, in years. It will mean spending days in the Arizona sunshine and nights in my parents' basement—at least for the short term, until we can figure out our own housing. It will mean reporting to my father while living with him just across a wall. Brent also wants it to mean starting a new ranch-supply store based on our ranch brand—building a future income and business for ourselves alongside the cattle business he'll manage for the ranch. But before we can start any of that, I'm afraid of what we'll have to finish: I will have no time or budget for our four personal horses, two of whom are youngsters I bred. Selling them will be parting with the closest things I've known to maternity.

As for recreation, riding will no longer be done for pleasure. What has been my escape will now be my workplace, possibly also requiring the sale of my mare and Brent's gelding. From what I've seen of the trails, asking our show stock to manage this footing would be as awkward as an ostrich on ice, and eventually just as cruel.

My emotional landscape is even more harrowing than the one we've been riding, and I am uncomfortably aware that moving to make this ranch profitable requires Brent and me to incur substantial personal losses.

"Yeah," Dad laughs. "I'm sure you want this to be profitable. But I really do too, for another reason. I think I had the realization about twenty years ago that I'd be the one to preside over the dismantling of almost everything my father built. I almost can't stand that."

Dad's working his jaw now in the way he does when he's particularly angry, and I rein away. I know he's thinking about the family partnerships—the business structures he set up for himself, his brothers, and their cousins to jointly own land planned for eventual sale. I am quickly learning that most of what we experience in life is not quite how it was represented in print. The rules of assessing value, for example, do not include splintered relationships, resentments, or the toll of carrying decades of baggage it could take a whole treasury department to sort through. Nor can any past accounting predict whether the market will swing to the value that's been reported on paper lo, these many years.

Several mountains' worth of rocks later, Dad's whistle pierces the air. I look over to where he's waving.

Glory be! The shiny black backs of the elusive ranch cows.

We ranch exclusively black baldies—Hereford-Angus crosses that tend to be birthed with black bodies minus some white pattern between the eyes and nose.

Excited, I nudge Shorty into a trot, but Dad waves me down. He gestures that he'll go farther around to push the cattle back my way.

I raise a thumb.

The cattle sense our approach, raising their heads like bread popping up from a toaster.

Shorty's ears prick at the motion.

"Easy," I ask him too late, as the cattle's alarm turns to retreat. I let Shorty have his head to follow them, and soon we're alternately trotting, loping, and hopping over the ground, trying to keep pace with the now-cantering herd of about six animals. Or is it eight? Maybe five? Black butts dodging trunks and shadows doesn't make for the most accurate count.

Shorty closes to within twenty yards of the herd. I look for Sage's white flanks or Dad's red shirt. Not seeing either, I pull Shorty up. He slows, scolding me for losing the herd by tossing his head. I can hear the crack and thud of hooves snapping branches ahead of us for just a few moments, then everything's still.

"Dad?" I call.

There's no echo, no anything except the sunlight streaming through an endless pine canopy.

"Dad!"

Shorty shakes his neck, then roots with his nose. In a minute he'll start to paw, if he's anything like my mare. Which he's not. Instead, he decides we must have been reassigned, so he simply stands and cocks a back foot, happy enough to wait for me to tell him when we have more work to do.

My pocket itches. I scratch at it, then feel it's vibrating. My phone! I fumble to get it out. It's Dad.

"Where are you?" I ask quickly.

"I've got about ten over here," Dad says. "I'm going to keep pushing them toward the road. You'll get to it yourself in a little bit. When you do, just go ahead and turn right and come on down, and I'll wait for you."

"OK. I think I've got six." I sign off, looking at the phone. Thank God Dad told me to bring it, or I'd be turning back to find him. Who knew it only took seconds to lose a man, a mustang, *and* a mini-herd in these woods?

Shorty and I recover two of the six-ish animals we'd been following, who are now lying in pine-needled shade. Figuring that a slower approach will bring faster results, I rein away from them, putting us at a nonthreatening distance to slowly close in.

"Hey, cow," I say, as we keep to a walk, about thirty yards away.

Brent and I had done some cutting work with friends this summer and fall, and I know that holding a herd together is best done from far enough away to seem benign but close enough to make the cows want to be elsewhere. The two layabouts track me with their ears.

"Hey, cow," I say again, using the popular cutting-pen phrase. I slap my gloved hand down on my chaps to get their attention. "Shhhh. Shhhht," I sound—the only other cow-handling vernacular I know—as I wave my free arm like I'm flagging down a cab.

Something about my half-windmill performance gets the cows on their feet.

I rein Shorty in a little closer, repeating my lines and choreography.

I can count six—maybe seven—butts turned my way as the cows stalk off, naps interrupted.

Progress.

A few minutes later, our scraggly bunch comes within view of the forest road, identifiable for its silty, dry S-curves and the whine of an approaching engine. The cows cross ahead of me, pausing at what would be a climb toward the next curve. I look left to see a dirt bike squealing toward us, its rider a blue-and-white streak. I take a firm hold of my saddle horn, not knowing if Shorty's bike-broke, but Shorty doesn't even flinch.

The cattle are a different matter.

In the time it takes me to turn my eyes back to them from the road, the bike's whine around the next turn has spooked them into a running reverse.

Frantically, I wave my right arm, trying to be scarier than their memory of the dirt bike. "Hey, hey, hey cow!" I wheel Shorty to trot back and forth before the charging line. The two leaders slow. Two more fade farther downhill. My arm and throat burn. I must look and sound like a wounded harpy.

I hear a rumble from the left, and my stomach drops. A truck-mounted camper chugs along the road, doubtless searching for a campsite.

Goddamn public on goddamn public lands!

My barely slowed herd reverses once more, galloping up the slope in a jagged line.

Spurring Shorty in a shallow angle to intersect, I will the herd to keep up the pace I'd been cursing just moments ago. Instead, they halt in the soft, loose dirt of the road shoulder.

I judge I only have a few moments before the camper appears before the next curve, and I don't feel I can trust it to stop.

The coiled lariat thumps along where it's tied near the horn as I smack an open hand on my leg, trying to be as noisy and insistent as I can be. My leg will be sore tomorrow; my kingdom for some rope skills.

The cattle amble along in the loose dirt, one of them nearly falling back down the slope. Not wanting any vehicular collisions, I rein Shorty into the middle of the road, then raise my arm, praying the clunky camper will see us through all the dust.

It does, the driver and front passenger waving as though we are a passing parade.

I bare my teeth in what smile I can muster as I wheel Shorty toward the herd which is, miraculously, now trotting along in a line along the forest road.

The passenger-side window winds down. A camera points at us from outside the crawling camper.

I can mostly take feeling foolish today.

I cannot take having it recorded.

Shorty and I plunge back down the shoulder to get positioned from an angle where we can push the herd off the roadbed and back into the woods. God love this twitchy-eared, opinionated ranch horse—he really knows his job.

Using the camper as a second point of pressure, Shorty and I close in. With a buck and a kick, one brave soul hops off the road surface to gambol toward the trees. The rest follow, Shorty in close pursuit, while I fervently hope there are no more reversals.

I can hear the camper start to roll again behind me.

"Some fun, huh?" the driver says, punctuated by laughter from somewhere else inside the cab. "Got some great pictures!"

I can't help but laugh: at the poor campers thinking they'd just come across something genuine enough to photograph, at my sudden violent dislike of all things vehicular, and at my now completely departed vegetarian sensibilities. I am suddenly a staunch supporter of eating hamburger as often as possible. Field dressing, in fact, seems like a brilliant idea.

Shorty sighs, pointing out that we have, once again, fallen behind.

I remember Dad, then realize the vehicles are headed his way.

I fumble for my phone, hoping I'm not too late. He's a determined but not confident rider. If the cattle turn back on him—

He picks up.

"Dad, you've got a bike and an RV incoming!"

"OK," I hear the phone rustle, then the whine of the bike engine before the call cuts out.

Oh. No.

I leave my herd to trot down the side of the road double time, hoping Dad's still in the saddle. If he's not, I don't know quite what I'll do. Put him in my saddle and walk? Assuming he can ride. What if he can't? I don't have anyone's number but his and Brent's. What if Dad's phone is crushed? What if Brent's is off? Would I flag someone down on the road? What if Sage is loose? Hypotheticals elbow at my equilibrium to the point that I feel clobbered by the time I see Dad, thankfully sitting tall in his saddle.

Cell phone to his ear.

The camper trundles along a few hundred yards past where Sage inclines a lazy ear toward our worried approach, dust whorling in its wake.

"We've lost all of them but you've got them there?" Dad asks into the phone, then checks, "You had six, Jules?"

I nod. "Or seven. I could never tell."

Dad speaks back into the phone. "And I had ten. OK, then we're good. See you at the gate." He reholsters his phone and turns to me, smiling.

"Chris and Brent just picked up our sixteen and put them with their five, so they're just going to push them all ahead and meet us at the tank gate."

"Sounds good," I say, reaching down to pat Shorty's neck. He twitches an ear, probably equal parts pleased and suspicious at the affection.

"So what do you think?" Dad asks, grinning as he nudges Sage forward. "Isn't this kind of fun?"

Fatigue is replacing anxiety. I feel foolish unto ashamed that I can't count cows and mortified that my human windmill routine might be caught on camera. That tender spot between my shoulder blades is barking at me, my legs are stiffening, and we still have over three hours before noon. Even so, there's only one answer. "It is!"

I even mean it.

HOW TO TAKE COVER
WHEN IT'S RAINING MEN

Woods wants to sell the horses Jake bought, saying they'll never make it on the ranch. Mom asks me to come look at the horses to assess their potential for sale, which is why I am in the musty cabin at Oldham Park, facing at least a half-dozen men who won't look me in the eyes. Brent and I are still running the pros and cons of making the move to manage the ranch; the longer we take, the more Mom and Dad need our help; and it's cattle shipping season, the ranch's biggest annual payday, but the Weather Gods either missed the memo or really despise cattle growers.

Having read more of the literature since our foray onto the range, I've learned that "cattle growers" is the term for the industry in which Brent and I may find ourselves if we go ahead with this crazy idea.

Which may not be so crazy, given a few recent events.

At home in Washington, I'm making green-chili shrimp for dinner when I hear the garage door, the scatter-scratch of dog paws on the tile of the mudroom, and the squeaky door hinge between the mudroom and the garage.

"Hi guys," Brent says, his voice tired and resigned.

Not a good sign for the evening ahead.

If the greeting were, "Hey Doc, my boy! Liberty, baby, I'm home—yes, I'm home!" there might be conversation and storytelling. This tone means he'll want to eat in front of the TV and let it do all the talking for the night. I don't mind TV, but I spend most of my days among things that don't talk back: dogs, horses, laptop. Human interaction is far more limited by working at home, and what I do get, I don't usually like, as it's either work- or bill-related.

"Hey, darlin'," I call out. Green-chili shrimp has become a go-to for me. Wash and peel; open cans; stir; take out tortillas, lettuce, and cheese; assemble.

"Hey, darlin'," Brent answers, shuffling into the kitchen to the wine beneath the counter. Also not a good sign. Usually he'd want to go upstairs to change clothes before he comes into the kitchen so he can wrestle with Doc, our Labrador.

I don't know what to say now. I want to ask about his day, but I sense he doesn't want to talk about it. If I ask him, and he doesn't want to talk about it, he'll say so, which will make both of us feel worse. If I don't ask, he'll know I'm not asking. Communications are a briar patch for us, and I've never found a way to be Brer Rabbit.

"Green-chili shrimp OK with you?" I ask, stirring.

"I don't know," he says, glancing over as he withdraws a bottle of red wine and a corkscrew from their places beneath the counter. "I might just make myself some ramen."

This isn't uncommon, and I don't take it as a slight on my cooking. I know what I make doesn't always sound good; I just feel bad that I don't have anything to offer that he wants. "OK," I say, getting out a pot.

He reaches across me for a glass. Not a wine glass—a tumbler. Volume must be important.

He's close enough to kiss, but he's not looking at me. I'm afraid he'd take affection as a sign of sympathy, then resent the sympathy as a judgment against him. A perceived weakness.

I try for a joke. "So . . . you OK? Want me to ask again? Want me to keep asking?"

Usually this would be good for a smile. Early in our marriage, I learned that Brent doesn't process things by talking through them. He wants me to think of him and how he must be feeling, but he doesn't want me to ask a lot of questions. Problems are to be borne out quietly until they pass. This is opposite of my family, where problems did not pass if we remained quiet about them. Silence was regarded as a cloak, not to be trusted or allowed to remain in place too long. So it's not that my joke was particularly funny, as that it was a means of communicating both my concern and my understanding that Brent prefers I not pursue the reasons for it.

Brent just shakes his head. "Remember how I told you I was applying for APTA Leadership?"

American Public Transit Association is our industry trade group and lobbying arm that reminds elected officials that transit is not only a choice, it's a necessity, linkage, stopgap, social service, employer, economic engine, development catalyst, and environmental remediation. The leadership program is an honor, educational opportunity, and network generator. Transit is a small community of professionals, but, as in any profession, there is an in crowd and an out crowd, and it's good to be in with as many people as possible.

"Mm-hmm," I answer.

"Dick stole my application," Brent says, pushing the counter away with both hands, jamming his shoulders next to his ears. "Stole it. Took what I wrote and submitted it for himself."

I can't see his face, as Brent's chin is tucked next to his sternum, his facial expression, like his aspirations, lowering.

"Unbelievable," I say, even though both of us know it's just the opposite. This isn't the first time, but it does sound like the most flagrant example of Brent's boss taking credit for Brent's work.

"Who does that?" Brent asks, offended. "Who steals an application? It might be one thing if he'd written his own and we'd competed for a spot, but to take my writing and submit it as his own? I guess we know now why I could never get the letter of recommendation back from him."

I shake my head. "I'm so sorry."

He pours a very full tumbler of wine. "That's the craziest part. He wouldn't even know about the Leadership program, except that I was applying."

It's so quiet between us that I can hear the dogs breathing, puffs and sighs exchanged with the night in the gentle conversation I wish Brent and I could have.

Conversely, I've been having too much conversation with my boss. For the past year, I've been able to work out of our house for a boutique transportation consulting firm. I've worked virtually for projects in Atlanta, Toronto, Cleveland, Washington, D.C., and Denver, and in person for a few projects around Seattle. The trouble is, most of those contracts are closing or stalling out, and my billable forecast is looking dry.

My boss calls to go over it together. I am the type who best processes information by reading it on my own; he best takes it in when it's being discussed, which means I repeat myself a lot. It seems redundant to me, and more than a little embarrassing, to have to tell him what we can both see on the screen, but this is what he's asked for. We've gone project by project through my billable hours for the next month, which all sum either zeros or single digits. For me that would be more than enough, but he wants to talk through the final step.

"So all in all," he says, "that brings you to, let's just add it up . . ."

Oh yes. Let's please add it up.

"So less than forty hours billable next month," he concludes. "Wow. I guess you've been telling me that, but I've had so many things going on I haven't really seen it until now."

Ouch. In one statement he admits to ignoring me and dismissing my problems because they're not his.

"That's what it looks like," I say, feeling the statement could apply either to the forecast or his inattention.

He assumes it references the former. "Have you been in touch with other managers to see if there's anywhere else you can help out?"

The answers to that are yes, and no, there isn't anything else. I've told him about that too. Taking a deep breath, I tell him again, trying to ignore the wormy sense of being nonessential to the firm's future. We are in the service industry, making our offerings subject to the needs and preferences of a client base we cannot control, especially because our clients are governments, themselves reactive to the decisions of changing policies and policymakers. We are also a small firm without any kind of research or development department. We cannot afford to invent products or services our clients might need during the slow times when nobody's calling. I know all this. I have a specific set of skills the firm bought to expand its offerings, but it cannot offer them if no one is buying. We're in the zits-and-braces stages of market development, when everything seems unknown, awkward, and deeply personal even if it isn't.

"We have a few options going forward," he sighs. "We probably can't keep you on full-time, but we could drop you to part-time. Or we could let you go to contract work—just work together when we both want to—if you liked that better. How about you think about that?"

I swallow hard. Why would I like an unpredictable paycheck better? And what thoughts am I to think that will have any effect on the immutable fact that I won't have a contract to charge to in less than a month?

"OK," I say.

"And I'll talk to leadership about this too, and see if they have thoughts. I'm sure the company owners will want to call you."

Oh, goody.

"Sure." I try to keep my voice neutral.

We sign off.

The next day, I get an email saying my boss talked to leadership, and they're switching me to part-time, effective immediately.

Woods has also done some offline conferencing. The ranch's former horse trainer has left a vacancy, and Mom and I are on our way to meet a potential replacement.

I have never seen it rain so hard, and I consider myself something of an expert on precipitation, having flown in from Seattle.

Now as we're ranch-bound from the airport, the northern sky looks like a bruise: gray to black skies hovering over a day tinted a nauseous green.

"Does the weather want to kill us?" I ask Mom.

She just shakes her head.

Seattle rains range from mist to dual-headed shower. No one except a visitor uses an umbrella because rain doesn't only fall straight down. Seattle rain is guerilla warfare, water coming from every direction, making a hooded raincoat the only effective form of defense.

The rain I've flown into in Arizona is cannon fire, a directional assault of massive force, splintering trees, windows, skylights, and building roofs. It may even get worse by turning to hail. Dad says the storm has been so bad on the ranch that the cowboys had to tie themselves to trees to keep from being blown off their horses.

A rustic log cabin warmed by a fire in an antique stove should feel cozy in such circumstances. The smell of onions frying, wet wool, and damp leather lend harmonic notes to a soothing haven melody, but walking in the front door with Mom, I almost prefer to take my chances with the storm.

Dad sits in a chair behind the sofa where Woods waits with Pete, a friend he wants us to meet to help the ranch sell the newly purchased horses. Ty, a ranch cowboy who is also a second cousin of mine, sits in a recliner watching *Lonesome Dove*, with the sound off as a concession to the business meeting taking place. Dad jokes that the cowboys quote *Lonesome Dove* so often he likely doesn't need the sound anyway. Chris sits in the cabin kitchen at the plank picnic table that serves as coatrack, boot jack, cutting board, and table and chairs. He looks up as we enter, then returns to a conversation with two other hands I've never met before. Dad told me it's customary for ranches to share labor during roundup. Neighboring ranches coordinate their shipping days so their cowboys can be available to gather up each ranch's herd from their pastures and get them onto trucks by way of holding pens. This is each ranch's one and only market day—the single paycheck out of which any future is to be made, meaning the workday won't end until the cattle are in place.

Fatigue hangs heavier in the cabin than the storm clouds outside, a kind of sick exhaustion not only with the work but with anything that doesn't reward it. Mom and Dad and I are outsiders, feckless dudes wanting to talk about how to handle horses that haven't earned their keep. This conversation is as uselessly misplaced to the cowboys as a parasol before a firehose, to say nothing of the fact that we are taking up coveted rest time with the conversation.

Dad clears his throat. "Julie, this is Pete, the friend of Woods I told you about, and I just thought it might be helpful to hear his ideas of what we might do with the ranch horses."

I have the list of horses with me, hoping to put faces to names, and, more importantly, ride each of them to get a sense of their skills. Not that any rides will happen today.

"Well, I was just telling Woods, there are lots of ways to get them horses sold," Pete opens. "I don't think you'll have a problem."

This is news to me. The horse market in my world is beyond depressed. Since the 2008 stock market plunge, what disposable income can still be found has been redirected away from the horse market. In the state of Washington, there have been record numbers of horses reported abandoned on Native lands—domestic horses dumped to do their best to survive with wild herds, the result being critical overpopulation.

There are many breeds and sports about which I range from ignorant to learning, but at least the horses we're talking about today are quarter horses—the breed I know best.

"That'd be great," I respond. "I've been hearing news that most people aren't buying anymore. Where do you see sales happening?"

"Well, you just said it," Pete says, stretching a flannel-clad arm across the back of the sofa. "Sales."

He and Pete look like an ad for chewing tobacco, a substance I know more about than I'd like because Brent is a user. Brent likes the brand of snuff whose tin top is easily distinguishable for its roaring bear. These two bearded, terse, suspicious, wily-eyed men before me may not be roaring, but they appear to be every bit as hostile and territorial as angry bears.

"I know there's one coming up in March," I say. "That's supposed to be good. Are there others you'd recommend?"

We've only sold a horse once through an auction rather than a private sale. My impression is that people who take horses to sales are desperate to find buyers because of personal circumstance or exhausted options, which usually doesn't speak well of the horse's marketability. However, I am keenly aware that we just acquired a half-dozen head through a livestock sale, so I am hopeful my impression can quickly be proven false.

"Colors of the Sun," Pete says. Woods nods agreement. "Coming up quick here. November, I think."

"It's a good sale?" I ask, knowing the question is vague. What I want to know is if moneyed buyers attend, expecting to pay a premium for quality stock. "They get good prices for what's sold?"

Pete shrugs. "You bring the value, you get the money."

I am in no position to know if what the ranch has to sell is valuable, and everyone in the room knows it. I haven't ridden the horses; I haven't even seen them, and that they have some proven bloodlines on their registration papers doesn't necessarily translate to value unless there are buyers who want to pay for that. What the ranch has now is horses with three months more riding experience behind them than they had at the time of purchase. Three months more in any market usually doesn't translate to much margin.

"I was hoping to get on them while I was here—"

I can't even finish for the laughter.

"You wanted to ride 'em here?" Woods guffaws. "Now?"

"Well, not today," I amend, watching the cowboys before me turn as critical as Statler and Waldorf, the Muppet hecklers, minus the good humor.

"You're not gonna ride out there for a week," Woods says, throwing a hand up dismissively. "And them horses don't need rode."

This will be ticklish. I don't want to offend the cowboy sense of horsemanship, but neither do I want to take their word for what the horses are and can do. "I just wanted to test a few things. I wouldn't ride any of them long—maybe ten, twenty minutes."

Woods snorts.

I recognize this as a signal of intolerance for any further conversation. Other signals I know to heed include changed subjects, excuses given for needing to exit, statements that it's time for me to leave, raised eyebrows, and other various facial expressions. Having spent all of my professional life and a good part of my married one around men impatient with questions, I am now fully fluent in the spoken and unspoken brush-off.

It doesn't occur to me to keep pushing for more information. Working with horses, engineers, and supervisors has taught me that getting angry, even getting emotional, is a sign of weakness, an immediate disqualification from any current or future respect. Being a sensitive type, I cope by avoiding confrontation: figuring out how to get out or get by with whatever I have when tensions begin to increase. I defuse, sidestep, delay, back up, re-characterize—pretzel my words, thoughts, or myself any way I can so as not to get emotional.

"We'll see what it looks like tomorrow," I suggest, hoping the storms will pass, taking the atmospheric sense of menace with them.

The next morning dawns dewy, with fluffy white clouds spotting the clear mountain sky. Dad is gathering cattle with the cowboys. Oldham Park is quiet: no dogs, no shuffle at the hitching post, no trucks grinding gears, readying trailers to leave. It's also walkable—the oft-libeled cinders making it possible to walk through the yard from corrals to trailers without slipping or soaking ourselves in puddles. The only trouble is that there's no one around to point out which of the remaining horses is part of the sale string. I consult my list: the new ranch horses are black, various shades of brown, and palomino. I scan the horses still in the corrals, seeing a palomino the color of buttermilk pancakes.

Freckles is easy enough to halter, saddle, and lead out to the arena. He doesn't flinch, doesn't twitch, doesn't react—his ears neither prick nor swivel. There's a broken sense about him, a depression, like a pro rodeo cowboy who's been told he'll never ride again. There's nothing obviously wrong—no cuts or lameness, no sensitivity to handling, no fear of people—just a resignation I've never experienced before. Even nose-to-tail trail horses I've been assigned on vacation rides usually have some spark—some character—a will to get free, to resist tasks, some stiffness or opinion about some part of the day. Freckles may as well be wet cardboard.

The arena's footing is dry at the top but altogether too wet to trot or lope in, making mine a short ride: a circle in each direction testing flexion and bridle skills, all of which Freckles offers after some hesitation, like a kid waiting to answer until he's sure no one's going to yell at him.

I stop and slide off, deciding we've both done what we can for the day.

"Nice guy?" Mom asks as I lead Freckles back to his halter. She's been using the time to clean and reorganize the remainder of her tack.

"Seems like it," I say, offering Freckles a face rub. He all but somersaults backward, tossing his head skyward and back, quick-footing away like I'd cracked a whip.

"Whoa," I croon, keeping hold of my reins.

He snorts, white-eyed.

"Poor baby," Mom comments.

I sigh. "That's sort of what he felt like to ride. Nothing that dramatic, but not comfortable. Not relaxed. Scared." I eye Freckles, looking to me more and more like a terrified kid pleading to be allowed to go home. "I won't even halter him," I decide. "Let me just pull his saddle and give it to you."

"Sure," Mom agrees.

When I turn Freckles loose in his paddock, he trots away a few steps, then stops, shakes, stands, squeezing his eyes shut.

"I think your dad said he was one of the ones caught out in the storm the other day," Mom remembers.

"That would explain some things," I murmur, thinking everyone and everything at the ranch is just saturated, unable to take in anything else. Both horses and people are overworked, overtired, overcome by the lashings of storms, long hours, short supplies, and the steady downpour always of more to do.

WHY WEED AND COWS
ARE INCOMPATIBLE

As a professional planner, it sits crosswise with me that the ranch can't forecast even five years' worth of revenues because its grazing permits are renewed on an annual basis. I want the ranch to have a predictable source of income. I want something less labor-intensive than cows. I want something with bigger margins, something that can capitalize on the fact that we have a lot of land in hard-to-reach places.

I don't want to do anything illegal—Dad's a lawyer after all. But I wouldn't mind being on the growth edge while the law is still being written.

Medical marijuana legalization is up for a vote in Arizona. I wonder if there's anything about ranch land that might prove medicinal.

I call my friend Will.

He and his contracting company once saved my house in Denver from a smoking attic fan when Brent was away interviewing for what would become his new job in Seattle. An entrepreneur by nature and experience, Will is a licensed electrician and contractor, self-made real estate magnate, and weed dealer. He dresses his hair and body like a surfer, drives a one-ton pickup worthy of an Iowa farmer, and prefers champagne over cocktails. He is articulate, jolly, metaphysical, and street-smart. I suspect he regards me as an amusement—a sweater-set suburban housewife-type who just happens to like farms. For reasons I can only guess at, he is kind to me and always returns my calls.

I'm going back to Denver for a visit. I text him a lengthy message explaining I want to ask him about his weed trade as a possible business line for the ranch. He texts back briefly that we can meet to talk.

Having never ingested marijuana of any kind, I am relying on the "you don't have to taste a donut to know it's sweet" mentality to guide me in this venture. I don't tell Dad. I don't even tell Brent that I'm curious about this. I don't want the warnings or the laughter, respectively.

That I feel a little cloak-and-dagger is completely at odds with the brilliant sun of the crisp winter Denver morning when Will and I meet to talk over coffee. He is in his characteristic flannel, laceless sneakers, and skater cap. I'm in Denver chic: jeans, running shoes, and a fleece. Despite the distinctive pungency of his most lucrative trade following him to the table, Will's eyes are bright as he seats himself next to me at the plain wooden table where the weekday has left us mostly alone. We will neither be rushed nor overheard.

"So that's not a message I thought I'd get from you," he opens, after deciding on tea.

"Yeah," I grimace. I know I am barely this side of ridiculous, doing the beginnings of due diligence research on pot. Making serious inquiry about entering a drug trade feels as misplaced as applying a chainsaw to cut a birthday cake. I reflect that maybe I should regard this as an indicator of how farfetched not only my weed idea, but also the ranch venture, actually is, but my curiosity shoves timidity aside.

"Sounds interesting, though," Will supplies.

Grateful for the safer ground, I tell him the story of how Mom and Dad's first invitation to come ride became a pending relocation plan.

Will laughs. "So, you're going?"

"We're going," I confirm, with more certainty in my tone than in my soul.

Brent sees the ranch as autonomy; a way to make something for himself and for us purely by his own efforts, without interference from corporate politics or hierarchy. I see it as reclamation of the wife, daughter, and self I'd hoped to be: constructive, supportive, indefatigable. We talk about it to my parents and grandmother as a great opportunity—an adventure we could never experience except by their invitation, one we don't want to regret passing. We don't talk much about what we'll do if it doesn't work. At some point, one of us mentioned "going back to what we're doing now," but my memory has blocked all but the kind of shudder that usually accompanies torture scenes in period war movies. Especially for two planners by training and profession, we are noticeably short of contingencies, metrics, or goals other than the general: ranch profitability. Perhaps the truth we don't want to acknowledge is that we've both been so short on hope for anything different, either professionally or personally, that the ranch feels like the password to the cave of wonders—something so improbably fragile but desperately welcome that we don't dare speak of it too much.

Even so, there's a coyote that's moved into my gut since Brent and I announced the decision to my family about a month ago. I've heard it howling at me more frequently since we decided to delay our start until spring. No one saw any use to moving before the holidays. With roundup concluded and the calves sold, the cattle will winter in pastures requiring far less rotation while the horses enjoy a much-needed rest. Mom and Dad couldn't muster the help required to get the new horses to the sale Pete had proposed, and no one was comfortable sending them with someone we barely knew, even if he was a longtime friend of Woods's. Plus, I think Mom and I felt the ranch owed the horses more than just a handoff to yet another auction. Given our druthers, we'd both prefer the horses go to homes, not just jobs.

"It sounds like you'll have enough to do without starting a whole other business," Will observes.

I flail for words, not wanting him to dismiss the subject so soon. I'm surprised at the instant feeling of desperation, starting to understand how much the cash-poor nature of traditional, and legal, agriculture scares me. For one thing, I'm already feeling the pressure of needing to develop and sell the ranch horses, which has become my task since Mom and Dad and I decided to hold onto them.

I clear my throat, trying to swallow my fright. "Well, it's a matter of choosing the most profitable activities, right?"

"Sure," he agrees. "I'd tell you that the first thing to do if you're going to do this is get a burner phone."

I blink back the sense of a sudden reversal, a mounting stampede.

"What you have to understand is that even if your product is legal where you're growing and selling it, you can't control where your customers take it, so you don't want anything that can be traced to you. If your customers take something across state lines, then you're in trouble."

I should stop now. Get a second latte and talk about movies.

"Got it," I say.

He raises his eyebrows. "Then, you want to have someplace you can secure. If it's a medical law, you have to grow for who you sell to, and you're probably only allowed a certain amount of plants per customer, so you want to control those. Do you have that on your property?"

Definitely not. Three-stringed barbed wire doesn't even stop four-wheelers wanting a joyride. Entitled recreationalists cut our fences all the time.

"Not right now," I answer.

"And, of course, you're going to want to control all the light and water," Will goes on. "An old barn could maybe work, but you'd have to make a lot of improvements."

We barely have any barn at all. Mom has installed a mare motel on the winter headquarters—stalls enclosed by pipe fence and half-covered by corrugated metal roof. The tack room there is a Tuff Shed, and the office-slash-bathroom-slash-kitchen is a parked toy hauler. No room at the inn, as it were, for plantings.

"We don't have that," I say, a white flag of surrender starting to wave in my mind.

"You'll probably need refrigeration most," he says. "A couple of 'refr' trucks, maybe."

The word sounds like "reefer." We both smile.

"No pun intended," he winks. "But then the next thing you'll need is a way to manage your cash. See, the banking's not legal. I've only found one place, one ATM where I can deposit the cash I get from my sales. I'm going there every day, and I still can't get rid of it. Some days I'm driving around with thousands of dollars just in my truck."

"I knew I liked your truck," I joke. There is no way this can work. No banking? Cash caches? I try to imagine how I could ever stand up straight in front of my grandmother again.

"So how's the ranch, Jules?"

"Well, the good news is I've found a cash crop . . ."

"Yeah," he laughs. "I spend most of my time feeding money into the cash machine."

That in itself is discouraging, as Will lives and works in Denver, with nothing like the mileage between grow and market locations that I would have to traverse for a ranch-based operation.

I try a different approach. "So that's the weed market, but what about hemp? I've looked into that a little bit too."

"Yeah," he agrees. "Eventually I want to get out of this and just get into that—it's more interesting. With CBD you can do lotions, tinctures, oils—the shelf life is a lot longer."

"That sounds good," I encourage, feeling hopeful again. "Why not go that way?"

"Because the prices are lower," he says. "CBD won't get you high."

"Oh," I say, reliving the time I went to see the movie *Traffic* with a boyfriend in grad school and had to lean over to whisper, "Is that heroin? Is that what they're doing?"

"Hemp is cool, though," he says diplomatically. "There are so many great uses for it. Paper, plastic, medicine, clothing fiber—it can replace anything."

I nod, grateful to get back to my research mode. "I saw that it even remediates soil. And that it's a low-water-use plant—that's good for us."

"Yeah, it would be," he says, "but you'd have to be really careful because even the hemp strain of the plant produces some THC, even more if it gets stressed by heat. If your plants get too hot and you don't have enough water at the right time, you can ruin your whole harvest. No one will take it if the THC is even a percentage point above the legal limit. Do you have irrigation out there?"

"Not right now," I confess.

"Maybe not hemp, then," he counsels.

I'm disappointed. I know I shouldn't be, that I was naïve to think I could find any easy way to make money in a new enterprise, but I couldn't help hoping that maybe with a little ingenuity we could find something that would pay better than livestock.

"So how much land are you working with?" he asks, his eyes turning bright with the gleam that usually follows the mention of ranch and cattle. Every child wants to be a cowboy or cowgirl at some point in their growing-up years. The same gleam lights Brent up when he comes home from work. He can't wait to give his notice. I already gave mine. My company didn't like how I did it, but I think their disapproval of its sudden nature was mostly to mask their relief.

"About three hundred acres," I answer.

His eyebrows rise.

"That's what we own," I say. "We graze several thousand—I don't actually know how many—that's Brent's department. I just know we can't grow enough grass on what we own to keep our cows fed."

"How many cows?" he asks.

"About two hundred," I say. "Half the year. The other half, after they calve, there are four hundred. We sell the calves in the fall, then turn the cows back out for the bulls to cover over the winter."

"Nice life for the bulls," he toasts with his teacup.

I shrug. I've heard that one before, but I don't mind the joke. "Our foreman asked my dad a couple of roundups ago if he'd met the environmental bull."

Will looks at me quizzically.

"Yeah," I repeat. "The environmental bull. The foreman said they call it that because it's so hard to flush out of the brush. It's a 'tree-hugging sonofabitch.'"

Will leans his head back to laugh.

I laugh too. "You think that one's good," I say. "You should hear what he told the neighbors who didn't keep up the fence between our pastureland and the golf course where they lived. Our cows ended up wandering around their houses, so the neighbors called us, all upset. Irate at the damage. The foreman goes out to round up the cows and says, 'Lady, don't you worry about them cows. Your flowers ain't gonna hurt them cows one bit. And you can keep the fertilizer. No charge.'"

"You're going to have fun out there," Will says, raising his teacup again.

I'm not sure. The living of it may not be fun at all—quite the opposite, I suspect. I just hope the looking-back stories will make the hard parts worth it.

HOW TO PACK,
AND OTHER BAGGAGE

Every road trip comes with its share of the unpredictable. In my experience, the amount of surprise inflicted is directly proportional to the size of the trip. Given that we will be traveling across four states from Washington to Arizona in two vehicles carrying three different species, with a volatile mix of early spring weather along the way, I shouldn't be surprised that even the packing comes with more upset than I might expect.

With just a few days left before the date of our scheduled departure, Brent figures out that the flatbed trailer he purchased will not balance when the tractor is secured to its top. Equally problematic—his Land Rover cannot tow the load. As the tractor's transport was the reason Brent purchased the flatbed, this is not a welcome discovery.

"How long is he going to diddle with that thing?" Mom asks, frustrated, as we pack the last of the office cartons. She'd flown up to help box, then drive, feeling that in a move of home, farm equipment, and horses, two more hands would not go amiss. Given that our planned convoy has some critical loading problems, I am especially grateful for her energies. Brent seems to be less so. I suspect that some of his "I'll be right back—I'm just going to load the tractor" statements are made at least partially out of convenience rather than necessity.

Neither of us is comfortable around our mothers-in-law. His to me is an almost perfect mismatch of interests and habits. She likes to shop just to be out in the stores. I loathe malls. She likes home décor and presentation. My understanding of a throw pillow is something else the dog gets to enjoy more than me. Worst for me, she is most comfortable with a constant presence of noise, from the television, radio, or her own voice. As much as I crave conversation, I need silence, and time with her offers neither, as talking for her is more of a pastime than a means of real communication. Brent bristles at my mother's suggestions, often made in the form of declarative to imperative statements. Rather than contradict her, he does things her way or stays away from her altogether. As her suggestions can be made on any topic ranging from our work superiors to what we should have for dinner, he tends to adopt the patterns of a flushed rabbit when she is around for prolonged periods of time, fleeing to the next-nearest cover before circling back when he judges she's moved on. Her view of how and when to expend resources, an unavoidable topic when one has horses, seems especially vexing to him. As the process of moving is all-consuming, with almost no topic that does not involve either time or money, Brent has been particularly quick to bounce these last couple days.

Doc, our aging yellow Labrador, sighs from where he had stretched himself along the wall to keep track of us. The gray of his muzzle flutters gently with his deep, even breaths. I would give a lot for his peace.

"If he can't get that thing loaded—"

"I know," I cut her off. By unspoken agreement, the house is mine to pack, the farm his, and I am unwilling to trespass on his territory.

We silently go back to our boxes, twisting paper around the few remaining fragile items, labelling them carefully. I wish I could similarly bubble wrap Brent's ego.

We've finished both bedrooms, the living room, and the office, and we've started on the kitchen when Brent tromps through the front door. "I can't make it work."

Mom and I stop and look at each other from over the top of the waiting glassware.

Brent's announcement hangs in the air like Doc's gaze, shifting to each one of us, patiently waiting for us to notice he hasn't been greeted. I'm more aware of him since we lost his companion right before New Year's Eve. Liberty, a black flat-coated retriever, had been timid, swift, and unfailingly loyal to Doc and to us in priority order, unless it came to food. When her usual supper-bowl-delay games, played to make Doc wait an agonizing few minutes more before rawhide chews could be dispensed for dessert, turned to genuine food avoidance, we'd gone to the vet. She had a heart defect causing internal bleeding into her abdomen. We'd gotten a night to say goodbye before returning to the vet for a final farewell. I hadn't left Doc alone since that wrenching day, assuring him we'd look for a new friend for him as soon as we moved to Arizona.

Maybe we're all counting on the ranch to complete something for us: for Brent, the realization of a childhood ranch dream; for Doc, companionship; for me, a homecoming and break from isolation. We had moved to Seattle from Denver as energetic newlyweds, confident our best days were still ahead of us, if for no other reason than that we would begin and end them together. Sometime since we'd moved, togetherness had grayed, and I didn't know why—realizing only that my efforts to be sunnier were growing more labored. We all needed some lightening up.

Doc sighs, the room quiet enough to hear the settling of his ear then nose against the floor.

"And?" I ask Brent.

"And, I don't know," Brent says, clumping into the kitchen in his wet boots to fill a glass with water. "The tractor just won't balance. I've tried loading it forwards and backwards, but the hitch is almost dragging the ground. The tractor's just too heavy for the trailer, and the trailer is too heavy for the Rover. There's no way I'll be able to tow that thing at more than 40 mph, and I can't fit the Gator on if the tractor's on. It's already too heavy."

I wince. The Gator has been something of a sore subject with me since the day of its purchase two summers ago. Brent has a thing for vehicles. When we bought the farm property, he pronounced we needed a tractor to combat slopes, stumps, and blackberry vines tangled as high as tree forts. After a few months of his work commute, he felt he needed a hybrid vehicle to save on gas. When we built the barn, he ordered a John Deere Gator—a dump truck built like a golf cart.

In his defense, all three vehicles had made the work they were purchased for easier on us, but I still wasn't comfortable with our household's legs-to-wheels ratio.

"Maybe you need another truck," Mom suggests.

Brent looks at me, his expression a bramble of resentment and curiosity.

I don't want a truck. Then again, I didn't want the tractor, Gator, or trailer. We sold the hybrid to pay for the move. At this point, I'd like to call the nearest John Deere dealer to see if they buy used equipment, and I'll throw the flatbed in if they'll come pick it up. I suspect that voicing even one of these thoughts would be like stripping Brent of his pants and drawers right there in the kitchen in front of my mom.

I shrug.

"Yeah, I'll need a truck anyway, but I don't know that we're in a position to buy one." Brent looks at Doc as he says this, the only one in the room without an opinion on the matter.

I hate debt as much as he loves vehicles. Every chance I've had, every gift I've received, I've used to pay off loans, both the ones we took out together and those he brought into the marriage. That many of those opportunities came from some form of my family's generosity is a reliable abscess in Brent's and my peace—a wound that can't get healed before something hits it just wrong and it blows, scabbing over once again in the raw silence between us.

Having to admit to less liquidity than either of us would like, and far less than my parents might expect given their gifts over the years, is tantamount to Brent's being subjected to the aforementioned condition while my mother applies a tape measure to make careful note of length and width.

"I don't know that you're in a position not to," Mom counters.

I remember the time I needed to size my mare for a winter blanket. I walked into her stall with a mechanical tape measure, the metal whirring as it extended. She flew back as though I had thrown a hissing snake, a reaction that now looks mild compared to the quaking in Brent's eyes.

"It doesn't matter anyway," Brent concludes. "We can't fit both vehicles onto the trailer."

My fingers slip on the glass as I sense the mounting frustrations. In my experience, anger is a gateway to nothing good. I am very much like a horse in this way, regarding angry people as dangerously irrational forces, even if they haven't wrought any damage yet. I feel myself wanting to shy from the room—bolt the whole scene—but because Brent would take my flight as a betrayal, I still my feet and nerves and stay put.

"Then call the movers and see if they can take it," Mom directs. "Or sell it and buy one when you're there. Either way, I think you need a truck."

Tension is so palpable, Doc sits up, his nails scratching against the floorboards.

Brent's jaw tightens to such a degree I'm surprised his words don't squeak on their way out. "OK, I'll go look for a truck."

I feel like I'm in a trash compactor under a press of powers I don't control. I can't make more money simply appear in our bank account, nor can I protect all the sacred cows Brent's surrounded himself with: the Rover, the Gator, our liquidity as our business, his feelings about all of that plus whatever else is stampeding inside him.

"Let me go with you," Mom says, seeing my face. "Maybe I just buy it for now and you buy it from me later."

The offer is salvation for me—an out from crushing additional financial pressure. It is the opposite for Brent: I see him recoil at the proposition. We are as opposed as we have ever been, except for the mutual sense that the ranch has become a promised land: if we can get there, all will be forgiven, fulfilled, or both.

He shrugs, striding off to get his keys.

"I'll call the movers," I say to his back. "See what I can find out about them taking either the tractor or the Gator."

No one responds.

Mom gets her purse.

It turns out that movers really can move anything.

"A tractor?" my agent asks. "It's not a request we get every day, but we'll take the whole damn barn for ya if you want us to," he says, laughing into the phone.

I appreciate the option, calling Mom next to let her know.

"Good, because I don't know what's wrong with him. They have a truck here that can do the work, and we could drive it off the lot but he doesn't like it," she tells me, agitated. "What's not to like? It's a truck that can do the work!"

Getting work done is valued unto celebrated above all else in my family. That it's uncomfortable, inconvenient, or unpleasant is beside the point. We're not expected to like it, we're just expected to do it. Work completed carries its own satisfaction, a dignity that's healing to any previous discontent.

Mom and Brent return—truckless and in chafed silence—the placement of Mom's purse on the counter and Brent's steps to stow his keys equally loud arguments of how wrong the other has been. I propose a truce by way of a convoy arrangement: Mom and Doc and I will drive my truck hauling the horse trailer. Brent will drive his Land Rover hauling the flatbed upon which the Gator will be secured. The tractor will go with the movers.

All parties agree. Peace in our time.

I have never said "flatbed" so many times in my life.

HOW RENO CAN
SAVE YOUR ROAD TRIP

Day One of our route will send us from Carnation, Washington, to Prineville, Oregon, where we will overnight with the same friends who trained Sage and Cheyenne. They have a buyer for my filly, making Prineville the end of the road for my maternal aspirations.

Examining that road not taken is more daunting than the one I have ahead, but I've looked enough to know that I didn't take it by choice. Neither Brent nor I had any family near our Washington home. We had made some friends, but I didn't have the kind of community I would want to bring a child into. Nor had it ever seemed right to me to "just try it." Had I failed as a dog or horse mom, I could rehome the dependent. Not so with a human child, whom I also simply did not want the way I know some women do, or the way I wanted to. I thought the want might come with time, but Brent and I were four years into our marriage, and no yearning voice had spoken up. Sometimes I took its absence as an abstention, sometimes as a kind of condemnation of my maternal aptitude. Brent's words on the subject were, "If it happens, it'll be great, and if it doesn't, I don't need it to." I have never been one for treating pregnancy like a lotto ticket, so I'd continued administering my own contraception, taking Brent's phrase to be a passive admonition that no matter what he wanted, the decision ultimately rested with me. Only it hadn't rested. It prickled and clawed and bit and, at best, stuck croaking between acceptance and grief.

Stopping for gas immediately down the hill from the house, I tear up. Maybe it's exhaustion. Maybe it's the physical descent from hilltop to valley, replicating the emotional one that, at last, the packing and prepping and fretting and fussing are over and now it's just us and the road and the future, come what may.

"Oh," Mom says, as I climb back into the cab. "Yes. Of course. I understand."

"I don't," I laugh through a sob. "I have mostly been miserable here. Alone and gray and wet and struggling, and so far away, and now I get to go home."

"But you *lived* here," Mom points out.

It's true. To live is to hope, and there are many, many hopes whose slumber I will never see wake.

The bright point of the day is that my filly is a dream come true for our friends, a realization that is as welcome as the opening horizons under a clearing sky the farther south we travel.

"Mom's always wanted a pretty palomino," the female half of our trainer friends says to me as she hands me the check. "She's so excited, she's already bought a halter and saddle pad."

I know that feeling. I've been culling office wear from my wardrobe and proudly adding jeans from every sale I can find. Looking at the pile grow feels like Destiny waving the checkered flag, signaling me to get on with it.

Bucking and twisting in her new pasture, blissfully unaware of my goodbyes, the filly sends a similar message: don't look back.

Day Two begins hauling south through the dry snow of Oregon and southwest through the wet rain of northern California, winding our way across highways that don't allow for much more than Brent's preferred speed of 55 mph, which is what he says the Rover can handle. Our destination is a horse hotel in Sparks—a spread outside of Reno, Nevada, built for overnighting horses. The people, I've booked in a casino hotel that allows dogs.

The weather is cold and gray, and my outlook isn't much better as we drive through the day. The enormity of everything we're doing seems to press harder at me with every mile that rolls by.

"Breathe," my mother advises from the passenger seat.

"Right," I acknowledge, then have no idea what to do except cry.

"It's a big time," she says, understanding.

I wipe the tears from my eyes.

"But we're so happy to have you coming to help," she says.

I laugh a little.

"Well, geez, Jules, your dad and I can't do this by ourselves. I mean, we've been trying, and you see how much work there is to do."

I nod.

"We're not up to it," Mom says. "I mean, we're just flat not up to it. We're in our sixties and your dad's had cancer. He doesn't need to be playing cowboy at his age. We're thrilled you want to take this on."

The encouragement soothes the flares of anxiety over housing, working with relatives, and figuring out everything we don't know about the land and cattle and cowboys. "It's a dream come true for Brent," I say.

"It's a dream come true for me," Mom says. "I'll be thrilled to have you closer."

"Me too," I say. My mother is and has been my best friend since college. We've shown horses together, driven cross-country, taken trips to New York and Paris and all kinds of places in between. We walk, we garden, we shop, we call each other every day, and in-between times, we email. We're keenly aware of the special friendship we have, and we cleave to it, because we just lost her mother to Leukemia a year and a half ago. We both feel that loss every day, but it's more than loss for her. It's a presence she's come to live with—a grief that's always around, announcing itself with every hummingbird or brightly colored flower or sweet surprise or remembrance that we associate with her mother.

Between that, my anxiety, Doc, and us, it's a very full truck.

Reno takes us by surprise as we haul ourselves up and over the grade that eventually descends into a valley of lights nestled between mountains. We can't see a lot in the dwindling light, but the landscape looks open, with squatty shrubs and a few tough trees as we make our way to the ranch where our horses are expected for the night.

Their accommodations are enormous turnout pens with plenty of bedding in their run-in shelters. After a long day of balancing on bouncing axles, it'll be a relief for them to be able to stretch and amble around.

My mare, Lena, does a lot more than that as soon as I turn her loose, and I grin, watching her buck and fart and spin and race up and down the fence line getting to know her neighbors. Marty, Brent's gelding, joins in the antics, high-stepping, half-rearing, baiting her into a game of tag. Seeing the horses are clearly happy, and after checking the gates, feed, and water buckets, we roll back into town.

Our casino hotel has a parking area for large vehicles that has attracted enough RVs to fill a football field. We gather our evening kit—Doc's food can, our bags, Mom's bags, horse papers, and a few other valuables—to stagger into surprisingly spacious and plush rooms and a lovely pasta dinner.

Breakfast has been to-go lattes and sandwiches for the past two days. Today is no different, prompting Mom to roll her eyes; a third day of Brent's and my preferred fare is still not a charm. Today's requirements will send us through a desert and past Area 51 to a stopover in Las Vegas. We've been moving, packing, and basically out of our minds with distraction for over a week, so we fumble the loading of both humans and horses. Brent had forgotten Doc's food can. I had forgotten my shower kit. Our lattes are basically gone by the time we actually roll from the parking lot, and long gone once the horses are loaded. Thankfully the driving will be straightforward: just one highway from Reno to Las Vegas, then a cut past the Strip to where we will stay for the night.

There's not much to that wide and dry expanse to recommend it: "barren" is a generous descriptor. The highlight of the day is stopping near a gas station that announces itself as being right next to Area 51 and gawking at all the green alien gear that comes in sizes ranging from dashboard bobblehead to full-size comic con companion. Perhaps it captured too much of our attention, because we arrive in Las Vegas just in time for rush hour. Between scrolling Strip hotel signs, freeway billboards, and brake lights, I need sunglasses and a stiff drink by the time we roll up to the horses' home for the night.

Our horse hostess lives in a suburban ranchette neighborhood south of the Strip, and she's excited to greet us and usher us in.

"You made it!" she calls, jogging out to the neighborhood street where we stop, afraid to drive onto her property without knowing the turnaround dimensions. "Welcome!"

Her enthusiasm is sweet and appreciated as we step, stiffly, out of the truck.

"Hi," I say wearily. "Thanks for making room for us."

"My pleasure!" she says. "We can settle up later, but I need to see your health papers, just to be safe."

Mom has leashed Doc so they can stroll and he can sniff. I dive into the now-empty truck for my horse papers file with the "proof of good health" paperwork that's required to haul horses across state lines. "Totally understand," I say, my hands busy.

I can't find it.

"Brent, do you have the horse papers?" I call, as I recheck the front and back of the truck cab again, switching on the interior lights against the dark.

"What?" he calls from where he's been banging around the horse trailer trying to get the horses unloaded.

I repeat myself.

"No, check the Rover," he calls.

I do.

No papers.

"Sorry," I say to our hostess as I hurry back to the truck to check again.

"Take your time," she smiles.

I don't want this to take time. I'm getting really, really nervous that I don't have the papers at all. Worse, I have no idea where they could be.

"Mom, do you remember seeing the horse papers?" I ask.

She doesn't, and now I am tearing out every loose piece of anything from truck, trailer, and Rover to locate them.

Our hostess has taken pity on us and agreed that we can stable the horses there anyway. She figures that no one would go to all the trouble I'm currently taking, just to pretend not to have papers. My bigger problem is tomorrow. How am I going to get across the state line with no papers? State agricultural inspectors are not known for their indulging sympathy.

"Well, maybe they won't check?" Brent suggests. "They don't always, you know."

"But if they do, they can hold us there or turn us around," Mom points out. "And then we're just in the middle of nowhere and have to find somewhere to get new papers."

I clasp my hands behind my head like a winded sprinter to take a deep breath.

"I can get new records faxed to us from the vet clinics," I say. "But it will take some time."

"Call Reno first," Mom suggests. "Maybe you left them there and someone's turned them in."

"Grand Sierra Resort and Casino," the honeyed voice answers my call. "How can I help you?"

"Lost and found, please," I say weakly.

"Sure thing," the voice assures me.

I hear a click and then, "Lost and found, how can I help you?" The voice sounds older, a little raspy, like a reliable auntie, frequently called to sort out the problems of extended relations.

"I think I left a binder there—a sort of black office binder with horse papers inside," I say.

"Horse papers?" she twangs.

Why is it customer service always sounds more reassuring with a drawl?

"Yeah, papers that have headings like American Quarter Horse Association and Equine Veterinary Hospital," I explain.

"Oh, sure, honey, let me look," the voice says. I wait, hearing rummaging sounds and voices in the background.

"You know, nothing yet, but let me check with security. We only get things hotel guests turn in, but security may always have found something. Can I call you back?" she offers.

Grateful, I give her my number, then turn my leaden arms and legs to the tasks of getting horses settled. Our hostess gives us her fax number to use for when the papers are recovered. She says she doesn't mind us staying longer if we need an extra day to let all the faxes come in.

Normally, an extra day in Vegas would sound like fun, but not when checking in means hauling in a can of dog food, the actual dog, laptop case, suitcase, and other bags that all seem to be getting more heavy and clumsy by the minute.

It's Friday night on South Las Vegas Boulevard, and no available trailer parking is the least of our issues—there's hardly any parking of any kind to be found at the complex of inn and restaurant our hostess has recommended. The rooms are spare and spartan but mostly clean, and the restaurant is busy, which we take as a good sign when we walk in.

The hostess hands us a pager. "Shouldn't be any more than an hour," she tells us cheerily.

Exchanging defeated looks, we brave the bar's clanging and flashing video poker games, thumping music, and clammy crowd to eventually find a table. Propping myself up against the wall beside the booth, I check my phone. Nothing. I call back to Reno three more times before the night is out, and we're all resigned to staying as long as we have to as we turn in for the night. Staying in South Vegas has to be better than being stranded on a state line.

"On the bright side, we have time for a real breakfast tomorrow," Mom says. "There's a sign saying the restaurant serves it."

It turns out that breakfast time is observed differently in this part of Las Vegas.

Awakened early by a fire alarm that went off because of the steam from Brent's shower, I decide to make the best of things and get us all coffee and breakfast from the restaurant.

No one is at the hostess stand at seven a.m., even though it's advertised as 24-hour, so I walk to the bar.

There's a couple with half-empty glasses in front of them, opposite a man clad all in black playing video poker. Another man with his sleeves rolled up sits at the bar with a beer in front of him and a cell phone at his ear. It's as dark as it was last night, but the music has been turned down a couple decibels to good-time '80s rather than the clubby hip-hop that had been blaring the evening before. I don't see a bartender as I pass a bickering couple whose profanities sound like the kindest things they have to say to each other.

I walk in farther, finding the kitchen door.

"Hello?" I ask, tentatively pushing it in.

"Hi there," I hear, turning to see a man carrying a gray bin full of glasses toward the bar.

"Hi," I say. "The sign says 24 hours. Do you do breakfast?"

"Sure," he says, already putting the glasses away under the bar. He straightens to hand me a menu. "What do you want?"

I glance at it quickly, choosing a few items I hope are least like our previous days' to-go orders.

"Sure," the bartender nods. "Simple enough."

Or not.

I look at my cell phone. I count its buttons. I scroll through my contacts. A half hour and an astounding check total later, I push my way out the door, the to-go containers stacked beneath the drink carrier. I make my way gratefully, precariously, and oh-so-carefully toward the truck where Brent, Mom, and Doc are waiting. We break open the Styrofoam and picnic on the hood.

"Oh my God," Brent spurts. "This coffee's cold. I think they made it last night."

"Probably along with these eggs," Mom says, picking through the contents of her box.

"Well," I say, taking a healthy slurp out of my own cup, and then raising it in a toast. "This is a fifty-buck breakfast, so eat hearty."

"Doc?" Mom calls.

Even I give up on the repast after a few minutes. Doc is delighted to scarf down his third cold and runny egg product.

The day's prospects brighten, though, upon our arrival at the barn.

"They're here!" our hostess greets us, jogging outside with a fistful of paper. "They called this morning and I told them which papers to fax and they're here!"

Enormously relieved and with only minor stomach pains, we hook up the trailer, load the horses, and roll toward Arizona.

Viva Las Vegas, but thank God for Reno.

HOW TO SING YOUR WAY
SAFELY DOWN A MOUNTAIN

"So, we have two choices," Mom says as we're approaching Kingman, Arizona, a study in arid. Pale sky and cracked gray of sun-beaten surroundings slip by like the silty earth. It's Day Four, the inedible eggs not a distant enough memory, and we've come to a fork.

"We can take I-40 to I-17 and go all the way around to the Sedona exit and come in that way," Mom says, tracing the long L-shape with a forefinger. "Or we can go south on this smaller highway and try and go east north of Prescott, which should be shorter, but it takes us through Jerome."

I have run two marathons, which is to say jogged, shuffled, and shambled my way across twenty-six miles in less than five hours. "All the way around" lands on my ears the way mile marker twenty-three appeared on the course: less an affirmation of what's behind you than the certainty of a lengthy trudge to go before the finish. "North" and "shorter" sound like bounce, feeling jaunty by comparison to their alternatives. Not having been to Jerome, I know it only by its reputation as a former ghost town. The fact that most ghost towns in Arizona are associated with mining, which usually requires mountains, is as wispy a thought in my mind as the scant clouds beyond the lizard-shaped hills.

"Shorter sounds good," I say wearily.

Mom agrees.

We turn south on State Route 89 at Ash Fork to roll through the deep green of juniper brush that dots the hard-packed ground, reddening the closer we get to Sedona. Or those could just be my eyes.

We call Dad as we pass through Chino Valley.

"Welcome to Arizona!" he crows. "Good for you girls!"

"Thanks, Daddy," I say, relieved the day is clear, the sky is blue, and there's still plenty of daylight left. "Our plan is just to stay on 89 and let it take us all the way to the ranch."

"Oh," he says, his voice an abacus of geographic memory and curiosity. "That means you'll cross over the top of Mingus."

"I guess so," I say, a wrinkle of discomfort creasing my consciousness. I went to a church camp on Mingus Mountain as a sophomore in high school. It was high, hilly, inaccessibly holy—approaching the area again today feels like an invitation to sit beside someone with bad breath. "Mom says it takes us through Jerome."

"Yes, it certainly means that," Dad says, half chuckling. "Well, that will be quite an adventure."

His amusement feels like assigned penance. *Say six Hail Marys and six Our Fathers.* Oh, Lord, have mercy.

"It will?" I ask.

"Well, yeah, those mountain roads really wind around," Dad says. "But I'm sure you can do it."

Oh. No.

"I'm sure we will," I say.

I've been sure about things with the trailer before: the time I was sure I could back in alongside a barn, the time I was sure I could get down the icy hill to make it to my lesson across the flooding river, the time I was sure I could get hooked up and drive myself to a horse show without a copilot. All three times I'd ended up stopping midway, engaging the parking brake, off-loading the horses, and abandoning the quest until I had more help.

About an hour later as we approach the base of Mingus Mountain, we see the sign: "Trucks over 50' in length prohibited."

"Does that apply to us, do you think?" I nervously ask Mom.

"We're going to pretend we didn't see it," she says, taking a swig of her Diet Pepsi and squaring her shoulders.

"Good plan," I say, mentally trying to compute the truck length—it's a short bed, so maybe twelve feet—and the trailer length—a three-horse slant gooseneck—thirty feet?

How do I not know this?

We spiral our way up the hill through scrub oak, juniper, and ponderosa with the occasional prickly pear sticking out from behind a boulder or clump of cliffrose. Up isn't so bad: it winds, it narrows, and there are people who'd rather be doing it faster than we are, but they largely keep their hands off their horns. We breathe a sigh of relief to be on the back side.

Then we see Jerome.

Originally a copper-mining town, from the Old West storefronts we can see that Jerome has now been populated by foodies, vintners, artists, and the tourists all the former attract. It's built into steppes along the side of Mingus Mountain, and its streets look to be about six feet wide with no shoulder, sidewalks crumbling to narrower widths in real time as we pass, and pedestrians oblivious to anything not on the other side of a shop window.

We are no more than two turns into our descent when my front right ankle ligaments begin to ache from braking.

Two more turns and my right knee has joined them.

I am in first gear, I avoid the accelerator as though it's cut glass, and I can smell the hot, acrid warning of failure if this continues much longer.

There is no place to go—nothing to do beyond what I am doing.

My hands are sweating. I rub them against my jeans one at a time.

There's a scene in the movie *Almost Famous* where the lead singer has come back to his tour bus in disgrace after a night away from the tour. Every look smarts with disapproval as he boards. Every normally fractious passenger is seated and staring at anything but each other as their bus gains the highway.

Why that scene finds me now, I don't know, but like them, I begin singing "Tiny Dancer."

A lifelong Elton John fan, Mom joins in, supplying the words I can't remember—an anthem to blue jean babies, sung by two ladies on yet another busy day.

My right ankle is actually shaking from its sustained flex on the brake pedal.

"Your Song" comes as a natural second act as we squeeze through Jerome. Cars, pedestrians, and bicycles clear toward any empty space as we wind through town. We are elephants in a mouse house: bulky, hulking, and commanding of the right of way. Our concern about coming into contact with any locals is in proportion to our size. It's a little bit funny, sighting their shocked hustle; it could also be a lot of other, less pleasant things if anything goes wrong.

We need a third song. This is no moment for "Crocodile Rock." We try for "Rocket Man" but don't know enough of the words.

The pedal under my right foot is vibrating and the trailer brakes grab, jolting the truck with the stress and the heat, bouncing our heads against the seats.

Whether we want to or not, we're bopping, which makes me think of the Beach Boys.

I bleat the first line to "Barbara Ann," thinking how absurd it is to sound like a harmonizing sheep. Ludicrous? Yes. Better than bawling? Also yes—and humiliatingly appropriate to this moment when only woolly-headed rationale can be blamed for ignoring the signs for steep grades and narrow curves.

Can this road even hold the weight of a horse trailer? If we crash, will Brent be able to stop before hitting us? How are his brakes doing? If he crashes into us, can I get Lena and Marty out? Is there a Jaws of Life for horse trailers?

This is no music for switchbacks. I try for a "Peaceful Easy Feeling," but there is none. Perhaps I can channel Mrs. Anna from "The King and I" and whistle a happy tune? Surely Broadway tunes on Mingus Mountain can be no more misplaced than our caravan.

We're about to try for some Doobie Brothers when another lane opens up, traffic pours past us, the grades ease, and we are delivered beyond the hairpins, past the twists, into the safe glory of a gas station—with a level entrance—at the bottom of the hill.

I pull us in, shift to park, then turn off the ignition. We're stopped.

"Good job," Mom says, patting my leg. I collapse against the back of my seat.

A moment passes. Doc raises his head in the back seat, the jangle of his tags reminding me I haven't opened any doors. That's because I haven't moved.

It's strange to see the day sunning past, the sky still blue, junipers still green. We are within a half hour of our final stop, and I marvel, as I did when marathoning, that there could still be more. I have covered every kind of mile. Surpassed the points of reason where someone else should take over. I am on the back side of madness, with only time and tenacity in front of me: open road for only a few minutes more if I will just keep going.

I can smell Brent's vehicle even before it gets off the road. He pulls in behind us.

Mom is apologizing for recommending the route, but her words roll off, as we will in a few moments when we cross the little remaining blacktop before the ragged dirt road that will lead us to the foothills of the Red Rock-Secret Mountain Wilderness and the owned plot in the wild that we call the McKinsey. I don't know the story of the owner behind the name. More than likely, he was someone else who once found himself in a quiet near a crossroads, perhaps with nearby feed store clientele rumbling by. Another recipient of unseeing glances as he pressed on, looking across the pink of a scrubby valley toward a new beginning.

BARBS

In high school, I was assigned an essay: describe the difference between signs and symbols and explain why I'd picked a particular one of each for myself. By definition, a sign is an object that indicates the probable presence of something else, whereas a symbol is something that stands for or represents something else. The difference is subtle, but what unites them is the requirement to know what you're looking at for either of them to be meaningful.

On first glance, barbed wire appears as a definition, a passive deterrent, a simple demarcation suggesting a difference in ownership and use privileges from one side to the next. What the first-glance observer can't know is how far those wires will stretch, how hard they are to see at speed; how unforgiving they are of chance encounter; and how any purposeful handling, even of those strands wound as gates, will come with entanglements.

Every one of my family's owned or managed ranch parcels is fenced with barbed wire for the obvious expedient that it is the cheapest and most easily replaced material available for keeping our herds within lands under our control.

Keeping things in and out is what barbed wire does.

Had I also known what barbed wire meant, I might have taken the barbs as a sign that Brent and I were about to get painfully caught up in hooks we wouldn't see coming, a requisite struggle with harsh cuts dividing any enticing appearance from its protected background.

WHEN TO RANCH
IN RUNNING SHOES

Brent and I embarked on this adventure hoping to become closer. So far, all we've done is spend more time apart. Separated by skill as well as necessity, our workplaces and interests diverge by miles, from the time coffee sluices into the travel mug until we stagger out of our respective vehicles at day's end.

I wonder if the nap of the carpeted steps to our basement quarters is eroding as fast as our intimacy. I had looked forward to our time in the lower level of my parents' mountain home in Flagstaff as a cozy hideaway, a burrowing into love rooted in our mutual passion for nature and its creatures. So far, it's felt no better than suspended slippage. When we're home, we sleep, shower, and change clothes—rarely simultaneously, and none of it together. I can point to where Brent and I spend our time, but I don't know where we are. My hopes of waking and drifting off pillowed by tender, earthy sensuality have shed and clumped like the dog-hair dust bunnies I hurry to vacuum up before they annoy Mom. I hadn't counted on Mom or Dad's almost-constant presence.

I thought they would spend the majority of their time in the home where I grew up outside Phoenix. Mom has pointed out that there's too much work to do for her to leave Flagstaff.

What I feel and cannot say to her, or Brent, and least of all myself, is that Brent and I have too much work to do for her to stay.

She's right in the observation that ranch problems have multiplied, popping up with daisy-fresh alacrity each day like an alarm clock that won't turn off. Our 300 acres is divided into four properties, one pair south of Flagstaff and one pair between Sedona and Cottonwood. One of the latter pair, the parcel we named "the McKinsey" for a former owner, is our winter destination, a seventy-five-minute drive from the house in Flagstaff one way. Summertime will bring more proximity as Oldham Park, the northern headquarters, sits just twenty minutes from our front door. It doesn't help that once Brent reaches the McKinsey each day, he has to leave again to reach wherever the cows are grazing. Nor does it help that getting to or from the McKinsey from the highway is its own adventure. It's accessed off of a series of unpaved and only irregularly maintained forest roads, popular with jeep tours, weekend RV campers, and archeological enthusiasts searching for petroglyphs. Squatters also favor the rolling ground with views of Sedona's mystical red rocks as well as scrub, washes, and gullies that can help hide them from view. Easy, mindless commute, it's not.

Thankfully, Mom has built and imported resources to our property, so once we reach it, we have some supports. Its improvements include: a roping arena; a small, four-stall open-sided barn; a Tuff Shed that acts as our tack room; and four gravel RV pads and hookups, one of which is occupied by a modest travel trailer. These are mostly grouped into the southernmost forty-acre fenced parcel nearest to the road. Two other forty-acre sections accompany it, providing ample winter range for our horse herd to stretch their legs—and mine when it comes to finding them. Water flows from two sources: a precipitation-fed stock tank about two miles away with gravity-flow piping to one of the metal livestock tanks on the upper reaches of our property, and a generator-powered well over twelve hundred feet deep that draws from the limestone aquifer beneath us. Water is distributed using the simple but effective force of gravity, as the upper corner where the well sits is easily over one hundred feet in elevation above the lower reaches of the property.

Besides the Billings horses that the cowboys pronounced useless, there are a few others too lame or unfit to work that accompany Mom and Dad's mustangs and Mom's filly, Bayley, in the herd. My job is to inventory all the ranch-owned horses not currently working on a cowboy string, then identify a path for their sale. The first stop for each of them seems to be either a psychic or a vet.

Cisco is cute and black, a color made popular from books and movies like *Black Beauty* and *The Black Stallion*, but he's lame on at least one side. I'm not sure which leg.

Freckles is still asocial, with a troublesome tendency for stopping dead at mid-stride.

Marvin is bay, brown body with a black mane and tail, chocolate-chip colors with just as lovable a temperament, but he's too young to be ridden, not yet being two years old.

Cali is a speckled and skittish red roan two-year-old, bred on the Babbitt Ranches—northern Arizona's largest and best-known ranch, with an annual colt sale that draws hundreds to its remote location. She is not yet saddle-trained.

Vegas is showgirl flashy, light gray with a black mane and tail, and built with classic quarter-horse curves—in the industry, that's known as "stocky"—but she's even more skittish than Cali.

Twolena, named for her resemblance to my mare, Lena, is small, brown, cow-savvy, and tough, but evidently not tough enough to hold up to either Woods or the ranch—we're not yet sure which.

Dozer is a palomino the color of maple syrup, rather than the buttermilk pancakes Freckles resembles, and as he's also that sweet, he's become Brent's go-to choice for his cattle-gathering days, even if Dozer is also as slow as syrup in the cold.

The herd may look intimidating, but its caretaker is fierce.

Cody is probably in his late twenties or early thirties in age but much older in miles, carrying a wicked knife and a dodgy outlook on life that are probably remnants from the military missions he occasionally refers to using a tone that discourages follow-up questions. He works for a neighboring property—a religious retreat center of dubious authenticity. He's hired on with our ranch to feed and water our herd on his way to and from his other job, but he's gone well beyond what we've asked of him. From the stories Mom has told me, this winter was unnaturally cold, and our pipes responded by breaking almost daily. Cody manhandled all of them back into working order, but sadly his fixes were more scrappy than sustained, presenting us with a lot more permanent work to do.

Flagstaff in March is mostly brown, so the descent to budding lower altitudes feels uplifting, the drive colored with new blooms each day. Hope seems to work the same way. Each morning dawns with fresh opportunity for gains: in our familiarity with our new world, in horse health, in calf births, and even with Brent and me, still newly enough arrived to thrill a little at pulling on work boots for the day. Yet, by evening, the steps we made by day feel small unto inconsequential compared to the mountain of work we have yet to undertake—an image amplified by the climb back home.

We don't even discuss living at the McKinsey. The travel trailer comes equipped with kitchenette, bathroom, and sleeping quarters, but my guess is we both see that there would be no room for avoiding uncomfortable topics, especially those caused by one another. We talk around the possibility of living there permanently, pointing out reasons why we'd rather not. Brent says he needs a reliable internet connection for the days he spends out of the saddle trying to plan and network. I mention not wanting to be left on my own out there should Brent have to be away. Neither of us spends much time brainstorming alternatives for our hesitations.

Which is why daily life develops a certain rhythm: wake before the sun, ascend from the basement, descend into work, smile at the blooms and the impossible views, run the generator to power the well, catch and work with two or three horses, catch and work with another two or three horses, clean the barn, check stock tank water levels and, inevitably, fix a new leak. It only took two days of this routine for me to exchange boots for running shoes when I'm doing anything other than riding. Within two weeks, I've dropped five pounds.

Lena and Marty have some special shoes as well, fitting like coveralls over their hooves on days we think we'll be riding through rough ground. The ground around the McKinsey is red and dense and mostly silty, but there are rough patches, and I'm taking no chances with Lena, whose show career was brief with me due to long episodes of lameness. We've opted not to shoe, but just trim them, figuring it will be better for their feet and save us money over the long run.

This is one decision of the few on which Brent and I agree since moving. I feel like we're cuckoo-clock figurines winding in and out of time but never touching. His mind is often somewhere else: the branding campaign he wants to launch to promote our cattle as local, natural beef; the contacts he wants to make within retail and merchandising to start a ranch store; the roping and rodeo events he wants to host to promote the ranch as both the place and the icon he wants to build it into. I want to see him succeed, but even more, I want to see him happy. I blame myself that he hasn't been—that maybe I haven't offered him enough love or affirmation, being so consumed with completing my own tasks that I've neglected helping him with his. I also suspect that I don't want what he does. Branded beef and rodeos would be fine with me, but I see the store in terms of a massive capital outlay and minimal upsides. If it were up to me, the events would come first, creating a community and potential test market for the store, but Brent wants it the other way around. I tell myself there's so much I don't know yet—that Brent deserves the chance to explore those prospects in the order that presents itself to him, just as I deserve to develop my herd in the way that makes sense to me. Most days, I'm talking to myself about him more than I'm talking to him, and I'm losing patience with the already tired conversation.

When Mom and Dad propose an exploratory trail ride, I'm a quick yes. All of us need a holiday from trying to fix what's broken—a list that populates faster than we can wrangle remedies.

Lena and Marty aren't tall horses; less than five feet at the shoulder or, in horse-speak, less than fifteen hands. They've also been bred for athleticism rather than sturdy platforms, but Lena's teeny feet still don't make fastening her overshoes on any easier.

One after the other, I work the stubborn, form-fitting rubber over the sole of the hoof, then tighten, adjust, shift, and tighten again. It's an ordeal that takes me longer than anticipated, and Brent, Mom, and

Dad are already mounted and finding little errands to do on horseback until I'm aboard.

My parents lead us out on their mustangs, stopping at our first gate to the horse pasture at the top of the hill. We have to cross through this to get to any of the choice of trails beyond the property. If we walk out the main gate, we'd have to walk through the "neighborhood" of proximate ranchette owners irritated at the increased activity on our property, then go down the road and through a "ranch gate" by a cattle guard. I don't love grappling with our metal gates, but the ranch gates would be far worse: wicked strands of barbed wire held together by wooden stays that have atrophied to eager splinters, with a loop at the top to wrestle over a narrow T-post, if you're lucky, or a thick, railroad-tie H-brace if you're not.

"I'll get it!" I call from the back, saving my folks the trouble of getting off and then on again. The gates are metal, hung from railroad ties pounded vertically into the ground to anchor the barbed-wire fencing that stretches in eight-foot sections between posts. As the ground shifts with weather and compaction from livestock feet, posts shift and gates get sticky. Today is no exception.

I flip up the keeper, then pull back on the handle.

It sticks.

I put some weight behind it, and the bar lock slides a little more.

Looping my reins in the crook of my elbow, I push up on the gate and then pull back on the bar, hearing the handle clang as I yank it home.

"After you," I call, before I see that the horse herd, interested in an open gate, is now on its way. "Quickly!"

"Go on!" Mom calls to the milling herd as she reins Sage through the daylight between the gate and the fence. "Go on!"

She waves her arms, but three horses in the coming herd advance and Sage pins his ears, rebuking their pushy approach.

Dad reins in behind Mom, trying to close the gap between her and the still-open gate. "Hey!" he calls. "Hey! Hey!" He too is waving his arms and slapping at his pant leg, trying to scare the herd back, but all he does is spook Sage, who crow-hops forward then sideways into the barbed-wire pasture fence.

"Ow!" Mom screeches, but Cheyenne is on a mission now, pushing past Sage into the herd's leading three horses, who retreat at the fold of her ears, almost flat against her neck.

"Move!" Mom calls as she reins Sage off the fence line, trying to dislodge herself from its barbs. Mom wears a kind of heeled tennis shoe whose laces get caught as she twists her foot to free herself from the fence.

There's scuffling, swearing, and pushing, but finally, Mom is loose, Dad and Brent are through, the herd horses have backed away, and Lena and I can enter the pasture, closing the gate behind us.

The whole process takes less than two minutes, but it feels like a week.

"You OK, Mom?" I ask as she pulls her leg up to examine the rip the barbs cut through her jeans.

"Yeah," she says cautiously. "I'm lucky it just got my pants and not my skin. Maybe boots next time—less to get stuck."

She and I trail Brent and Dad, who are climbing over the next hill. We relax into the ride as we get farther into the pasture, variously following old game trails and picking our own ways through the juniper. Then I see Brent dismounting.

Another gate.

The good part is that we don't have to fend off a charging herd. The bad part is that this gate is secured by exceptionally heavy chain and a lock that's too small for the links.

"Maybe we add the gates to the list of things to fix?" Mom suggests after another lengthy fight to get us all through. "We'd have a lot more fun if they were more user-friendly."

⊂━⊃

At this point, fun sounds as likely, transitory, and potentially dangerous as sighting a mountain lion.

⊂━⊃

We follow an old forest track out to the backyard-size seasonal pond known as Black Tank, north of our property by about a mile. The scents of cool morning, damp conifer, and warm horse surround me as we ease across the gentle red hills. Lena's ears prick. She flips her nose a few times, enjoying the spring air and the other horses in the new surroundings. She and I haven't been out much because of the move, and I forgot the healing sway of her gait—she ripples. I can't help grinning as I feel the miraculous sensation of power and grace in the fluid motion beneath me.

Nothing feels like this. I have ridden horses of all kinds for almost thirty years. I have ridden in a Cadillac—even a Ferrari. I have zip-lined, hot-air-ballooned, whitewater-rafted, canoed, and kayaked. I've reveled in sensations ranging from lust to love that are the stuff of all the Freudian jokes about being a horsewoman. With respect to all of them: Nothing. Feels. Like. This.

The area around the ranch is known as a "chaparral forest." High desert—about 4,000 feet in elevation. Plants are squat: prickly pear and hedgehog cactus paddle horizontally against the gritty earth; oak, juniper, and coarse grasses tuft rather than spread. I raise my head to the cry of a hawk, spotting it circling in the distance.

Black Tank opens up in front of us, a shimmer beyond clumpy clover and vining weed that spring's frolic presents as parklike.

Letting a horse water sounds pastoral, but it involves pushing and prodding to get the horses to step through the ooze of mud at the tank edges to where they can reach the green and brackish fluid. Giant suction sounds echo each horse's step as we urge our horses out of the pond, which is sort of funny, until I realize that Lena is missing a boot.

Great—I get to go wading.

Lena watches me curiously as I walk to the edge of dry ground and remove my boots, then my socks, roll up my jeans, and ease into the muck, soft slime squirting up between my toes. I forbid myself to think of water snakes, crawfish, leeches, or other creepers as disgust crawls across my skin.

I plunge my hands in, mixing and stirring to search, but despite my effort, the boot just seems lost, sucked down into the spring mud, not to return again until the dry spells of summer, if ever.

I step back onto dry ground, then pretzel my legs to wipe my feet as best I can on the legs of my jeans.

Tank Pilates, the latest thing in exercise for ranchers.

Once I pull socks and boots back on, I remount, and Lena and I pick our way carefully back toward the ranch.

Midway, my thigh begins to itch.

I keep rubbing at it off and on over the hour it takes to get back to the barn. When a necessary biological break time allows me to examine the area, I realize the source of the trouble.

Ants. I must have sat in an anthill back at the tank.

Red welts and black smudges dot my quadriceps and inner thigh.

The next day, scratching, I call the farrier to schedule Marty and Lena for a shoe job. From now on, they will wear horseshoes. Mom will wear boots. Only I will wear shoes that can be tightened by straps, ties, or anything else adjustable. But never horseback through gates.

HOW TO PRACTICE
RANCH YOGA

It is a true and humbling part of life to realize that, at some point, one's body simply will not do all that one might ask of it without some additional support. This becomes quickly true of my own body after only two months of ranching, but it is equally and more alarmingly true of several of our herd: Bayley has uneven hips, Cisco can't hold a right lead, Lena is still off on her right front, and poor Freckles just seems to hurt all over.

Mom has told me about Susan, an equine bodyworker she found to help with Bayley's particular physical challenges. Bayley and Mom have hip and spine issues in common, though Bayley as a filly was diagnosed as having a twisted pelvis—something that likely happened as the result of a bad fall when she was a yearling on the range of northern Arizona. Mom bought her at the spring Babbitt sale, where the practice is to buy a foal, then come back six to nine months later at weaning time for pickup. When Mom and I trailered in, Bayley had loaded resentfully into the trailer. She had played as any weanling would with my filly when they pastured together to grow up to training age. Only, when my filly was ready for a saddle, Bayley was much less so, needing months more to be able to bear a rider's weight. Years and moves and careful administrations by vets and chiropractors later, Bayley's hips are almost level, and she and Mom enjoy their rides.

I was prepared to already respect Susan for her skill in helping a horse past its pain; I was not prepared to be intimidated by her strength and badassery. A firefighter by profession, Susan has leg muscles that show through her jeans, and her arm muscles dance as she moves horse legs around as though they were swimming-pool noodles. This after finishing a twenty-four-hour shift, driving the hour and a half it takes to get to our ranch, and sustaining herself with a whole two bananas.

In Susan's skilled hands, I see Bayley angle and lift her knee into a kind of "pigeon stretch," balancing on her forehand as Susan lifts alternate rear hooves to mobilize the hips. Susan presses her thumbs into Bayley's gluteal muscles along the hamstring, and Bayley arches into a "cat/cow stretch." Susan stretches a foreleg out in front, reaching Bayley out almost into "child's pose," and Bayley's shoulder drops into even carriage with its other side. Susan stretches the same leg back, a "crescent pose," and the neck and shoulder stretch, forgetting the strain of days long past. I hear audible pops as joints release while Bayley sighs into a flat and sleepy pose—her old hurts stretching into smooth tissue.

To complete the session, with Bayley still in a relaxed state of bliss, Susan walks her out to the arena, removes her halter, then slaps its lead against her leg or the ground with a charged "Ya!"

Bayley startles alert, but Susan doesn't give her time to think.

"Ya!" she calls again, sweeping both arms up.

Bayley crow-hops before trotting off, snorting.

Susan is there with the lead rope before the mare can stop: *Slap!* Bayley is off, running, racing down the fence line.

"Yes!" Susan calls, running after Bayley. Now they're jogging, turning to run the other way, Susan chasing, Bayley stretching out stride, delighting in unlimited range, painless movement.

"They have to know they don't hurt anymore!" Susan calls to me as she jogs toward the horse to slap-start her into another run. "I want them to run because they know they can!"

It's amazing to watch the difference in the horse that initially walked uncertainly toward Susan with a timid and uneven gate, now sporting around as though she has never known soreness nor strain.

Susan laughs as she joins me at the fence. "This is what makes horses so fun." Her breath comes fast, but she's hardly winded. "They don't hold on to their pain. Once it's gone, it's gone, and they just move on."

"Wow," is all I can manage, wondering if she does marriages. "Do you ever work with people?"

She shakes her head, chuckling. "I used to, but—" she waves off the idea. "Horses are a lot easier to work with. They smell better too."

I concede both points as we take in how Bayley plays—truly plays—because now she can.

It's on Susan's advice that I next engage the services of a horse dentist—specifically a dentist rather than a vet.

"Most vets don't really believe in dentistry," Susan says. "They just want to fix what's broken. But a good dentist can really help you get the tooth and jaw angles right. I mean, it's just like people. Everything begins in the mouth. If you get the jaw right, everything else will fall into place."

She traces the angle of her own jaw with a forefinger. "See, if the teeth are too sharp and the horse has to hold its head a certain way to keep from cutting himself on the edges, then the angle's off up to the poll," she says, motioning to the top of her head as I envision the point between the horse's ears. "Holding his head in that way to stop the jaw pain next stresses the spine," she points down her back. "Then sometimes to try and relieve the spine, or if the angle is also crooked, a hip will go out," she gestures along her side.

I feel myself leaning on my own hip and self-correct to stand up straight. Susan's posture, I notice, is perfect.

"Feet are a big deal too. If a horse is standing too tall on its ankle because you cut the toe and not the heel, or too low on the heel because the toe's too long or the heel's too shallow, they change their movement to compensate, and that binds everything up." She's been gesturing to the horse's body parts. Now she casts her hand as though trying to toss away the possibility of an irrevocable problem: "Of course, some things just go out, like they do on people."

The metaphor is almost too powerful to touch. If our foundations are flawed, if too much has been allowed to develop off-kilter, we can never grow what we want. Likewise, none of the structural components of a life or relationship can operate without affecting the whole; pain in one place will eventually spread. I had never before thought of pain as a kind of cancer, the inevitable diffusive atrophy of all it touches. Now, it seems I can see little else, as emotional and physical pain manifest in the ranch, with its stuttering management causing such headaches for Dad, Brent, Mom, and me—likely the cowboys too. What the horses show us are micro-examples of how untended hurts will only grow, and, conversely, how comparatively little it takes to heal them.

Susan works on Cisco next. He'll take his right lead only under a lot of pressure, and he can't hold it. In no more time than it took me to utter this background, Susan has explored every joint from withers to hock.

She steps back to his right-side rib cage, running both hands together along the line of each rib as though trying to pry open a door with no handle. Her fingers pause, settling into contact with something that makes her crinkle her brow, before kneading in to grip and pull back once. The precision of the move is almost percussive—the exquisitely timed strike of a master against timpani. Cisco shifts, testing his weight on all four feet before standing solidly, licking his lips, a gesture in the horse world most closely akin to saying, "Yep, you've got it."

"See, this horse just had a rib out," Susan says as she rubs, nudging along each of his vertebrae, checking for any other issues. "He couldn't lope to the right because it hurt too much to push his hip in to where the rib was squeezing back."

"I thought it was maybe a behavior problem," I say, shuffling my feet, feeling a little embarrassed. "Then I thought maybe he didn't know how to take a right lead, so I should take some time and really get him set up, really kind of muscle him into it." I wince at the memory. "But when he kept not taking the lead, I thought something must be wrong."

She laughs. "It was!"

I swallow. I hate the idea that my own puny understanding might have caused a horse greater pain.

"It'll be interesting to see what you find with Freckles," I say. "The first time I rode him and stopped him, I barely touched my reins and he tossed his head up, then flew backwards like I had jerked on him to shut him down. I've never seen anything like it."

She furrows her brow. "Maybe teeth," she muses. "Maybe a hot nail in his shoe. Was he limping?"

"No. That's why I didn't know what was wrong." I pat Cisco. "Same thing with this horse. He wasn't favoring a leg, so I didn't know."

She nods. "Yeah, it's hard sometimes."

Anxious to contribute something helpful, I spell Susan off from the post-therapy sprints. She watches as I do the release-and-chase with Cisco. Just as Bayley did, when Cisco's halter is off, he bucks and plays, racing down the fence.

On the right lead!

I jog over to head him off, sending him down the fence the other way.

Again, he picks up the right lead!

"Funny!" I shout to her.

Susan is laughing. "Yep—guess we fixed it!"

Cisco, very proud of all the attention he's getting, canters around me, tail high in a right circle on the right lead.

"OK, boy," I call out to him. "I'm happy for you too."

Susan works on Lena and Freckles, but with not quite the same brilliant results. Lena still has a hitch in her forehand, and Freckles still seems sad. He keeps his neck low as he trots off, but mostly what he wants to do is roll around in the arena dirt.

Susan laughs. "That's great!" she calls out. "He's working his spine himself! It's healthy!"

Freckles seems to agree as he rolls himself from vertical to one side, to vertical, to the other side, his legs kicking into the air, his tail sweeping beneath him on the ground. He rolls himself up to stand, sneezes, shakes, then pricks his ears.

It's the first notice I've seen him take of anything outside his own body.

"He's better," Susan assures me. "Didn't you see his whole energy shift? Like he just woke up to the world. He doesn't have to focus on how bad he feels. Now he can be interested in other things."

I wonder if that's also how it works with people—if pain is so selfish in any species as to demand all attention be paid to its voice. How much do we miss by only listening to its keenings; but then again, how much can we blame ourselves for what goes by without our knowledge?

I am not trained as a pain specialist. In my life and career, both my training and experience have been to evaluate future options by a set of metrics generated today. While that evaluation absolutely seeks not to cause harm, it gives only a cursory look into each option's cumulative effects, and then only with an eye toward incremental impacts. I know that the pain I'm observing, both in these horses and in my relationship, didn't start with me, but I also know that mid-trauma is no time to try to differentiate the specific bit I may have caused.

Oh, sorry—but you know, most of that hurt is because you've been hurt before. I just accidentally hit a sore point.

Taking responsibility had been emphasized in my lessons from church, school, and family. When I was old enough to ride, the first lessons were in taking and remaining in control. I was nothing if not a devoted student, trying each day to demonstrate mastery of what I learned. Now, I wondered if I'd missed the point of the lessons. Yes, personal responsibility is important, but shouldn't it stop at the limits of the next student's desk? Of course I must control my horse, but do I also expect myself to control the circumstances by which it comes to me or how its needs or body might change just because life changes the living?

How could I not recognize that I have been in a world of hurt applying the lessons I know, only to find that what I know doesn't apply?

Freckles is the one in the herd I judge to need the most help, so I have him in the barn when the horse dentist arrives.

Greta is a horse dentist who has been practicing for thirty years. She spurns power tools and has affixed her tools to the grip end of golf clubs to provide length and leverage to do her work by hand. Arriving exactly on time, she climbs from her red sports car, a tall and strong-looking woman with short, dark hair and a crisp collared shirt. She shoulders her golf bag and asks, "Could I have a bucket of water?"

I scurry to fill a bucket, watching her identify an empty stall with some shade, set her golf bag on its stand, and don a headlamp. Next, she withdraws a bottle of, no kidding, Listerine.

"Right here," she says, gesturing next to the bag. I place the bucket where she points. She pours a healthy dollop into the bucket as I snatch a halter and hustle off to move Freckles into the stall where she can work on him.

Docile as he is, he walks placidly along beside me, giving Greta an ample study of his movement.

"How long has he been sore?" she asks.

"I don't know," I answer. "I've been here a few months, and this is how he was when I arrived. Maybe something happened to him when the cowboys had him out?"

She nods, walking to his left shoulder. She lets him watch her as she rubs his shoulder, neck, then reaches for his poll. Within seconds, she's standing in front of him, hands grasping either side of his head below the ears.

"I'm feeling where his jaw connects," she says. "I can see why he's sore. He's all bound up in there."

Without meaning to, I work my own jaw as I stand to the side.

She steps in to take off his halter, then loops white cord around his neck. Freckles drops his head, compliant and completely unconcerned.

"It's better if they're free," she explains. "If they want to step here or there it's fine—I'll go with them."

The last dentist I saw do his work used tranquilizers to keep the horse completely still, so this is new to me.

I have no one to ask about the last time Freckles or any of the other ranch horses I am now caring for had their teeth "floated." This is an odd term that someone must have picked at random to substitute for its meaning: a wet, awkward, and labored process of filing the sharp edges off a horse's teeth. Naturally, the horse does not love the idea of someone sticking her arm into his mouth, much less running a file over the edges of his molars, though Greta appears surprisingly free of resentful chomp marks. This may be due to the jaw-locking halter Greta uses: the horse takes the metal part of the halter into his mouth, much as he would a bit on a bridle. An adjustable mechanism allows the dentist to adjust the hinge to progressively open the jaws until the horse stands, agape, ready for work—a posture not unlike my own the first few times I see this done.

I step out of the stall as Freckles obediently takes his jaw piece. Greta adjusts it once, and Freckles shakes his head. She raises a hand to adjust it once more, but he jerks his head, backing up as though she'd cracked a whip.

"OK," Greta says calmly, "we'll just ratchet that back a little." She adjusts the hinge, allowing Freckles' mouth to close. "Let's just take a feel."

She works her hand into his mouth along the side of his teeth. I cringe, thinking that at any minute Freckles is going to shake the headpiece off and bite down.

"Ah ha!" Greta crows. "Well, that would be the problem."

She retrieves an iron from her bag headed with a palm-size file as though selecting a club for her next shot down the fairway. In one practiced motion not unlike a professional's backswing, she inserts the file end into Freckles' mouth, sites it along the cheek side of his teeth, and pulls. The file grates with a resonant sound reminding me of kids skinning their knees on a lacquered gym floor. She pulls a second and third time, then tests her work with a finger. "Big ol' hooks. Huge. Poor guy. They were so sharp he couldn't move his head without poking his cheek into them." She resumes her filing, each pull deliberate and measured.

Not having Greta's fearlessness when it comes to testing teeth, I have not inserted my fingers into Freckles' or any other horse's mouth. This is the difference between an amateur rider and a ranch owner, I realize. The privileges available to a hobbyist hiring scheduled care from a boarding stable's list of contacts cannot apply here.

"I had no idea," I mutter, gutted again by how much I've missed.

"Yep," Greta says. "Most people don't."

I want to explain myself—to absolve myself of the guilt that I've damaged someone else undeserving of it. "I was riding him and I pulled back a little to stop, and he completely flipped out, so I knew—"

"Oh!" Greta cuts me off. "He would have gone into orbit! See, out in nature horses eat all kinds of things that wear down their teeth, but domestic horses don't. Without that grinding, the tooth grows out and up into these pointy spikes we call 'hooks.' So now, imagine biting down on a fork with your tooth shaped like a piece of barbed wire that cuts your cheek every time you close your jaw. It would have been torture for him!"

"Yeah," I say, sickened. "We didn't ride long."

I remember that day so clearly, shuddering as I recall the details for her. "He'd been so light to ride, so easy. We loped along a few strides and I'd said whoa, raising my hand a little. He ducked his head and flew backwards. The overreaction scared me, so then I overreacted—"

She chuckled. "Yep."

"And spurred him forward," I winced, ashamed of myself now, "which meant he couldn't help hitting the bridle again, so off he goes backwards another time. Now I understand what was happening, but I had no idea then—I just thought he was being willful enough to have to correct."

She shrugged, still focused on Freckles' mouth. "We do what we learn to do."

Got it in one.

In my family, marriage is forever. No one, on either side of the family tree, has ended a marriage by any other means than death by natural causes. Besides which, I have been a devoted, if not practicing, Christian all my life, and the day I said "I do," I said it before God as not just a personal promise but a sacrament of the church. It's through these fully committed, unwavering lenses that I have viewed Brent's and my relationship, which is looking like the marital equivalent to Freckles, an unseen or unacknowledged backstory spearing us into hasty retreats. The only response I will accept from myself is to keep trying, never mind the setbacks, though, in our case, going probing to find the source of the anguish sounds like sticking my hand in an unhinged mouth.

About forty-five minutes after Greta finishes filing down the hooks, Freckles is actually trotting around in the arena where I've turned him out. I jog with him, petting him when he stops. His ears are up, his eyes are bright, his tail swishes, and his coat sparkles, losing the grayish tinge that had reminded me of a buttermilk pancake flipped into campfire ashes. Now he's a surfer, blond highlights catching the breeze and the sun as he coasts through the remaining afternoon.

What a difference when we get the care we need.

HALTERING AND OTHER
ILL-FATED RECKONINGS

When the calendar turns to May, Dad wants to meet at Oldham Park to plan the move there for the summer season. I look forward to the meeting not only for the planning but for some time with Brent on a shared task.

Days are getting hot down on the McKinsey, even without the friction building between Brent and the cowboys. He's never invited to ride with them, and when he decides to join, either his presence is barely tolerated or he's assigned to more distant trails. He hasn't learned enough to feel authoritative about either the herd or the grazing lands, but even if he had, his comments make it clear that his authority would be resented.

"I think the only reason they haven't pushed me off a cliff is because I buy lunch," Brent says when I ask how things are going.

For me, the move to Oldham feels like the "real" ranch promise being realized at last—the last few months of separate tasks and geographies just a prolonged warm-up. Judging from Brent's defeated expression, though, moving to the higher pinelands doesn't represent a chance for cooling off as much as a simmering pot about to boil over.

Dad has already opened the tack room by the time we arrive. A bay and a chestnut horse are standing in the yard around where the trailers were parked last fall.

I notice the chestnut is limping.

Dad had said the cowboys might drop off a couple horses early, but I can hardly fathom the idea of leaving livestock where no one is yet living full time. Still, the stock tank is full of water and there's grass in the park, so I suppose these two have been left resourced.

"The cowboys are accustomed to using all the saddle racks to store their gear," Dad says to us as he gestures inside the now-open tack room. "I've never seen any empty slots in here by the time they move in."

Brent and I look around, nonplussed. The tack room has one bare bulb at the top, eight saddle racks to the right of the ancient refrigerator humming at its center, and filthy metal shelves along the facing wall next to the door that accesses the feeding manger on the building's other side. It's clear that mice are very fond of everything the cowboys have stored inside the small building, as there's evidence of them everywhere.

"We've got portable saddle stands we can bring up," I say. "Brent and I have some that we used in Washington, and we bought a set this spring when we moved to McKinsey so we could set up that tack room. We can bring all that up here."

Because what we really want to do is move a bunch of stuff again.

"Oh, good!" Dad says, obviously relieved. "That's great, then."

"What about the bridle racks?" I ask, mentally inventorying all the tack we'll be moving. "Do the cowboys use all of them, too?"

I try to keep the edge from my voice but can't help feeling that Dad is overly deferential to his ranch employees. I wonder if the orientation he intended today was to cowboy norms rather than to facility layout.

"No," he says thoughtfully. "I think they only use a couple. I've never actually seen them full. So, you could probably share them."

I nod.

Brent does not respond, which worries me. I know he hasn't enjoyed his exchanges of ranch information with my father. He's said they've been pretty one-sided, with Dad speaking and Brent listening. He also says Dad hasn't sounded interested in any of his marketing or merchandising ideas.

"When will the cowboys move in?" I ask.

"Woods usually starts moving in a little bit at a time before Memorial Day. I don't know why, because he always leaves that weekend to go to the rodeo in Williams."

Dad's words drift off, and I know he's thinking about last summer when Ty, my second cousin, employed by the ranch, insisted on participating in the wild horse competition. Horses that have never been touched by humans before are let loose into the arena, and the competitors have to rope, saddle, bridle, and ride a horse across some distance to be declared the winner. Ty broke his leg in the process, which would have been bad enough, but it was made much worse because he never purchased the health insurance Dad had paid him to buy. He'd come back asking to make a workers' comp claim to try and defray some of the hospital costs. Dad refused, pointing out that Ty was not actually working when he was at the rodeo. The recovery had been slow and painful, and Ty hadn't been able to ride again until early this spring, which is why he hadn't been around when Brent and I rode part of roundup last fall. From both Brent's and Dad's stories, it sounded as though the leg had healed faster than the grudge Ty still had that Dad wouldn't pay his hospital bills.

"Anyway, they'll probably start moving a few things in here and there in between now and that weekend," Dad finishes, his jaw tight.

"And the two cowboy horses already here?" I ask Dad. "Is anyone checking on them?"

Brent's jaw tightens now. This should be his information to share, but he doesn't have it. He is supposed to be managing the cow part of the ranch, including the cowboys, but Woods never calls Brent back. All cowboy questions are always directed to Dad, and Dad and his business manager, Rachel, control the ranch purse strings.

Brent and I have tangled a few times over horses too. The last couple times Brent went gathering with the cowboys, he wanted to take Freckles, Vegas, or Twolena, but I refused, saying they weren't ready for ranch work. He'd argued they'd never be ready for it if they never did it. I told him it was thinking like that that got them hurt in the first place. Since then, relations between us had been chilly enough to cool even the most sweltering sun, but I'd gathered from Brent's few comments that by comparison to his time with the cowboys, our interaction was positively toasty.

"When he called to tell me he was dropping them off, Woods said something about one of them being sore," Dad says, reaching for the memory. "I think I remember that."

"I saw one was limping when we drove up," I say carefully.

"Oh, really?" Dad asked.

We're approaching tender ground. I have told Dad all the work I've been doing and hiring in to get horses back to full health and utility. It's involved chiropractors and dentists, but also farriers and vets, and the bills have been substantial. They were also avoidable, in my mind, if the cowboys had given the new horses some time, care, or conditioning before just taking them out on the range. I may feel bad about my ignorance, but I judge the cowboys should feel worse. At least I'd seen that things were seriously wrong after just one ride. Either the cowboys hadn't noticed or hadn't said they'd noticed problems, which was why I arrived to a herd of surprises—the least of which being the story I'd finally heard of why Dozer was available to Brent. On his tryout day on the range, the cowboys had ridden him so hard Dozer dropped to his knees, trying to lie down.

I take an old halter from where it was dropped, forgotten on the floor. The two horses, curious, have wandered into the yard between the hay barn and the tack room. There's grass out in the pasture, but they're used to eating alfalfa, and I wonder if they're hungry. The cowboys hadn't left any hay when they dropped the horses off. At least there's still water from the stock tank—a pit with built-up sides about twenty-five yards square that fills with water from rain and snow runoff.

I step toward the pair, casually carrying the halter. Both horses prick their ears.

Brent quietly strolls along behind us, hands in his pockets.

I shrug my shoulders, unsure as I think back through all my files. "I think the red one's Slick," I say, referring to the tall chestnut with the white sock leg markings and the limp. "I don't know about the other one."

"It might be Buster," Dad says, stepping over to get a better look.

Buster or not, the bay horse raises his head and backs away warily. The chestnut raises his head, too, but doesn't move.

Looking closer, I can see a lump and a gash on his foreleg. I point to it. "That would be the problem—he must have cut himself."

"Oh, dear," Dad says. His tone sounds the same as the days he tried to help me balance, the first few times I rode a bicycle without training wheels. Falls on the gravel didn't just hurt, they bled, and so did Dad's voice when he got to me.

Buster wants no part of our concern, wheeling into the red horse to push them both off to a safe distance near the far corral, the red horse limping the whole way.

"Yeah, that would be Buster," Dad says. "Everyone says he's hard to catch."

"Stay here a minute, will you?" I ask Brent and Dad. "Maybe they just don't want to be ganged up on."

I walk slowly toward the two horses, keeping my hands low, my body quiet.

Buster watches my every step with swiveling ears, as though any minute I could blast him with a bullhorn.

Slick inclines his ears as though I'd played a few bars of a song he knew once and might like to hear again.

Step by step, I get closer. I let the halter hang from my hand, making no move to raise it. A few steps later I am at Slick's side with a good view of the gashed leg. I rub his neck and shoulder, noting swelling and dried blood but nothing oozing yellow.

I keep crooning and rubbing, slowly raising the halter to Slick's head, wanting to clean the wound if he'll let me.

With a snort, he backs away, turning to Buster, who's only too happy to put more distance between himself and anything that might trap him into work.

"See if you can stop them on that end," I call behind me toward Dad and Brent as I run around the hay barn, trying to cut the horses off from galloping into the open pasture.

When I look again, I see we're all running in some kind of scatter-shot defense pattern to close, block, approach, and regroup as the horses wheel and turn and quickly outdistance and outmaneuver us.

Flagstaff is over 7,000 feet in elevation, and despite the miles I've been hiking over McKinsey's hills each day, I'm soon sucking air.

"Hold it!" I call to Dad and Brent.

The horses trot off around the chutes toward the open pasture. We follow at a winded walk.

"Maybe we could push them into the arena," Dad suggests. "Brent, if you'll stand by the gate and get it as soon as they're in, maybe that would work."

Brent shrugs, but walks for the near gate as Dad and I continue south with the idea of pushing the horses back up to the northern enclosures.

Let me just say that there is no sneaking up on a horse, especially in open territory. As casual as we might try to appear, the horses know very well what we're up to, and their ears track our every move. They do allow us to get on the south side of them, but it's an easy game for them to split Dad's and Brent's and my coverage until we're tired, frustrated, and winded again.

Never try zone defense against an experienced horse.

"The saddest thing for me," I say after we concede the scrimmage, "is that the horses associate being caught with something they don't want. I've never had horses run from me before."

Removing his hat, Dad says, "These horses know that when they're caught, they'll be working all day. And the ground we've got isn't good to work on. It's rocky and craggy and hard and it hurts."

I nod, remembering that Ritter Pasture, where we rode together over Labor Day, is one of the better parts.

"But then they hurt," I point out to Dad, "and they're just allowed to. Why would Woods put a lame horse up here with no attention? The horse is bleeding, and he turns him out anyway?"

Dad shrugs. "Well—"

"And the other horses I've been trying to help," I continue, too indignant to stop. "Some have been badly shod or haven't had their teeth done in nobody knows how long. I get that the choices are hard work or extra expense, but why not let you as owner know there's a problem and then ask you to pick one?"

"The cowboys have always been told not to spend any money," Dad says. "It isn't their fault."

"But that's stupid!" I say. "They may have been told that before, when you weren't running things, but now you are! Have they ever heard 'Don't spend any money' from you?"

"No—"

"No! And the horses are what makes this whole place go, so why wouldn't they take care of their stock?"

I'm near shouting now. I've had it with seeing animals broken and busted up, then abandoned to "heal themselves."

Dad rounds on me. "You cannot expect that the ranch horses will or should receive the same kind of care you've given to your show animals."

Unwittingly, I take a step back. Dad is first and foremost a kind and thoughtful man, deeply committed to justice and compassion. We have been running buddies and carpool partners, united by faith and family. Always, he has been "Daddy" to me. He has olive skin, and hazel eyes that go dark and moist when he's tender and blazing hot when he's mad. They crackle now, and their intensity is a little frightening.

"I don't," I say, swallowing.

We start walking again.

I try for a more measured tone. "The cowboys may be great at gathering and branding and fixing fence and everything else involving the cattle, but they're poor horsemen. I don't think they take good enough care of their horses because more of them keep showing up for me to fix. I think it's avoidable, and I know it's costly."

Dad shakes his head as he works his jaw. "I think you need to respect the job they do," he says. "They go to work at three in the morning and don't stop until every cow is in. They work in the snow, they work in the rain, they work in the heat. They work in the worst of the storms. They had to tie themselves to trees to keep from being blown away in the storm last fall, did you know that?!"

I nod, remembering the story. I do not ask what the hell they were doing out in the first place if a storm was coming. Cattle must be moved. This is the first, most immutable law of ranching, superseding any horse-husbandry sensibilities I've imported.

We walk back to the yard in silence.

I hang up the unused halter back in the tack room.

Brent still hasn't said anything, and I suspect he's fuming. I shudder at the flat, one-word answers I'll get later if I try to ask him about why he didn't want to speak to my father. Or me.

"We wouldn't have a ranch if we didn't have the cowboys," Dad says to us. "You don't have to like them, but you do have to respect them."

Brent and I exchange a look. Brent blinks and looks away, conceding not just the chase or the point but, I'm afraid, his role on the ranch.

"We do, Dad," I say quietly. "But we have a job to do too. I can't sell any of these horses if they're all broken."

It's the last anyone says on the topic: Brent and I climb into the truck, and Dad gets into his car. The trip back to Flagstaff is far too short for the long talks Brent and I need on the lengthening list of cutting topics that silence will only leave to scab.

HOW TO READ
A SHRINKING BUDGET

B
rent and I have joined Dad to examine the ranch's condition on paper.

Files and binders are stacked in the middle of the kitchen table in a scene reminiscent of three students cramming to finish their term papers. Several taped-together spreadsheet pages stretch across the piles in a numeric accounting of what's in the tomes' fine print. Had I been faced with a scene like this in college, I might have changed my major.

The first line is encouraging: the ranch is capitalized for the next two years of operating expenses.

Then come the expenses—payroll, insurance, vet fees, shipping costs, accountant and legal fees, insurance, fuel, taxes, workers' comp, health insurance—all which explain the predicted operating losses.

Then again, the paper version is based on assumptions, any one of which could change and all of which are beyond the ranch's control. The math estimates that 490 year-round cows are bred by ten bulls, with a live birth rate of about 80 percent in the spring yielding 390 darling black calves to sell to "backgrounders" wanting to feed them to slaughter weight. The math further assumes a selling price of two to three dollars per pound per calf, both extremes requiring planning. The market really can flux that much depending on drought: if ranchers are forced to sell their stock because there's no grass on their range, the market floods and prices tank. Of course, the next year, prices jump because of the shortage. The calves are about 300 pounds when they're sold—maybe 325—making annual sales of hundreds of thousands of dollars.

The revenues look good until the ranch subtracts the cost of restocking old, deceased, or missing cows, plus the steers that comprise the extra summer herd, plus all the related operating expenses, which have outpaced the revenues for the past three years. There are no earlier numbers to reference despite the ranch's longevity, because the ranch as defined by today's units and boundaries only began three years ago with the estate splits.

Our numbers are also not helped by being unable to choose the size of our crop. The Forest Service sets our grazing allotment each year by dictating how many cattle the ranch may graze on the leased pastures. That number is subject to annual review, making long-range planning impossible.

A few weeks ago, Brent and I met with the Forest Service range conservationist. He had tried to be a nice guy while breaking some unpleasant news.

"You know," he'd said, pulling at his collar. "We're starting to hear that Sierra Club is real concerned about that range over by the Rim."

We looked at him blankly.

"I might be looking at my herd numbers there, if you catch my meaning," he said, a little more intently. "A lawsuit could mean they might change in the next few years."

"What's the nature of their concern?" I asked. I've dealt with public process when working on big transportation projects. It doesn't immediately scare me: somebody somewhere usually has some concern with government doing something instead of nothing.

"Overgrazing," he said. "They're just concerned that if we put cows out there every season, the plants can't grow like they're supposed to."

"But," I said, looking at Brent, "we only graze one part of the year. Maybe a month at most."

The ranger smiled. "I know."

"Our cattle leave, and the grass grows back. Which is why we're able to graze there the next season," I said.

"Yep," the ranger agreed.

"So, what's the problem?" I asked.

"Well, not everybody sees it that way," the ranger said. "Not even here in the department."

"Wait." I shook my head. "You're telling me there's debate within the U.S. Forest Service about whether or not grass grows?"

Brent smiled. He enjoys catching people in the silliness of their own arguments and hadn't had a lot of success with it lately. Cowboys tend to only acknowledge the truth and weight of their own pronouncements.

The ranger choked. "I guess you could put it that way, yes."

Now, looking at the budget forecasts, I can see that the way to a sustainable future is not through more cattle. Permissions for greater herd sizes will not be forthcoming. Dad has looked for more grazing land, but it would require more labor, making it a break-even proposition at most.

"Can we get more value for our calves?" Brent asks.

Dad recites a detailed history of research pertaining to herd health, breeding, and vaccinations.

The ranch breeds "Black Baldies"—Hereford-Angus crosses that produce black calves with white faces. No one has done more than the Black Angus industry to convince the beef-eating market that Black Angus is the best-tasting beef available for consumption; but, as a practical matter, Black Angus tend to be lazy while Herefords tend to be wild and skittish, which is why herding turns out to be such an ordeal. The ranch has also tried "Brangus"—Black Angus crossed with Brahmas. The Brahma strain means they grow bigger, faster, and they tend to range better, but for whatever reason, the market doesn't reward their grade of beef.

Dad has also made lots of calls, trying to sell into forward contracts with backgrounders looking for certain cattle types with a certain vaccination history. Success has been limited: when it comes time to sell each October, folks who expressed interest on the phone have never shown up.

"So," I consult my tally. "We can't change the number that we sell, and we're not likely to change the price when we sell. Can we introduce any new revenue streams?"

I already know horseback rides will not be among them. It seems like a home run to me to offer public rides in the pines during the summer and fall and near the red rocks in the winter and spring, but permissions are problematic.

The permits manager for the forest district around the McKinsey said, "We don't even have enough staff to process the permit applications, let alone grant or monitor them. So, don't even apply. We stopped accepting applications two years ago, and we don't know the next time we'll be open to them."

The Flagstaff district rep said, "We could give you a temporary permit for one season only. We've done that before. But if you want a permanent permit, we'd need to do an environmental assessment, and we don't have budget for that, so you'd have to pay for it, and even if you do, there's no guarantee that the assessment will find we can grant the permit because there might be impacts, and then you'd either have to pay to address the impacts or, again, just not do the rides." I know from my transportation work that any environmental study is likely to cost tens of thousands of dollars, and my back-of-the-envelope math doesn't suggest that we'd recover the cost of producing one—assuming the study concluded that rides can be permitted.

"How about horse sales?" Dad asks hopefully. I wince. Dozer is sweet enough to do for a family—Freckles too, now that he's feeling better. Cisco is coming along over the jumps, Marvin is still a good reining prospect, and Twolena will make a great cow horse. The trouble is, all of them have needed unbudgeted help and none have sold yet.

"Best I'm hoping for is break-even," I say.

Dad frowns.

"What about a boutique beef operation?" Brent asks. "Arizona Beef. We raise it all the way up, butcher it, and sell the beef instead of just the cattle?"

"Friends of ours have tried it before," Dad says, sighing. "I think it sort of broke down over marketing, but you should learn about that. Maybe things have changed."

Brent makes a note on his follow-up list, frustratingly bare until this point.

"I've looked into a couple other things," I say.

Dad poises his pen.

"I called a local distillery because local vodkas and local gins were really taking off around Seattle—I wondered if they would here too. I found out that gin takes a special kind of juniper berries—probably a lot more of it than we could harvest off McKinsey and Grindstone—and that most distilleries don't even use actual botanicals anymore. They're using synthetic flavors because they are a lot more reliable."

"Hmph," Dad grunts.

"I also called a winery in the Cottonwood area. The person I talked to said there are all kinds of tasting rooms and wine bars in Jerome, and I asked them where they get their grapes."

Dad raises an eyebrow.

"She said California," I say. "Can you believe it? She said the biggest secret is that Arizona wine comes from grapes grown somewhere else—it's the minority share of the wine that's made from anything in Arizona, and what's Arizona-grown comes from down south. She said grapes just don't grow in the Verde Valley."

Dad exhales. "Well, that's disappointing."

"Really disappointing," I echo.

"What about beer?" Brent asks. "Does anyone grow hops?"

I have no idea.

"I think that takes too much water," Dad says. "And we don't have anything like an irrigation system that could deal with that."

Brent nods.

"But Sedona breweries make beer," I say. "And they have leftover grain. We could feed it, if we were feeding and finishing our own cattle to market."

Dad nods. "The VBarV Ranch does that," he says. "They're close to Sedona. I think they pick up everything Oak Creek Brewing Company will give them."

"I'll find out if anyone's working with Lumberyard," I say, thinking of the newly expanded brewery in Flagstaff. "Might be good for us."

Dad nods approval. "Awhile back, the VBarV tried to introduce a new kind of beef to market, a mix of cattle that range well in Africa crossed with the Wagyu cattle that are made for Kobe beef. They bred a few of those crosses and raised them and processed them—when they shared some of the beef, I heard everyone said it was great, but they couldn't get anyone to work with them. I guess it was just before its time or something."

Brent scratches a line off his list of new business ideas.

"Where are you in your thinking about Arizona Ranch Life?" Dad asks.

I tense.

This is Brent's vision: a brick-and-mortar store selling everything you'd need on a ranch—saddlery, clothing, hardware, fencing, all kinds of things. It'd be a place we could sell what our own cowboys use and a place to sell what we grow ourselves, as well as a bunch of other Western-style merchandise. Brent thinks we could start, staff, and grow it large enough to retire from. I don't see how we would possibly be able to run the ranch *and* the store. Moreover, I have no idea how we'd fund the start-up.

"I think we need to know if it's a business venture the ranch wants to invest in," Brent says neutrally. "Is the ranch looking for another business line, or would this be Julie and me on our own?"

Dad taps his pen. "I think this would have to be on your own. The ranch is held by my mother's company, and it's tied to her estate plan. We've done a lot of work so that we can liquidate everything and dispose of everything quickly to be able to pay taxes at the time of her death, so

I don't think it's a good idea to complicate that any further by adding in another business."

Brent sets his jaw as he crosses another new business item off his list.

"So, what's the role of that estate plan?" Brent asks. "At the time of death, you have to sell the ranch to pay the taxes?"

"Probably," Dad says.

Brent nods in resignation.

It's not that this is new information. We knew before we moved that the ranch is among the assets held by my nearly ninety-year-old grandmother, many of which require disposition by her estate plan. There was a chance that if the ranch was prosperous, or even solvent, the executors of her estate might want to keep it running, but today's numbers have dashed those hopes.

It's not that the numbers are new, either. Dad sent us annual reports before we moved—they're what inspired all the ideas we'd had for change. But there's a big difference between seeing losses on paper and incurring them in real life. What had felt academic once, variable by chance or choice, now feels both as corroded and entrenched as the peeling red metal that comprises the Oldham Park corrals.

Brent slumps like a defendant awaiting verdict, his expression known only to the scratched pad of paper under his tapping pen.

"So, to recap," I say. "The plan needs to be to sell the cows for as much as we can, maybe try to earn more by feeding beef for the finished market as long as it doesn't add to operating costs, and maybe see what else we can do with the owned land and facilities without incurring additional expenses."

Dad nods.

Brent shakes his head as though I just read out a life sentence.

"OK," I mumble, never having heard of a product that doesn't cost anything to produce.

By the end of the study session, no one is making direct eye contact.

Dad doesn't want to see us discouraged.

Brent and I don't want to see that we chose to relocate to a failing enterprise that, actually, we can't help.

It's as though all three of us are stumped in different wings of a carnival fun house where every mirror is a misdirection to the truth that could lead us out. We keep seeing ourselves—our hopes, our efforts, the possibilities we're willing to venture that no one else ever has—but the questions we ask just add to the noise and disarray that keep us seeking clarity in places where nothing is either as it seems or how it should be.

KICKS
AND OTHER BODY LANGUAGE

Before we move north for the summer, I want the two younger horses to be halterbroke.

Marvin, a sweet bay yearling, and Cali, a red roan two-year-old, have been basically left under Cheyenne's care until now. They eat when she eats, drinks when she drinks, and range not far from her in the herd. She's established herself as Alpha Mare, and the two youngest revere her as leader. To get the youngsters down to the arena to be worked with, Brent and I halter Cheyenne and Sage, leading them out of the top pasture at McKinsey. The youngsters immediately fall in behind us, and we parade down the hill and into the arena, where Mom closes the gate behind us.

Step one complete: containment.

Brent leaves to fix yet another broken pipe. I beckon Mom into the arena with me.

"Bring the extra halter on the fence, will you?" I ask.

Mom has always loved young horses, and Marvin and Cali seem to know that. They step toward her as she approaches, sniffing at her arms.

I hand Mom both Sage's and Cheyenne's lead ropes. They stand placidly, only mildly curious about my activities as I loop a lead rope around Marvin's neck, then quickly slip a halter over his nose and head.

Step two complete: capture.

Marvin is one of my favorites. He's been known to follow the Gator around, even climbing into its passenger seat with his front half once.

He's a "pocket pony"—giving the feeling that he's affectionate enough to want to crawl into one. Given his breeding, I'm hoping to get him sold to a reining or cutting barn, but first things first: he must accept wearing a halter, then follow where he's led.

Now he mouths at the lead rope then tosses his head, delighting as the rope bounces. Nodding and nosing the rope become the giggle of a sound wave. I laugh out loud as he incorporates twists and loops into the improvised broadcast.

As the haltering part of the lesson has come and gone without incident, I move on to leading. I walk forward, holding the halter end of the lead rope with my right hand while waving the tail end behind me with my left. The idea is to engage a mild startle response to encourage the horse forward as I gently tug with my right hand. Marvin spooks away from the rope tail, his ears busy sounding out its threat level.

I repeat the twin cues of tug and wave, praising Marvin each time he comes forward, repeating the cycle a good half-dozen times. Feeling we only need one more round, I tug and wave once more for the sake of mastery—and sweet Marvin stands on his hind legs to paw at the air. A hoof connects with my lead arm, then as I turn away from the blow, a foreleg kicks me square in the butt.

"Shit!" I call, gripping my arm and dropping the lead rope.

Marvin swivels his ears toward my cry, backs up a couple steps, then wanders toward Cheyenne and Sage at the fence line.

"Jules!" Mom calls over. "Are you OK? Did he get you?"

"Yeah," I answer, trying to swallow tears. I don't specify which question I'm answering. "Just give me a minute."

I turn my back on the horses and arena, latching the gate behind me as I surrender to a nearby straw bale. Even the gentlest horse in my herd has now mutinied from my leadership.

It's too much. I have lived with months of feeling inept as a rancher, atop years of feeling inadequate as a wife. I can't make my husband happy, can't make my marriage go, and have been forced to face the fact that it's not the fault of Washington's weather, Brent's job, my job, or the isolation of being far from home. We're just not working. Actually, we are working—all we're doing is working—just not for each other. We haven't had a real conversation in months. Maybe not even in years. I've been too afraid of his disappointment, his anger, his shunning me with any further retreats, to ask the questions or make the statements, much less the changes, that I've needed and haven't known how to find.

Somewhere in my consciousness, I've equated the ranch with the home I want Brent and me to have, Marvin and Cali with children. I know in my brain that not everyone has to be a mother—it's an expectation I would never dream of assigning to any other woman. But I wonder what's wrong with my heart that I am without this fundamentally human and feminine desire. Moreover, I wonder what's wrong with me that I've felt nothing but fatigue and dread where desire should be.

Now I feel that our attempted home and family are pushing us off, bucking our adoption.

I sob.

I've replaced so much with the hope that I can create new possibilities for these beautiful innocents who've just had a rough start, but I will never be a mother. I'm not actually a rancher. Evidently, I am not even much of a horseman.

I feel I have utterly failed everyone I've tried to love.

"Oh, honey!" Mom calls, still holding the mustangs. "Just . . . oh dear."

She removes the halters from the mustangs. They immediately turn to sniff at the youngsters who have been lipping at their hindquarters, shoulders, and legs. Marvin is still wearing his halter, wagging his lead rope like a happy puppy.

I cry into my hands, not even capable of cogent speech. I wonder if this is how worms view the world when a rock is turned over to expose them: everything they sense is higher, greater, bigger, and absolutely a reason to crawl back into hiding.

"I'm doing everything wrong. I am a disaster."

Mom sits beside me on the bale, the palm of her hand circling my back.

We're quiet for a time, letting the morning and me settle into each other again.

Our arena looks up toward the ochre and plum of the Red Rock-Secret Mountain Wilderness. Not for the first time, I wonder what the big secret is behind the name. Maybe how people manage to find anything in these vast spaces, least of all themselves. Maybe how to just keep going.

Mom pats my leg, inviting me out of my head.

The horses nuzzle each other under a warming, wispy sky.

Doc and his new puppy friend, Lucy, regard each other from opposite sides of the shade in the barn. Creature time does not have minutes nor milestones—it expands and contracts like the push of a pulse, without defining moments so much as the shaping from alternate peace and pressure.

Lucy is remarkably mature for a young dog, taking to Doc right away, then willingly settling into his more senior pace. Brent heard a radio ad for the Sedona Humane Society the day we arrived. The very next day, we went to visit the featured year-old Rottweiler mix, who found her place with Doc, in the truck, and in our lives, all in about the space of an hour. I'd named her Lucy, her sweet nature reminding me of the character in *The Chronicles of Narnia*.

Like her, I am in no world I control or can predict. I can only make my most loving response to what's right in front of me.

Mom keeps patting my leg, and I enjoy the sense of physical safety and comfort I have just sitting next to her. I haven't felt either for, it must be, years now. Nor am I likely to with either of the men in my life.

Neither Mom nor I have made any headway with Dad regarding changing the ways of the cowboys or ranch spending. The ranch's finances are dictated by the governance of an estate plan, and my father is its trustee. There is no extra capital to do anything new. Any change Brent and I want to bring has got to be from how we manage things, which we would do except that our management is on paper. On the range, the foreman manages the cattle moves and the labor needs, moving horses into my care only after they can't hold up to his lack of it. As a result, neither Brent nor I feel as though we've been managing much at all.

"I didn't know it would be this hard," I say to Mom.

She shakes her head. "None of us knew it would be this hard."

"I'm afraid I'm making things worse," I confess.

She sits back. "How could you be making anything worse?"

"I have a dozen horses to sell. My job is to bring in some money for the ranch. Instead, I'm spending money on vets and teeth and feet—"

"None of which are problems you caused," she says.

"No," I concede. "But I'm spending money, and Dad's made it clear it's not in the budget to spend. And he's right—I've seen the budget, and it's not there. Not for the horses, not for anything, either individually or as a whole. Even if I sold every horse at a substantial profit, I couldn't earn their way back into the black, and we both know with the amount of care they need, none of these horses will be sold at a profit."

"No," she agrees, smiling gently.

"And now the sweetest, gentlest, most promising colt we have just turned into a monster," I say. "He's never done anything like that before. I don't know why I thought I could help—there's too much I don't know."

I have a master's degree and ten years of professional consulting experience. I have a wall full of blue ribbons and trophies from a lifetime of equestrian sports. None of that is helping me.

"Who else could do more than you're doing?" Mom asks.

I shrug. "I don't know that there are better options. I mean, we could take all the horses to the next auction just as they are. It'd stop the spending and get them off the feed bill."

Mom shakes her head vehemently. "I don't want to do that."

"I don't want to do that either. I don't think it's fair. I don't think it's ethical, but mostly I don't think it's humane. If the horses were hurt on our ranch, they should heal on our ranch."

She nods. "Yes."

"Maybe they won't, and what we do won't make a difference, and they'll end up at auction anyway, but I feel like I have to try other things first. Only, right after I feel that way, I remember I don't have a lot of things left I can try. We can't put them all with professional trainers—we'd never get the costs back, and we tried hiring Jake, a trainer of our own, but that didn't work. We can give the horses time to get healthy and sound and fit, then advertise around online and with folks we know—at least give them the chance at good homes when they're ready," I say, getting a little of my focus back.

"Yes," she says again. "The auction has to be the last resort."

We sit for a while, watching the youngsters play with Sage. They nuzzle his hip or shoulder, he pins his ears at the annoyance, they back off, then repeat the very same sequence. Should they not reach out again, Sage reaches out to nuzzle at them, restarting the game.

So go the games of our lives: pretending nonchalance, then inviting annoyance because nothing is as bad as being ignored.

"Brent's miserable," I say. "And I don't know what to do."

Mom nods.

"We're not talking." Tears blur my vision as I finally air out the nightmare I've been afraid to voice. "When we get here to work, he goes off to do whatever he thinks he has to do, and when we get home, he goes to his computer or the television, then he goes to bed."

"I know," Mom says. Living in the same house, she, too, has observed the behavior.

My world has been spinning since well before we moved, my job and life and marriage all separate planets to which I have felt more and more a dysfunctional satellite, unable to do other than drift, pulled along by the inertia of my commitments. To view them all from this straw bale beside my best friend is to dock safely into a stillness, a quiet, in which I can examine the pull of each source of gravity that's been working on me.

"I thought Brent wanted to come here to lead. He's the ranch manager. He could fire Woods. I think he wants to, and I wish he would, but he won't talk to Dad about that."

Mom sighs. "I don't know why your dad thinks there isn't anybody else who can do that job."

"I don't either," I reply. "I mean, Brent just had to lay someone off. So clearly there is now at least one more person around who could take Woods's place."

That had been an ugly day. Brent had drawn the responsibility of firing the cowboy who had been working for us while Ty recuperated, a task he not only regretted, as he liked the cowboy more than either Woods or Ty, but resented, as it seemed to be the first and only discrete task he'd been allowed as ranch manager.

"Which isn't actually my problem to solve," I acknowledge. "I don't know if Brent doesn't want to try to change things anymore, but I know nothing's changing except he's getting more and more withdrawn and less and less communicative—"

I can't say any more.

I would be too embarrassed to say as much as I already have, except that I feel so stripped of dignity there's nothing left to feel the shame.

Mom, ever ready with tissues at exactly the right moments, draws one from a pocket. "Was he like this in Washington?"

I shrug. "Things have never been quite like this before."

Mom chuckles. "Well, that's the truth."

We've never worked for my relations, nor have we lived with them. Certainly, we've never done both at the same time. We've never earned so little, never had to deny ourselves so much. The consumer-based coping mechanisms afforded by a two-income household without debt hadn't been available to us for months. It frightened me to have to acknowledge how much we must have relied on them without my notice. Ironically, as little time as we've spent together, we'd seen much more of each other without our past distractions, and neither one of us seems to like the view.

I summarize, "When things are bothering Brent, he just goes quiet. If I try to ask him, he gets mad at me."

"That isn't fair," Mom says.

I wince. I don't know what's fair, what's healthy, what's helpful. I don't know what tool to apply because, so much like Brent with the ranch plumbing, I can't find the source of the problem. We seem to spend so much time spraining and patching up the small stuff, there's been no energy left to go looking for the main cause. Perhaps it's as fundamental as language. Anything I say seems as inscrutable to Brent as it's been to the horses.

Mom stands up, interrupting my woes' orbit. "Brent's going to have to figure out his stuff. As you say, it's not yours to manage. And there's plenty of other work to do without you dealing with Marvin. Let me try to work with him a little."

I don't want to task Mom with work that could hurt her. If one of us is going to get her ass kicked, it really should be me. "You don't have to—"

She holds up a hand. "If it's bad, I'll stop. I know I can't do much, but maybe I can do something. Why don't you get on with the rest of what you're working on, and we'll see how the day goes."

A half hour later, I lead Cisco to the makeshift jump course I've constructed using branches, stumps, old poles, and boards laying around from some decades-long-forgotten construction project. He's athletic, with a long stride unchecked by pain since his session with Susan, giving me the wild idea that maybe he'll like jumping.

I snap on my helmet, then use an inverted bucket to climb up into my small English saddle. I'd stowed it away in the trailer until now, thinking I would never need it for cattle-related activities. As we warm up, I see Mom walking the length of the arena with Marvin following sedately behind her on a loose lead.

Magic Mom, purveyor of clarity to the confused. All species welcome.

I nudge Cisco into a trot. Immediately I feel the lift of his stride, my own heartbeat, and my hopes for the day in the buoyancy of his gait.

We canter next, and I rise in the stirrups. Cisco's stride is springy and adjustable—every step collected beneath us with no wayward motion. He could so easily be leaning or careless, with the sloppy, indolent carriage some horses adopt when they've given up on people, but he gathers and spreads his body with the grace of a conductor's hands. We canter a few rounds around the course before I ease him back to trot, sighting a few of the branches I've laid out.

I consciously relax my shoulders, my back, my hips. I will my body into neutral readiness: to encourage, to shift, to sit, whatever his reaction might be.

Cisco's ears, already pricked, flex attentively toward the branches as he raises his neck, then shortens his strides.

I press my lower leg against his sides, holding encouraging pressure.

We're strides away from the branch pile, steps away, then he canters a step and pops over what's now our first jump, cantering happily away from the branches. My heart and hands soften, relaxing into the lilt and roll of the rhythm sweeping me up. I'm floating now—having relaxed my grip—on the saddle, the reins, maybe even life. I bask, allowing myself to just feel, to savor the sensation of shared triumph.

I glance toward the arena: Mom has Marvin lunging. The yearling is confidently trotting a circle around her on a long lunge line, stride checking and ears flicking in response to her clicking cues to trot, or steady voice to walk.

"Good boy, good boy!" she calls toward him, flashing me a thumbs-up.

I flash her one back before stroking Cisco's neck, the predatory sense of playing a game of inevitable gains and losses shifting to the tentative joy of an impromptu dance, each one of us reveling in finding our way through some first steps.

NEIGHBORS, DOG BITES AND OTHER RANCHING ACCESSORIES

I remember when I used to dream of being loved by a cowboy. I'd watch the men and boys roping at horse shows, hands quick as they reined, roped, or tied off dallies, eyes intense. Their smiles were bright, if rare. They barked laughter at rookie mistakes, winking when they admitted their own. I wanted nothing more than to have anything from them directed at me.

For three decades, I held that fantasy in my heart, and in barely two months of ranching I can't fathom how "romantic" could ever be used to describe either the work or the workers.

Romance is the sweep of possibility, the swoon of emotional fascination, the pleasure of anticipating what's to come.

Ranching is mud, rocks, early mornings, and scarcity of everything but soreness.

As for cowboys? Let's just say the girlhood daydreams grew up.

First there were the wannabe cowboys living around the McKinsey.

Some people have neighbors who bring over casseroles, stand across the fence sharing news, and maybe volunteer to pick something up at the store. The McKinsey is bordered on two sides by private five-to-ten-acre ranchettes, with more across the forest road. In the patchwork pattern of public and private land that is the forest in Arizona, a wildcat development had sprung up around McKinsey with residents regarding our previously undeveloped property as a kind of private park. When Mom began improving it, the neighbors called meetings and spread rumors. Mom shared some of them with me by phone.

"The Wilsons are going to plow it under."

"The Wilsons are going to put up stadium lights for rodeos."

"The Wilsons are building a helipad."

My mom's letters to each of the neighbors explaining the proposed development of a roping arena, trailer hookups, and small, open-air barn made no difference. The rumors continued.

One irate neighbor, shotgun in hand, stopped Cody in the middle of the road to demand explanation of the property's increased activity. Unfazed, Cody told him he'd heard the rumors too; they spent about ten minutes comparing fictions.

Another neighbor sued us over the placement of our ranch gate, located nowhere near his home, outbuildings, or access points. We had placed our gate on what the surveyor said was our property, behind the community dumpster collecting the neighborhood's trash.

We received a cease-and-desist order and a letter informing us we were being sued for trespassing.

The surveyors had evidently got things wrong, but rather than speak to us, the neighbors lawyered up, then rolled a boulder in front of our gate, making it impassable to vehicles.

We installed a new gate farther down the fence line to be able to get in and out while the matter was negotiated.

Cody wished us well for the summer season, likely very grateful not to have to visit our property or our neighbors again anytime soon.

The one thing the all-too-real ranch cowboys have in common with the weekend version around McKinsey is disgust with us as owners.

Woods and Ty are local—they grew up in the Verde Valley of Arizona and have been working ranches in the area for most of their lives, barring times out for broken bones or seasons joining a construction crew for the steady paycheck. Woods has a family. Ty has a girlfriend. Neither has pets, though both have cattle dogs that live in chain-link kennels except for when they're working.

Their rules are that no one eats until the boss eats, your saddle belongs on only your horse, beer comes in two kinds: free and cold, don't come inside the cabin if there's a bottle or can on the fence line lest you embarrass yourself walking in on intimate company, hats are to be worn at all times, gloves are to be worn at none, happy hour begins when the work is done, and coyotes and Democrats should be shot on sight.

New to their customs, Brent and I stumble into many a cultural misstep in our first few days of being collocated with the cowboys at Oldham Park.

It's locally accepted truth that after the last snow, it never rains in Flagstaff until after the Fourth of July. Until then, May and June bring red-flag-warning winds and rising temperatures—perhaps nothing like Phoenix, but with actual danger of fire as overnight campers with scant outdoor skills begin packing the forests the moment Valley temperatures top 100 degrees. Late May to June days can feel like new sunburn, inflamed and constantly irritated, with nothing that really soothes so much as makes things feel sticky.

Relations with Woods have certainly gone that way since Brent saddled Slick. Woods was away at a rodeo when I noticed Slick's left eye was weepy. A closer look showed me the incessant watering was due to a few dozen fly eggs in the eye, acting as a constant irritant. This can happen to horses with a certain eye physiology—some are more prone to it than others—though it's easily avoided with regular eye flushes and copious amounts of fly spray. Under Woods's care until then, Slick had been missing one or both treatments.

I called the vet, and Brent saddled Slick for a quick ride to get a feel for him while we were waiting, which would have the added benefit of keeping him moving and not itching for the twenty minutes it would take the vet to get to us. When he returned, Woods was as furious as if we'd stolen his paycheck, though it was unclear whether the vet's presence or the recent saddle marks were the bigger transgression.

A few days later, Ty was trying to catch a horse. Halter in his right hand and grain bucket in his left, he approached the horse he wanted, about to swing the lead rope up around its neck to catch it.

"I have some extra horse cookies here," I said from the open door of my truck where I'd been watching. I retrieved then rattled the full plastic bin, delighted to finally have something to offer Ty. "Would these help?"

Both Ty and his horse startled, and the horse pulled away. Ty stormed to his ATV, gunned it, wheeled it in a circle, and chased that horse from fence line to fence line, not caring what was in the way as he tried to run it down. It was no wonder ranch horses went lame—Ty pursued his target over cinders, boulders, loose fence posts, and the uneven ground in between. It was also no wonder horses didn't want to be caught, if halters were associated with motorized trauma.

From Woods and Ty's venomous looks following both counts of unintended outrage, I sensed we would be uneasy co-tenants in the tack room this summer.

One midmorning, after the cowboys roll out and well before their typical return, Mom and Brent and I saddle up for a trail ride. Doc and Lucy sniff at corral corners and into holes in the hay barn. Mom sings songs as she grooms Bayley. I'm enjoying some time with Dozer, the big palomino I've elected to try out on the trail. Brent croons to Marty, who couldn't be more pleased to be called upon for an exploratory adventure.

Brent hasn't been out for a while, having given his notice to Dad. While Mom and I have been in Oldham's arena and park acreage, he's been rapt at his laptop seeking another job. He told me there's no reason for him to stay at the ranch when there's no future in it for us. He also said if he stayed, he'd endanger every family relationship we have. Hearing the words out loud felt like seeing Halloween decorations in August: premature and yet inescapable.

I hear the cinders crunch—the cowboys are returning early. I call to Mom and Brent to untie from the hitching posts, clearing space so the cowboys can unload.

My hands are full of Dozer's lead rope when there's a rustling, a scuffle, and a pack of four cattle dogs are out of the truck, racing toward Marty's hind legs. White-eyed, Marty dances in place, prancing to avoid jaws snapping at his ankles. I step past the scurry, clicking to both horses to move with me, when I feel a sting below my left knee. A mottled gray dog retreats, eyes expectant, mouth bared toward a return attack.

"What the hell?" I yell, trying to keep ahold of the squirming ropes as the horses hop, plant, and prance against the milling dogs.

Three dogs. Where's—

I hear a yelp, then a whimper. Brent scoops up Doc, trying to simultaneously keep our eighty-pound Labrador aloft and the leaping gray dog off his own legs.

At shouts from beyond the hay barn, the cattle dogs retreat.

Brent staggers to our truck, depositing Doc in the back seat.

I shakily retie Marty and Dozer to the hitching post, then bend to look at my leg. The jeans are ripped and the skin broken—the area around the bite already sunset shades of red and purple.

I limp to the tack room, grope through my vet supplies for rubbing alcohol, uncap a bottle whose label and sides are smeared with what I hope is hoof oil, and douse my lower leg.

Brent storms through the door in a palpable rage. He takes in my leg and the alcohol without speaking. Without pausing. Without asking.

I register the keys in his hand. He must be leaving.

My stomach flips in panic that this could be the last time I'll see him. Doc is his alter ego, the best and most reliable friend in his life across moves and a previous marriage. He's been joy and solace and sacred to Brent; in his words, "If Doc don't mind, it don't matter." On some days I think nothing has mattered more—not me, not our marriage—and I am petrified that Brent will never want to see the ranch or me again. I must look as scared as I feel, because his eyes change from lightning bolts to emergency flashers—urgent, but blameless. I breathe again: of course Brent would have his keys in his hands. He has to get Doc to the vet.

"Is Doc OK?" I ask.

Perhaps it's a mercy that we can't say what we mean in times of trauma—that pain reduces language to the simplistic, more a conduit for tone and volume than any meaningful lexicon. I hear the prayer in my question—not only for Doc's safety but for my own. If Brent were to leave me, he'd be throwing me to the wolves in more ways than one—a pack I can't take on by myself.

I can handle that he's left the ranch.

I can't handle that he might leave me.

"They drew blood," he reports. "I don't think he needs a vet, but I'm taking him home. This is ridiculous. We can't stay here."

Strange what registers in these moments. *We.* It sounds cleansing, like the iodine scrub I wish I had. It doesn't change the wound to Doc, nor does it change the hurt that Brent has asked neither about me nor if I want to go too. There's been no "we" for much too long until this moment, even if it's been said with a finality about what we're doing here that's been unspeakable until now.

Cinders fly as Brent guns our truck's motor to make his way toward town.

Mom inspects Bayley, then Marty. Their legs are clean—no wounds.

Woods walks over. "Got 'em penned up now—didn't think you'd be here."

His voice sounds like an abscess: layers long damaged from a small wound rotting away, ready to blow. Apology, fear, entitlement, defensiveness, outrage, and concern are all in there festering with one another.

"We were going to go for a ride."

I wish I knew how trauma chooses its words—of all the things it could respond with, it chooses the obvious? The irrelevant? Maybe they're the only words available. Maybe my pain and fear are redacting my speech in real time to keep me from saying things like "you scare me" or maybe "I hate you." Maybe it's me who's incapable of speech. The words are all there, it's just me who can't say them.

"It's better if we don't have to share the space," Woods says with a glance from under his hat.

Shame bristles like sparklers across my consciousness. He's saying we brought this on ourselves. He's saying we're wrong to be here. He's not saying he's sorry after all. He's saying he shouldn't have to be.

"Yeah, sorry. I saw you were coming, and we tried to give you room." I am right and wrong and achingly adolescent, powerless before Woods's disapproval to do anything but plead. "Then, your dogs started biting, and I don't know what happened."

"Oh," Woods looks directly at me for the first time to scan my legs. "Did they get you?"

"Yeah," I point to my ripped jeans. I hear teenage girl in my voice: her desperate need for accomplishment, legitimacy, understanding, acceptance.

"Damn dogs," he says, grumbling off toward the cabin.

A moment ago, I would have shot the dogs myself. Now I want to turn them loose. Tell them to run, flee, go as far as they can and never come back. I cringe more from what I fear Woods might do to them than from my own pain.

The horses shift where they wait, the morning having gone back to normal for them two conversations ago, sunbeams glinting off the metal roofs, pine air, leather strapped to their backs. I feel the adrenaline pull back like a tide receding, revealing all the tiny lives hurrying to burrow lest they be exposed, easy prey to hunting monsters. I sit down in the tack room doorway, feeling I've been caught up, chewed on, spat out, and flung away—chum for even scarier monsters trolling in deeper waters.

"Are you OK?" Mom asks, joining me from where she'd been checking the horses. I sense that there is diplomacy rather than pain or assumption behind the question, like an open door: I am free to walk in, or out, to any interpretation of the question as I choose.

"I got bit," I say, running cinders through my fingers rather than probing at my own wound. "But I disinfected it." I feel wobbly, as though the alcohol entered more than my jeans. It's the "one drink too many" feeling without the nausea—just the sick knowing that I've gone too far.

"You need to have that looked at," she says. It's her "mom voice." Authoritative, concerned.

"Doesn't hurt that much," I say. "And nothing's broken."

She shakes her head. "Still, I think we should get you into urgent care—"

She stops speaking when I look up. If I weren't already in shock, knowing I'd just surprised or frightened my mother into silence puts me there.

The cinders I hold sound like raindrops on account of my shaking hand.

The past few months have seen my parents and Brent and me running sprints in a game of shifting goalposts, from discovery to disbelief and back again, trying to find some chance at reward. I feel breathless and light-headed. We have winnowed our way down to so little: epic-scale visions of riding the range diminished to a few circles in a cinder-sand arena once in a while. Still, even that was something, and much more than most people would ever know. A remnant of what we hoped for might be enough, might make our effort worthwhile if it could last, but now it's been not only shot down through study but attacked on site.

I can feel my reason dissociating like snaps of worn rawhides as I mentally survey all the wreckage.

"We haven't had a ride yet," I say slowly as I stand to turn for the bridles. "We've really wanted one. I think we go anyway."

Mom doesn't argue, and I don't think too hard about the fact that she doesn't. I don't care about my leg. I don't care about infection. The pain and the sickness can't be any worse in my body than it's been in my heart.

I unsaddle Dozer, opt to take Marty, and we ride out into the woods.

Where we promptly get lost.

Turns out a bunch of rocks over here looks a lot like a bunch of rocks over there, and barely used forest roads all look alike. We have to cut a fence to get ourselves back to a place we recognize, a fact that gives me a small and evil glee, thinking the cowboys would really hate that, and maybe I won't tell them we did it.

At two hours out, my leg is on fire, but my back is worse, so I dismount, limping Marty down the rutted road. Marty looks at me curiously, as if wondering if he's done something wrong. I look back at him sadly, sure that I have.

HOW TO RANCH
ONE-HANDED

A famous line from the classic film *A Lion In Winter* follows the Fool's being asked why it should matter how we fall. His answer is, "When the fall is all that's left, it matters very much."

Re-homing the horses is all I have left to do now, and I approach the task with nearly religious devotion.

Mom and I drive in around eight o'clock in the morning to start on the day's horseback rotation: the youngsters, mustangs, and Bayley for Mom, the rest for me.

When Brent visits the ranch, he varies his time between Marty and the new herd of barely weaned Jersey calves we rescued from a dairy in Phoenix for the nominal cost of their mothers' feed for a few weeks.

The dairyman we got them from works specifically with Jersey cows because he likes the quality of their milk as opposed to what one collects from Holsteins, the much more common black-and-white cows made familiar through clever commercial packaging by Shamrock and others. Intended or not, one of the consequences of the dairy industry's going primarily with Holsteins is that the beef industry has too.

One of the "useless byproducts" to a dairy is male calves. Dairymen typically sell their male calves to beef producers, which is why processors scale and size their operations and equipment specifically for Holsteins. Jerseys, being smaller than Holsteins, don't fit that standard. Before we met him, the Jersey dairyman euthanized his male calves as a least-cost option because he couldn't get any beef processors to work with him.

Seeing an opportunity for a low-cost feeder crop, Dad arranged for us to pick up a few dozen and bring them to the ranch to feed. Stumbling off the trailer, the fawn-colored Jersey calves squeezed and blinked their liquid brown eyes, beneath the chocolate-rimmed ears that made them look like Bambi—only smaller. We hope they'll grow quickly off the spent grain we've arranged to pick up from local breweries.

Brent is enamored of the calves. Like a kid with a science-fair project, he is determined for them to grow by a deadline. This gets a rough start when we learn that, despite what we'd been told by a fellow cattle grower, the calves, being just barely weaned, cannot digest the brewer's grain without bloating dangerously. Husbandry and pride push off cost concerns as he makes weekly trips to the feed store for calf manna, distributing it among the calves as a mother hen might to chicks.

I don't have time for nesting.

My day usually begins with working Cisco, then either Freckles or Dozer, then perhaps Slick, who's been added to my sales string since he's coming up lame too often for the cowboys to rely on, then Twolena. Vegas, a flashy, light-gray mare with black mane and tail, and my Lena both mainly need rest before anyone can think about riding them. Both have been consistently sore, and there's nothing to give them but time. I don't like that they're hurting, but I do appreciate not having to exercise them—riding four to five horses a day, plus grooming, saddling, washing, and cleaning out pens, is taking its toll. My feet hurt almost all the time, and, but for some devoted use of gel insoles, I might join the mares being assigned to stall rest.

Oldham Park is beautiful to ride in, but it has its quirks. First, for a flat piece of ground, some parts are flatter and smoother than others. The south end of the park is best, with a long and wide swath between the tree line on the east and the drainage course shedding seasonal thaws, rocks, stumps, and other detritus on the west. Because the summer rains haven't started, the ground is cracked with fissures, making it look like a jigsaw puzzle that won't connect. Still, there's a large-enough area to put all the horses through their paces outside the confines of the roping arena, and I have also managed to construct a jump course. Straw bales form two of my jumps; actual poles and standards another three; and I've also made creative use of a few spare trash cans—a sweet and fun beginner course that Cisco and I both look forward to.

For a former ranch horse, he looks the part of a Hunter/Jumper: sleek and spirited, he could be a seal arcing through waves rather than a horse jumping fences. Even better, Cisco has been willing to jump over even the most unnatural shapes. One of the things I've read is that horses identify things by familiar shapes—not necessarily by motion or color—which explains why Dozer always looks twice at the trash barrels we've placed by the arena (round cylinders don't occur much in nature), and a hat on my head was grounds for Cali to panic.

I'm very pleased with Cisco's progress, and we've become something of a mascot to my old training barn where I'm working by phone with Nell, my favorite and trusted coach, to increase Cisco's skill and confidence over the jumps. Nell is one of only two horse professionals I have met in thirty years of horsing who can be trusted with not only client safety, but client money. She is honest, plainspoken, unflagging, kind, selfless, and wise.

Nell collects horses and dogs in need the way some people collect Beanie Babies, and they're all the better for it. We've taken lessons from her for a few weeks now, driving to Phoenix for instruction, then meeting her at horse shows. Nell feels the best thing I can do for Cisco is get him exposed to all kinds of jumps and all kinds of shows, in that order, as she has confirmed that he could have a future in the Hunter/Jumper world for an intermediate rider wanting to do mostly local events.

It's a bright and beautiful morning, with the sun just barely over the ridge and the morning cool still in the air as Cisco and I mosey out to the jump course. Mom and Dad are out of town on vacation, and Brent is home on his computer, but we have a new staff member starting today, and I want to ride Cisco before it's time for Heidi's orientation.

Not that she'll need a lot.

Heidi is petite, blonde, curvy, and tough. She needs a job because the track is closed; otherwise, she'd be hustling to get through her usual lineup of ponying and exercising racehorses. She is sweet, knowledgeable, and easy to talk to, and her references love her. I am thrilled to have her help for the summer, because I can't keep up with the physical demands of my growing horse herd.

I'm thinking about the last show Cisco and I competed in—how he hesitated at some of the lattice gate–style jumps. I wonder if I might be able to build something like that. I gather my reins. Cisco pricks his ears in response. This is one of the things I love most about him—many horses take some pressure on the bit as an insult or a threat, their ears twitching or even pinning back, whereas Cisco seems to take the feel of the bit as an invitation.

We've walked past all the pens, the roping arena, and the long line of trees that borders the park's eastern boundary all the way up to the beginning of the flats where I've set out the jump course. I can see that the elk have been chewing on the straw-bale jumps again. Dad mentioned that the cowboys reported elk hopping the Oldham Park fence at dusk to chew on these bales as though we're offering happy-hour specials. I've just nudged Cisco into a trot when a bird flies out from the messy straw pile at the bales' base.

Cisco leaps to the right—sliding completely out from underneath me.

I feel myself falling left, my left arm bracing before I can stop it.

I hear a thud, realizing after impact that it was the sound of my body hitting the hard-cracked earth. I'm dazed, the wind knocked out of me, the world indiscriminately spinning except for the burning pinch in my left wrist.

I'm still on my left side, blinking and reorienting myself, when Cisco comes sniffing back, head down, ears pricked, wondering at my supine posture.

Several body parts scream at me to roll to a different position. I gather my legs, then shove upward to a kneel. I test my left hand, wiggling it from side to—no. It will only move to one side.

Cisco is grazing next to me as I half-crawl over, reaching for his reins with my right hand. The move startles him and I fall, twisting to land on my butt instead of my side.

That's when the tears start, dislodged not so much by pain as by an overwhelming sense of disability. Uselessness. I am flat on my back in the middle of the pasture, with an arm that is very likely broken, over half a mile away from the tack room, ice, water, or anything else that could help me. My best horse just dropped me on my ass, but my biggest problem, given the tension between me and my husband, is that my closest help is likely to be Woods.

Hating my life, I work my cell phone from my front pocket, relieved to see it's undamaged.

"Hello," Woods gruffs.

"Hey—are you guys close? I just came off a horse, and I think I have a broken arm," I say, trying for a tone more like road construction than emergency vehicle.

"Ah shit—no—we ain't. What happened?" he asks.

I don't know if it's harder to sit there through the pain or to admit, again, that I fell off. I take a ragged breath. "I'm at Oldham Park, and I just had a bad fall. I think I've broken my arm. Do we have any ice in the tack room?"

"Ah shit—well—ah shit," he says. "No—no, I don't think—ice?"

I know I need a lot more than ice. I need a hospital. But I am doubtful enough of both Woods's and Brent's willingness to help that I figure I should start with what's easiest to deliver.

"Don't worry about it," I say. "I'll call Brent. I'll figure it out."

"OK," Woods says, sounding relieved. "I—we ain't anywhere around there—"

"Yeah, I've got it," I say. "I'll take care of it. Thanks anyway."

God—I just thanked him. For not helping me. Clearly, I am a fucking mess, and my broken arm is the least of what I need to fix. I pocket my phone, stand, then push the dirt off my pants and shirt with my good hand.

Cisco raises his head.

"Hey, pal," I say, walking toward him. "Don't birds suck?"

He pricks his ears as I hold my left arm against my chest the best I can while reaching toward him with my right. The burning has turned to a kind of radiant heat, like I caught a curling iron to myself, scorching at my forearm.

"I really, really hate birds," I croon, wanting to keep Cisco calm. "Birds are awful, hateful bastard beasts, but you are a good, good boy."

He stands still, letting me grasp the reins, then lift them over his head so I can lead him.

He follows meekly.

Thank God. I love this horse.

My legs are more and more solid as they step underneath me, walking regularly, if not quickly, toward the tack room. After a hundred feet or so, I muster enough strength to withdraw my phone and call Brent.

"Hellooooo," he answers, surprisingly playful.

"I fell off," I say, the truth of it hitting me as though Cisco himself broadsided me.

I won't be able to ride. I certainly won't be able to jump. My main joy just crashed and shattered into silt of the kind I just pushed away from me. I sob—the tears burning my eyes. "Cisco spooked, and I think I broke my arm. Can you pick me up?"

"Oh no," he says. "What happened? Where are you?"

I don't know why "What happened?" seems to be such essential information. I've just said I broke my arm and need a ride. How does it matter if I did it arm wrestling or skydiving? I don't need questions right now. I need a groom, a driver, and a doctor in that order. I also probably need my arm set and put in a cast, painkillers, and a change of clothes because I am filthy and the dirt on my face is fast turning to mud.

I suppose shock works both ways, and people usually need a minute, even in an emergency, to process what it is they're being asked to do. Perhaps hearing "what happened" is a verbal equivalent to the time between flipping the switch on the machine and seeing the first widget pop out—processing time.

"I'm at Oldham," I say.

"I'll be right there," he says.

"Come to the tack room," I direct.

"Don't you need me to come out into the park?" he asks in the tone of a man trying to evacuate while his wife keeps packing suitcases.

I rankle at what feels like an implied correction. "No, I'm walking in." As I say this while walking, I feel if anyone should be making corrections it should be me, and right now I want him to correct his ass off the phone and onto the freeway.

"You're going to walk all the way back to the tack room with a broken arm?"

I have never wished so much that I could hand my phone off to my horse.

"Yeah," I say, allowing myself a tone. Strategically this is perhaps a bad move, as I am reliant on Brent for a ride, but there's also nothing like righteous anger to fuel moxie, and if this continues, I'm going to unsaddle Cisco and wave down a trucker on I-17.

"I have to get Cisco back in."

"I'll be right there," he says, a tone now in his voice.

Thoroughly pissed, I pick up my pace. There is no one here but me, my horse is still saddled in a part of the park where he has no access to water, and if I leave him, he could trip on his reins and get himself hurt. Unlike some people, I have no intention of leaving the ones who have shown me the greatest try, the greatest effort.

I hear a righteous anger in my words and thoughts I have never allowed myself, and I crumple, ashamed. Anger in my world has only ever pushed people further away. It has never been redemptive, as natural fire might be to a prairie or forest. It has only ever been a nightmare—one of the worst things that could happen to a household.

I cry, not for the pain but in profound frustration from loving in such different ways. My instinct is to step in, show care, do what I can to heal hurt and share burdens. Brent's is to step out. Mow some blackberries. Build a barn. Fix broken pipes. Show love through projects rather than offer it heart to heart. We just don't love the same way. Between the thought and the pain, I weep every step of the almost mile back to the tack room in a pathetic ratio of walking to wiping my face and nose on my sleeve.

"Oh no!" a voice says over the rapping sound of a closing truck door.

I look up to see Heidi has arrived early. Over time, I will come to understand early as on time for her.

"Yeah," I snort out a choked laugh as I trudge to Cisco's halter at the hitching post. "I got dumped. Not my best day."

Heidi is wearing a snap-front, long-sleeve plaid shirt over a bright tank top, jeans, a belt and buckle, and well-worn riding boots. Dressed for a first day, but also dressed to work. Her face, so openly cheery on previous meetings, now looks like a crease in a ribbon. I want to hug her like I would a dolly, tell her I'm not usually like this, that she hasn't come to work for embodied disaster.

"Are you all right?" she asks, taking Cisco's halter from me as she sees me fumble. "Do you—oh."

She sees my arm with the hissy inhale that follows presumed pain.

"Yeah," I say, looking down at my misshapen wrist. "I don't think it's good."

She starts stripping both saddle and bridle from Cisco. "Go sit down. I'll take him."

I cannot tell you the relief that comes from her declarative statement.

"His name's Cisco," I say, stepping out of her way. "He spooked at a bird flying out from one of the straw bales. If you're up for it, it could be great to take him back to the jumping course and at least walk him around everything."

"Sure," she agrees, now taking my helmet, which I have disentangled from my head while we've been speaking. "But you need to get to a hospital. Do you have—?"

"My husband is on his way," I say.

"Good," she says. "Now stop that and sit down."

Out of habit, I've started fumbling with Cisco's splint boots—the protective gear I wind onto his front legs before jumping. This doesn't make any sense for several reasons, one of them being that I had just asked Heidi to take Cisco out again, so he may need them.

"Good idea," I say, sitting down in one of the plastic chairs my mother has insisted be imported into the tack room despite the space constraints. Heidi's making sense, speaking all directives, and asking no questions. Her confident clarity is emotional morphine.

Heidi untacks Cisco and steps through the tack room door. "I brought my own saddle," she says. "I'll use that."

I nod, inclining my head toward the empty stand where my saddle belongs. "Good idea," I say again. Smart girl to come prepared. We hadn't discussed tack. I had just assumed she'd use ours. I'm impressed she simply brought hers without any prompting or questions.

Heidi looks at me with a critical eye. "You should drink some water. Where's water?"

I point at the refrigerator a few feet away and idly view the contents as she rummages through the cowboys' alcoholic contraband, then withdraws a plastic bottle.

"Hand me a beer as well, will you?" I ask as she uncaps the water bottle.

I can see her reassessing her estimation of what kind of boss I will be as she complies, then chuckles as I use the sweating aluminum can as a proxy for an ice pack.

I trap the icy can between my wrist and resume sipping water. Satisfied, Heidi returns to work, saddling Cisco with her battered Western saddle.

I hear the familiar sound of leather flaps slapping, creaking; latigo sliding past metal. Ravens caw, horses shuffle, snuffling for leftover feed. I realize it's still early. The sun has not yet cleared the cabin roof in its journey across the sky.

After Brent pulls up, it's a long and weepy drive to Flagstaff Medical Center—a distorted duet of my sobbing and his saying, "You'll be all right." I don't believe him. I am impatient and insulted by every red light. I deeply resent stopping for people crossing the street. I rage at whoever decided the hospital should be at the top of the hill instead of right in the middle of downtown. I am grumpy and sad and embarrassed and scared and literally snotty as we arrive.

Brent rolls past the emergency room overhang, not pausing to drop me off.

I am so shocked, I cannot even utter the word "stop."

Maybe he feels if I can walk myself down the park, I can ride the extra minute to a parking space. I wonder if this is punitive: I wouldn't stop, so now he's not going to? I wonder if he has ever, in our lives, truly understood me. Does he not get that people have limits, that I have limits, that I can only take so much? That when the adrenaline is long past gone and there's only pain, I might want some relief as soon as I can get it? I am disgusted that I have needed him, needed his help, needed his car. I open the door before he can help me any further. I am beyond exhausted and outraged with our misunderstandings. I wonder if the ER will still admit me if I enter pummeling my husband with my one good arm.

A series of sympathetic nurses get me checked in: more questions.

No, I don't need a rabies shot.

No, this was not domestic violence (though I am fantasizing about inflicting some. Yes, I know that's not funny. No, I don't care.)

Pain makes me selfish. I revel in its ugliness.

Yes, I am insured.

Pain level? Compared to what? They're referring to the arm, right? Not the psychic sear of hating myself for hating my husband while he sits beside me ready to assist.

"High," I tell the nurse.

I'm asked to wait.

The shame of angry selfishness confronts me, and I can't stop crying.

Mercifully, the nurse calls me next, and I am wheeled into triage. I sense Brent following and don't know if I want him there or not. Maybe I just want to be broken. Left alone to puzzle out my shattered fragments so I can see them clearly enough to figure out how to knit them back together.

The nurses start me on morphine, and the rest of the day is a fuzzy mix of people—doctors, nurses, all kind, all compassionate. Mom and Dad arriving. Hadn't they been somewhere else? Auntie Mac coming with a gift. A stuffed dragon.

Brent looks in from time to time.

I prefer the dragon's company. I like dragons. *The Hobbit* gave them a bad rap, but that's not their fault. Nor is it Tolkien's . . . people have Tolkien all wrong too . . . dumb drinking songs about miserable marches over rocks . . . Oldham Park is rocky . . . except where I fell . . . fell off of Cisco . . . Cisco!

I cry again.

Someone asks me if I'm in pain.

I nod.

A nurse comes to give me more morphine. I let her, not trying to explain my wrist is the least of what hurts.

I nap, only to be woken by the alarm of the blood-pressure machine, soothing compared to my own thoughts.

I don't know how I'm going to help the ranch now. My one contribution was getting some horses ready for sale, but now . . . Heidi is likely to do that. Thank God for her.

Devil take me: I went from moderately useful to useless in the drop of four feet.

Hello, dragon.

I suspect Brent wants to leave everything: the ranch, Flagstaff, proximity to my family, all of it. I don't know if he wants me to come to wherever he'd rather be. I don't know if I'll want to go.

Oh, dragon.

I nod, the machine bleeps. I wince.

My father and I are not doing well. Whether he is or not, I feel he keeps choosing the cowboys and the way things are over me—and Brent—and the way things could be.

Dragon, I'm sorry, there is no treasure here; I am only hoarding sorrows.

Hours go by.

The nurses are kind.

I am rolled to X-rays and back to triage, then a doctor confirms the break. He explains they're going to put me under so they can straighten me out.

I nod, wishing they had a similar procedure for life. I drift off, tearing.

Then I'm awake, my arm suspended above me.

Brent tells me I invited everyone to come ride horses, before the anesthesia kicked in—that I didn't understand why nobody wanted to come.

A different doctor appears at my gurney. A surgeon. Tall and soft-spoken, with glasses. I will need surgery in a week. The break is worse than a mere cast dictates. But they want the swelling to go down before they operate.

I agree. Everything is too inflamed.

I drift off.

More nurses . . .

My dragon and I regard each other.

The re-setting didn't work to the surgeon's satisfaction, and it's long after nightfall when they roll me into an operating room to try some other alignment procedure. I have no more tears, or I might sob that even the professionals can't get me straightened out.

They'll have to do a general anesthesia.

I nod, accepting.

Then I see the anesthesia mask. Terror rips at what's left of my calm, and I am horrified, a horse to a snake, panicking at the coils and mold that will close itself around everything that allows me to breathe and press against me, pinning my senses, tail arcing up into the heights that hold my breath. I can't look.

Someone from the hospital makes me sign a waiver; in case I die, it's not their fault.

I tell the nurse I am afraid.

I don't have the words for not wanting to be squeezed out, to be constricted, to have my breath, my soul, trapped inside the tubes of a black rubber snake.

The nurse says she will hold my hand. My good one.

I feel her fingers twine with mine as her other hand pats at my knuckles. My tears come back. I want to come back.

The black snake may drag me into nightmarish depths of unconsciousness. May even hiss that I don't have to leave. May tempt me with the release of all this pain—all my torments. But I want to come back. I *will* emerge to free myself of these coils and pressures. I am surprised by the intensity with which I want to awaken. I *want* to *know* I will come back, and I am strangely excited to get to try. How long has it been since I wanted to wake up?

The nurse says she will stay with me.

It's the end of her shift, and late at night, but she says she will stay.

She has kind eyes.

She smiles at me, patting my hand. Her eyes are the last things I see as I pray to the God of Black Snakes that He won't let me fall and stay down, that He will allow me to at least get up; get up and get back on, because that's the only way to ever redeem a fall.

The next few days are a hodgepodge of learning how to dress myself, feed myself, and do other rather personal things one-handed. Those involving the bathroom are a particular challenge.

My left arm lives in its own beige cocoon—wrapped and bandaged and slung across my body, its weight dragging at my neck. I will have to wait two weeks for my surgery. Until then, I am to keep my casted arm in a sling, or keep it elevated. Always keeping it dry.

Pain meds are awful—causing nausea and constipation—two new conditions I do not welcome. Worse is the throbbing pain that cheats me of sleep.

Surprisingly, surgery itself is a nonevent compared with the daily adjustments required to navigate the world with one less able limb.

I quickly ditch the meds and try (with limited success) to sleep on my side, hurt arm steadied against my opposite shoulder. Mom has bought me shoes that lace up with a pull tab. I have a new appreciation for elastic waistbands and plastic hair prongs. I go out to the ranch every day to talk to Heidi about the horses and say hello to Marty and Lena. They sniff at my arm, examining my limp left hand for possible treats. Happily, I discover that feeding treats is one function my hand can still perform.

Progress.

I have been counseled that I should absolutely not ride again until I am fully recovered, as another fall could damage my arm permanently. Forget riding; I might not even be able to hold someone's hand. Assuming there's one being offered, which I don't. Brent hasn't moved yet, but he's interviewing now, and it's only a matter of time before he gets hired into a job that will most certainly not be in Flagstaff. He didn't even apply in Flagstaff.

If I stay out of the saddle, do not fall again, and get well, the doctor tells me I'll be healed up in three months and really back to myself in six. Back to myself. Who or where is that?

Two weeks later, I still don't know, but I do know it's with horses. I also know it's time for them to help me overcome at least one of the fears that has been with me ever since the fall.

Marty is a thoughtful horse: stocky, strong, and intentional about his work. He was a national champion as a three-year-old, and where most horses burn out and sour, even at the age of fourteen Marty stands a little taller at the sight of an approaching saddle and still pricks his ears at the sight of the arena. He willingly fields rider requests, then is affronted if his performance does not seem suitably pleasing. He is cautious—his feet always firmly on the ground—never allowing himself to step somewhere until he's satisfied himself that it will be stable. He has great respect for having a job, and he is accustomed to performing it the very best that he can.

He stands solidly as I mount, ears swiveling, waiting for a cue.

I gather my reins into my right-hand fingers, feeling them quicken past their first, dull response to the unfamiliar objects. I have only ever saddled, mounted, and ridden left-handed, keeping my right hand and side free—in the tradition handed down by centuries of equitation—for swordplay.

Feeling a bit like a knight riding out to turn back a darkness, I nudge Marty into a walk.

Blessedly, any dragons leave us be.

HORSE SALES AND
OTHER TEMPORARY CONDITIONS

Ty watches my one-armed saddle-shuffle from the tack room door and juts his chin in the direction of where Doc and Lucy are flopped out by the truck.

"Heard your dog has cancer," he says.

I'm surprised he's taken notice of anything in our lives, but I smile a little, grateful that he'd offer condolences.

News of Doc's cancer had been another unwelcome event to Brent's and my struggling family. Doc had been eating dirt as though it were peanut butter, and when internet searches didn't surface an answer that fit, we'd consulted the vet. A few blood tests later, we had our answer.

"You can treat him," our wise and weathered vet instructs. "Chemo, radiation, the whole deal. But he'll stop eating and be sick and be skinny, and he still might not make it."

Brent and I just shake our heads. We don't want to put Doc through all those procedures.

"I wouldn't either," our vet says. "Or you can go the other route, which is to just keep him comfortable. Watch him close."

We nod, stroking our oldest friend. He is supremely unconcerned as our hands slide through his pale gold coat, thick, lustrous, and always, always shedding. Even now. I smile a little.

"How long?" I ask.

The vet shrugs. "Maybe three months. Dogs are all different. He'll let you know."

We nod again.

"Thanks," I say as he collects his clipboard and steps toward the door.

The vet shrugs. "Thanks for the trust," he says. "We'll do our best for him."

I really appreciate that neither he nor any of his staff wish me a good day. They just say goodbye with knowing looks.

Ty doesn't have that look now, nor is it quite a smile on his face.

"Yes," I confirm, hoping I won't have to say much more. Platitudes, even in the nonranching world, have always felt limp to me, and here, surrounded by grit and iron, they seem downright flimsy.

"I know what to do for that," he says, grabbing for his rope.

He must be going out to water the horses in the pens. He always takes his rope when he waters—walking up and down the corrals spinning it, winding it, throwing it, never mind how it spooks the horses.

"You do?" I pause, still holding my saddle. This is not an easy thing: my good arm grips the saddle horn, balancing it on my hip to displace its weight.

Marty sidesteps where he's tied, questioning my pause.

"Feed him some antifreeze," he grins, grabs his rope, and strides off.

My jaw drops, as unhinged as I feel. Who jokes about killing a dog? A family member? Even as I remember that Ty is a second cousin, I answer my own question: maybe me. I clap my mouth closed against speaking profane and murderous curses and limp toward Marty, both the saddle and Ty's parting words too heavy to bear easily.

It's as though clocks changed once they hear the word "cancer"—hands and faces soften. Moments tiptoe past whispering condolences, ignoring the indolent demands of the outside world with its bills and its goals and its hurry. Time for us is now defined as the emptiness when Doc doesn't want to eat, or play, or walk, or nap. Brent and I orbit our dog as though the centrifugal force of our constant spiral can catch the tiny grains slipping through the hourglass.

The ranch remains as gritty and indifferent to us as ever, though the same cannot be said about the horses, around whom business is picking up.

True to his butterscotch coloring and nature, Dozer has been purchased by a couple wanting to use him as a saddled escort to the two cart ponies they already own. When Brent and I trailer Dozer to his new home, we are welcomed with a party of cake and soda in the barn while Dozer acquaints himself with his two mini-me roommates—dark palomino miniature horses exactly his color.

Marvin has also found a new home with a training barn in Texas, where his buyer wants to start him as a reining prospect. The man who bought him has an endearing Texas twang, and, far more importantly, uses it to ask professional questions about vet care, hauling papers, and the groundwork Marvin's been taught to date. I feel good about Marvin's prospects.

Twolena's picked a new owner too: Beth, a precocious twelve-year-old from a New Mexico ranch, who has driven over with her mother to try her out. Beth is a hand with the truck, trailer, and all its trappings, handling cords, ratchet straps, gears, and levers the way most preteens would handle bubblegum wrappers.

"She's beautiful!" Beth says as I lead Twolena out to her.

This amuses me, because Twolena is a lot of things—smart, quick, responsive, hardy, gentle, even sweet—but beautiful seems a stretch. "In the eye of the beholder" works its magic both ways, though, as horse and new rider seem smitten with each other in less than half an hour.

"If you shorten your reins a little, and bump, just a little bit—raising your hand straight up over her neck—yep—like that," I coach. "She'll soften up her step and round her back a little in the circle. Do you feel that?"

"I do!" Beth calls, delighted. She should. Twolena is flexing her neck, drawing her nose in as she pushes with her hips, stretching her step farther underneath herself. Then she holds it as gracefully as a Pilates coach might pause mid-pose, looking relaxed as she does so.

"Great! Now make sure you sit straight on her back—keeping your own shoulders square—don't lean," I call. "And don't let her lean either. A little inside leg—yep!"

"I feel it!" Beth calls back.

"You look great!" I say as she goes by, her face its own sun of smiles.

"I *love* her!"

She and the mare are radiant.

Cali's gotten some calls too. She's a flashy red roan, in demand for both her color and Babbitt Ranch breeding. She's been learning quickly, taking to work willingly, though she hasn't yet graduated past her own jitters. Nothing about her is mean, just skittish and prone to flight. A seasoned, patient horseman will understand this as the equivalent of typical kindergartner meltdowns—quick to start, but easy to stop. A less patient rider could make the problem worse by overreacting, which is what I fear when Dad tells me Ty wants to buy her.

"Under no circumstances," I respond, unsurprised that the offer came through my father instead of directly to me. The cowboys and I don't exactly seek each other out. "Ty is a hothead—they'd be a horrible match. Tell him I have someone else looking at her."

Fortunately, as it happens, I do.

A New Mexico rancher wants a horse his wife can bring along for his two young daughters.

"Well, Cali's just a two-year-old," I tell him.

"That's perfect," he says. "The girls are seven now. And my wife wants some time for a project. She won't hand her over for four, maybe five years."

I smile, thinking of Cali around three horse girls—a *My Little Pony* reality show.

"Sounds good," I say. "But I have to ask, what's the ground like where you are? Cali has pretty small feet, and I just worry about her in really rocky country, you know?"

"We've got silt and sand," he says, chuckling. "We do a lot of riding in the sand dunes."

The placement sounds ideal to me. We agree on a price, then set a date for him to see her.

"She's perfect," he says to me while his wife fawns over the filly, both as lovestruck as teenagers when the adults turn their backs. "I'll be back tomorrow with my trailer. We're just gonna stay overnight in Flagstaff—go out to dinner—make a night of things."

I accept his cash, then wish him a good visit. I notice as I drive out that Ty is walking over to the man's truck, but I think nothing of it. Visitors are a novelty to the ranch, and both Ty and Woods like to hear where people came from and what brought them in.

Early the next morning, Mom and I are back out at Oldham Park to load Freckles and Lena in the trailer to drive to a specialty vet in Prescott. Despite their progress, both have injuries we can't seem to find to fix, hitches and halts in their gaits that rest and care haven't been able to solve or smooth. We have an eight a.m. appointment and a ninety-minute drive.

I thought there might be a chance we'd run into Cali and her new family if they, too, wanted to get an early start, but there's no sign of them. Any of them.

Cali's not in her pen.

Panicked, I look again.

No Cali.

I call the buyer.

"'Lo?" he asks, sleepily.

"I'm sorry to call you so early, but I don't see Cali, and I didn't think you were picking her up until today. Did you already come out to get her?" I ask.

"No," he says to some rustling noises in the background. "No, I—well, that guy came out to my truck when I was leaving. Ty? He came out and bought her from me. Said he'd give me five hundred dollars more than I'd paid. Said he really wanted her."

"So, you sold her?" I all but screech.

"Yeah, well. It seemed like a good deal." He clears his throat, perhaps only now registering my outrage. "He said he was gonna tell you. He didn't?"

"No," I state with the tone of lake ice splitting. "He didn't."

I turn as we ring off to look toward the pen where Ty keeps his horses. Sure enough, there's Cali, munching on some hay. She bobs her head over the fence gate as Mom walks by with Freckles.

I feel like someone's burgled my house. I see all the same things that were there yesterday: nothing appears to be missing, but nothing is in place. An intruder snuck past me, violating all sense of privacy and order. That nothing is broken is immaterial. It's as though I've seen a snake in my house: the terror is knowing one can get in.

Despite being one-armed, I mechanically take the lead rope from Mom to step Freckles into the trailer, then have to step out again so she can tie him. "I'm going to kill him."

Mom glances at Freckles in alarm. "Who?"

With my good arm, I slide the divider bolt home with far more force than is necessary.

Freckles flinches.

"Ty," I say. The word feels like cut glass in my mouth as I raise the good hand to Freckles' side, stroking reassurance for both myself and the horse.

Freckles settles. I hold my hand against the biscuit color of his coat: warm, soft, comforting.

"Ty bought Cali back from the guy I sold her to last night."

"He what?!" Mom questions as I hop down from inside the trailer to retrieve Lena from where she's been tied waiting.

I focus on keeping my hands steady, my voice suede instead of sharp.

"Ty offered my buyer five hundred dollars more than he had just paid, to buy Cali back. She's there in the pen with Ty's other horses now." My fingers are as stiff and curt as the words I can no longer say, trespass choking off any further speech.

Lena snuffles, sensing.

Horses are gifted therapists, not caring what emotional state you present to them so long as you are honest about what it is. Try to deny what you want to saddle them with, and that's when a horse flees or fights.

"You've got to be kidding," Mom says, her voice communicating exactly the opposite.

Lena shifts her weight, eyeing me.

I swallow, stroking her shoulder. "I swear to God."

I trace Lena's neck, feeling the sinews of her muscle, reminding me of a rope—how snakes and ropes both coil, lash out, striking across space to immobilize their target. I've heard stories of horses stamping out snakes, but flight has been the instinct I've witnessed. Nostrils flaring, a bit like Lena's are now, they'll scent the snake in a hole or shadow, stop with an emphasis that usually leaves marks, and suggest in every way possible to their rider that anywhere else is a better place to be.

Lena blows, the release quick, purposeful, like a sprinter's, just before a start.

I stroke her neck again. Today is supposed to be about her care, her comfort—finding a future for her without pain.

I rub her withers, kneading the flesh above the bony ridge humans use like we would a car's passenger-seat grab bar—the quickest purchase we can get in "oh shit" moments. It seems unfair that horses have no such handle on us.

I take a deep breath, watching my hand loose Lena's tie rope, watching my feet take steps across the cinders, feeling the extraordinary creature beside me follow, these simple acts feeling momentous in a world where surprise attacks can happen at any time.

As we bump down the frontage road to the freeway, Mom cuts across my silence. "Call your father. He needs to know about this."

I dial.

"Dad?" I say when he picks up. I can't even manage a hello.

"Hello, sweetheart," he says, his voice softening as he registers my tone. "How are you?"

It occurs to me that he could be asking about my arm, which only aches now. It's an alarming metric for the morning that my most broken part hurts less than anything else.

"Pissed," I clench, then begin to tell him why, my voice sounding like the wailing of an acidic guitar in a solo more metal than music.

"I was going to call you about that later this morning," he says. "I didn't think you'd be up so soon."

If I'd been a volcano before, now I am an earthquake, my interior structure crumbling in on itself as I realize Dad not only knew Ty had bought the mare back, but he had allowed it.

"What?" I shout, the road before me blurred with tears and fury. "You knew about Ty buying Cali?"

"He called me about it last night, honey," he says. "He knew you'd be upset—"

"You think?!" I shout. I never, ever shout at my father. In a law of honoring parents and respecting elders as immutable as gravity, my whole life I have never raised my voice to him. In moments of misplaced teenaged vanity, I've screeched about homework or boys or teachers in peacock-worthy wails *around* him, but never, ever *at* him. Something twinges inside my consciousness as I do so now, a tether holding me accountable to our familial law.

"He called me," Dad says in a firmer voice, "which I give him credit for."

"I don't!" I blast. "He went behind my back!"

"He doesn't see it that way," Dad's lawyer voice informs me, the tone evidence enough that Ty has already been judged and acquitted. "Ty said he'd been trying to buy the mare, and he doesn't know what you have against him, but he figured this was the only way he could get her, and he called me to let me know what he'd done."

This outrage is an alien feeling, superpowered by an indignation I have never allowed myself in my work, marriage, or family. It feels summoned—called to me by the force of my care for the ranch horses, for all horses, for their role as the sacred and unchanging in my life. That

Cali could go to a brute is an injustice I cannot stand for, a wrong I must right or lose myself to cowardly complicity.

"I told you," I rasp through teeth gritted against sobs. "I told you Ty would be unsafe for her. I told you she was not suited to work on this ranch because her feet are too small and the rocks are too big and that Ty is a hothead and that they are not a good match."

"Well," he says, judge and jury reluctantly denying the appeal. "You did your job. You sold the horse and got a good price. What's done is done."

Oh, no, it's not. It can't be. I cannot live in a world where this is dismissed. "This is OK with you?"

"Well, no, of course not," he says, the judge in chambers now able to be candid. "You're obviously deeply upset, and Ty's clearly not communicating with you, and now I'm in the middle. So no, none of this is OK with me. But I don't think I should fire him, if that's what you're asking."

I feel the weight of reason wedge itself home, locked, leveraged against me.

"It is."

"I'm not going to do that," he says, a judge now contemplating contempt for misplaced appeals. *This matter is closed. We all have other work to do.*

"I see," I say, ice in my voice, the jagged edge of betrayal against my throat—that Dad would find on the side of He Who'd Made an End Run, going straight to Management rather than working it out with his peers.

Ty doesn't know what I have against him? How about the fact that he suggested poisoning my dog? Or that he'd never so much as acknowledged me or my work with any of the horses, let alone Cali? How about that he would so discount my role and my person as to not only move the mare to his own herd without telling me, a flagrant violation of his precious cowboy ethic, but buy her out from under the deal I'd made? If I'd been a cowboy, it'd be grounds for lynching. I wasn't shocked that I didn't rate the cowboy code; I was devastated that Dad didn't uphold a different one.

"I'm sorry it's happened this way," he says. "And I'm sorry you're hurt."

"Yes, I am." I click off the connection. Another first, as I have never hung up on my father. I sob, at how I have now betrayed him, betrayed myself, my own rules. This is not how a daughter treats her father—not how I want to treat my daddy.

I know he's sorry.

I know he doesn't want me to feel this way.

I also know that understanding is a different capacity from forgiveness, and while I may still be capable of the one, I have nothing of the other, and there, finally is the lasting pain I have been searching for: I have been forgiving hurts from Brent and work and change and the ranch for so long, it is a part that has atrophied past exhaustion to brokenness.

Mom takes the phone from my hand as I crumple into myself, hugging my slung arm to my chest, the cradle too small for everything damaged. I turn into the seat, pulling my knees up and chin down. I wrap my good arm around the huddle as if to hold anything left together.

Mom gently places her hand on top of my good one, holding it there for long, long miles.

I wonder if she feels the shards of my heart as they fracture, splintering to float within our silence, indistinguishable from the dust motes that we haul along through the morning.

BOOTSTRAPS

I like the story I've heard about Picasso, sketching on a napkin while enjoying an outside coffee at a café. A woman realizes who he is and what's about to be lost when he stands and makes his way toward a trash bin, napkin in hand. She stops him and asks, please, to buy the napkin from him. He agrees, saying it will cost her tens of thousands of dollars. She's aghast—this for a sketch that took him a matter of a few minutes? Not a few minutes, but decades, he corrects her.

My family likes to reference the punchline from a greeting card my father gave to Mom when they were dating: Charlie Brown is standing under the words "Everything's coming up roses!" with an astonished smile on his face, the wobbly one that looks like it could have just as easily been a doodle from a pen being tested for ink. When the recipient opens the card, there is the confession: "I planted tomatoes."

The point of these stories forms the spectrum of why I suppose things got better for me at the ranch, and why they get better at all. Effort and still more effort may eventually yield, if not mastery, at least familiarity, maybe even competence. There is also an alchemy of time mixing with opportunity that brings change.

To pull ourselves up by our own bootstraps is among the most compelling of Western myths. Of course, we can set ourselves to the required tasks for a harvest. We can return again, and again, perhaps for decades, tending to what we hope to create, but the truth is that we'll rarely be alone. Others, regardless of footwear, will have tremendous influence on what and how and when we plant, and especially on what we reap.

FRIENDS, WATER,
AND OTHER ESSENTIALS

"I just want to make sure I'm clear," I say into the phone. "You want me to come on a trip to Oregon, and I don't have to pay for it?"

"Right," the cheerful voice of the trip's coordinator says back. I'm so startled at the offer of a truly free trip I can't even remember her name. "You'll be part of a group the Water Resources Research Center is assembling to go tour water management in several river basins in Oregon. It's part of a grant for studying collaborative water planning among water managers and agricultural producers."

"Oh," I say, disappointedly realizing they must have the wrong Wilson. It's my father who's the water expert: he's handled water-rights contracts, litigation, and legislation in Arizona for thirty years. "You're sure you want *me* to go?"

I don't mean to sound thick. Or pathetic. I'm just at a loss to understand why I've been called.

The voice laughs. "Yes. You met Dr. Dalmedge at graduation, right? She said you had a nice conversation."

"We did," I agree, remembering back to the ceremony when Dad was presented with an honorary doctorate by the University of Arizona. Those months were lifetimes ago now: when Lucy Puppy was smaller, when Doc didn't have cancer, when I was happy to be moving to Oldham Park, when I had the use of both arms. "Wow. Well, this is really nice of her. Yes—yes, sure I'll go."

The ranch can spare me: Heidi has the remaining horses well in hand, and the Jersey calves salvaged from the dairyman are eating and growing. Brent hasn't asked for my help on that project, nor on any other. I want to ask him about going. I want to go to give us both a break.

The voice promises an email to confirm all the trip details before I ring off, still feeling stunned.

Two weeks later, I'm at the airport participating in priority boarding, as I am among those who need the extra time to get both myself and my bags situated on the plane. I am equal parts relieved and self-conscious, as the special needs designation reminds me of the new medical information I've learned that is both less obvious, and more permanent, than my broken arm.

When pain from the break kept me up night after night, I gave up on hoping exhaustion itself would be enough and went to my doctor for help.

Much as I trust my veterinarian, and grateful as I've been for the hospital's care, I don't equate doctor's offices with safe places. Well before leaving Washington, on the advice of my counselor, I had asked my general practitioner if he could help my emotional struggles with an anti-depressant. He consulted my chart.

"I can, but it says here that you're twenty pounds overweight; now, can you lose that?"

The question shattered me. At the time, I was running four to five miles four to five times a week, plus riding horses, plus walking dogs—I wasn't sure I could do more. Plus, I was on my own, without friends, without society, and with diminishing security in my marriage—I wasn't sure what else I could give up.

When I devolved into tears, the doc prescribed the meds—which caused me to gain weight and made sex painful, so I'd stopped them after a few weeks.

Someplace in the depths where all memories mix, I had equated medicine with entrapment: aid will be dispensed only conditionally, and its administration will create new problems I will feel similarly powerless to address.

It was only because of a bigger, more debilitating trap posed by postoperative sleep deprivation that I had approached my doctor to plead for help. In this case, another condition had been imposed before treatment: bloodwork, which had led to being diagnosed with hypothyroidism, likely a contributor to not only the sleep problems but the weight gain, fatigue, and emotional struggles that had plagued me for what felt like ages.

Steadying my steps as I make my way down the ramp, I recall how I limped along on emotional crutches for months, even years, trying to appear able-bodied when in fact I was not. I'd known I was depressed, but when I couldn't find a medical regimen that would help without creating other problems, I resolved to manage my symptoms by either powering through or dismissing them as illegitimate. My new information entitles, even compels me to accept that I struggle because my physical self cannot produce the necessary components to make me either wake or sleep properly, and the related depression has been such an enfeebling state that even without the additional challenges posed by an unsympathetic doctor, I couldn't admit to the hopelessness I've been living with, even, and perhaps especially, to myself.

Now, I know the medications are helping, but the things they're helping me with aren't words I'm ready to say publicly. Hypothyroidism. Depression. They may be blameless descriptions of my physical state, but I still feel they are flaws, and my experience in both the horse and the consulting world has taught me that imperfections diminish worth.

Even more frightening, I know how hard and costly and frightening it has been for me to advocate for treating the imperfect ones in these worlds with compassion, and I'm not sure how much advocacy might be available for me.

It occurs to me that accepting help for my broken arm might provide me with valuable practice in acknowledging my physical state fully and without shame, especially when the admission results in new forms of assistance.

I meet the rest of the water group at a Mexican café in Redmond, Oregon. Right away I feel like the lone weed in a bumper crop. I'm not a hydrologist or water manager. I'm not an agricultural professional, consultant, or expert. I do know how precious water is to our ranch, and I know how much we've invested to be able to access it, but this feels like chaff among the seeds as I look around at nametags referencing utility companies, irrigation districts, and universities.

Dr. Dalmedge asks us each to introduce ourselves: our name and a little about our backgrounds.

I don't want to share most of what's defined me.

I decide I can focus on what I have to do with water. "I'm Julie. My family has a cattle ranch in northern Arizona and very little water. We have a food-truck-size generator that powers a twelve-hundred-foot well at a property between Cottonwood and Sedona. Our other water comes from stock tanks or water haulers that replenish potable water tanks aboveground every week."

This isn't much of a crowd-pleaser. Thankfully, I also have a story.

"I think people assume that water just happens, and whatever is there will happen again once they take what they want. My husband was out herding cattle a couple weeks ago and came across a man who'd set up camp for himself and his eight horses next to one of our stock tanks. He was not only watering all the horses, but he had set up a pump to pipe water out to fill up his trailer tanks."

"Seriously?" a man asks. He's tall and soft-spoken, and he works for Farm Bureau. His nametag says *Bob*.

I nod. "So, Brent asks, 'Hey—do you have permission to be taking that water?' And the man just says, 'I don't need permission—water's free.'"

Bob shakes his head.

"So, Brent explains that the water belongs to us as the leaseholders on the land and that we're the ones who have to keep up the stock tanks, and we do that so our cattle can drink when they come through," I go on, "and the guy just says 'Yep—water's mighty important.' Doesn't stop what he's doing, doesn't apologize, nothing!"

"People just don't get it," Bob says, as others in the group nod agreement.

"Well this guy didn't," I agree, relieved to have something relatable to share.

The first day of our excursion, we load into a plush coach to motor east for the John Day River. The countryside around Redmond and Bend is arid juniper scrag under blue jay skies: a Flagstaff doppelganger feeling so familiar I squeeze my toes inside my sandals just to remind myself I've traveled. Unlike in northern Arizona, an hour's drive here delivers us to lush meadows—pastures of dense, foot-high grass—grass enough to roll into bales the size of tractor tires.

I could weep for grass envy.

"These ranchers we're going to meet have sold their hay by the cutting," we're told by a local conservation agent. "Most of them have sold us the water they'd usually use for a third or fourth cutting. They don't actually need the hay by that time, and the money's the same, so they sell their water to us and we keep it in the river for the salmon."

I raise my good hand. "How is the money the same?" I ask. "Most alfalfa-hay producers charge a lot more for third- or fourth-cutting hay—it's a lot more desirable."

Although my own family grew alfalfa in the fields around the house where I grew up, I didn't know the difference in price until I'd started buying hay by the squeeze for the ranch's horse herd and by bales for the Jerseys. The only characteristic in common is that the ranch is looking for the lowest price, but where I want the third or fourth cutting for the greater amount of leaves and stems for the horses, I want first-cutting alfalfa at best for the calves, for its fibrous bulk.

"Well—most people aren't growing to sell," the guide explains. "They're growing for something extra to feed their stock during dry spells."

I wonder what a dry spell comes to in this comparative rainforest.

The farm we visit feels like a holiday scene: fields fit into river bends the way my grandmother places her copper cutters along the curved edge of rolled cookie dough.

The owner apologizes that there's not an open path to the river's edge. "We planted all these shrubs a few years ago for the salmon. You know—they need shade."

I try and fail to keep a straight face.

"Really—the fish need shade to keep the water cool enough," he says earnestly.

"I know the feeling," I grin. "I could use more shade on my ranch too, but my stock tends to eat it."

The idea of grass-fed beef is a joke among most Arizona ranchers, grass being the one plant source their cows can't find. Understandably, no one has tried to launch a "scrub-fed" or "cactus-fed" label, as it sounds like it should come with toothpicks.

The rancher looks at me curiously.

"You have livestock in Arizona?" he asks.

"Sure," I say, more shocked at his surprise than I was at the idea of fish-cooling landscaping. "We're a cow-calf operation."

"I didn't think you had enough grass for cows in Arizona," he says.

"That's the challenge," I agree.

He smiles understanding as another of our group asks a question.

I listen to the questions posed about in-stream flows, retired water rights, and other things I don't follow, feeling like one of the salmon might when encountering sandbar shallows.

"A little different from back home, isn't it?" a feminine voice says beside me.

Large, brown eyes shine from above a genuinely welcoming smile.

"Yeah," I agree. "There's so much water here they build ladders in it and shade over it. There's so little water at home we have to use ladders to get to it."

She laughs. "True enough. I'm Nancy—I've wanted to talk to you the whole trip."

"Oh?" I ask, surprised. Bob and others have been kind in the well-mannered way that people adopt among the pitied, and I've appreciated it, but I haven't exchanged more than pleasantries with anyone. Of course, I also haven't tried that hard. Travel with my arm is a bigger pain than I had expected in every sense of the word, and it doesn't help that the discomfort is fighting for stage time with all my insecurities.

"My husband used to run the Apache Maid," she says. "And you're—"

"Really?" I interrupt, excitedly. The Apache Maid is an extensive ranch in the Verde Valley—closer to Camp Verde than Sedona. The story I've heard is that my great-uncle actually wanted to buy it, and the hodgepodge parcels and permits in the Verde Valley and on the Coconino Plateau that constitute our current ranch were a very distant second choice.

She chuckles. "Yep. He was their construction manager. He's got lots of great stories."

"It'd be fun to hear them," I say as the group gets called back to the bus.

Nancy defers the request, feeling her husband would make those stories' best narrator, but indulges my interest by telling me about how she moved from Washington to Arizona for college and ended up married to a cowboy and working ranches all over central Arizona. That roller-coaster life got a little rough for raising her son, so she divorced herself from her cowboy and his endless migrations to become a ladies' shop owner, then a development officer for the main community college in the area.

She knows more cowboys than I do.

She knows more ranches than I do.

She's ridden far more ranges than I have.

Thoroughly humbled, I tell her a little about what we've been up to, but it turns out she's already been all over our website and wants to know about our Jersey calf project.

I'm embarrassed unto intimidation. I hadn't even thought to research the other trip participants. Attempting to stumble through a new round of self-judgment, I describe who's doing what. She interrupts, "Ty's your cousin? Are you a Wilson?"

I grimace in anticipation of her reaction. "Theodore's my dad."

She seems as impressed as I had just been hearing about her. Most people are. Dad's been a fighter pilot, farmer, lawyer, and priest, and many people call him to run boards and businesses for one area of knowledge, not knowing the many others he carries with him. Public service is more than an obligation to my dad—it's a calling.

Nervous to be found even less impressive by comparison, I return to an earlier comment. "So, you say you're working on the Southwest Wine Center? I thought winemakers in Arizona use California or New Mexico grapes."

She looks at me like I'd reported that in Cottonwood, Arizona, Christmas is celebrated in August. "Who told you that?"

"I called a winery in Jerome." I tell her the name.

"Oh, those people are the biggest grumps," she says.

"They told me grapes won't grow in the Verde Valley."

She laughs, the sound reminiscent of the water we'd just seen spilling over river rocks, ample with play. "That's hilarious! Grapes won't grow? Grapes have been growing in the Verde Valley for over two hundred years! We're planting our own vineyard at the college. That's just—well, it's just—well, there are people you need to meet." Her words trip over one another, crowded by her intention to reassure me.

A few rows back and several hours later, I am befriended by Nancy's friends and acquaintances: the mayor of Clarkdale, a reporter for the Camp Verde Bugle, and the president of the Friends of the Verde River, who all assure me that grapes grow just fine in the Verde Valley, thank you very much, and are more than happy to introduce me to people back home who can tell me if they'll grow on my ranch.

I could be running though sprinklers, splashing through fountains, boogie-boarding in the surf I am so happy: friends and opportunity, all in one day?

My voice sounds buoyantly adolescent, an eighth grader asking permission to stay an hour longer at the water park, when I call Mom at the end of the day. "Want to be wine ranchers?"

PINK AND OTHER FRIGHTENING COLORS

When I left for my trip, northern Arizona conditions had been like a hand-lotion ad: dry and crusty, with a high chance of itch. Since I've been back, a late monsoon season has transformed Oldham Park into a slice of what I toured: stock tanks full to brimming, puddles rutting out roads, and velvet pastures rippling in the summer breeze. Unfortunately, moisture also brought along flies, and though we try to keep them from our horses with spray, ultimately we rely on fly masks.

These molded mesh masks with fuzz-lined ear holes strap close under the horse's jaw, giving the effect of overly large, wraparound sunglasses. Sage is the first to need one, followed by Lena.

Sage has been getting all kinds of special attention lately, as he impaled himself on something sharp enough to tear out a chunk just beneath his back muscle. Puncture wounds are very prone to infection, so I call the vet clinic—again—requesting a ranch call. It's Dr. Eastman's partner, Dr. Crosby, who will come to stitch him up. They both know me by my first name now: I'm a regular caller, what with Doc's cancer, cattle vaccinations, Vegas and Lena's lameness, and, most recently, rattlesnake vaccines for the dogs. Flies aren't the only things that like moisture.

Like everything else at Oldham Park, the hay barn has been segregated into "cowboy" and "outsider" territories. I had placed grain and supplement bins for my herd on some pallets along an unoccupied wall. One morning as I was doling out rations, I happened to look down at the dark spot between bins and saw a coil. A moving coil.

I jumped out of there with an agility worthy of a high school track star and ran to the cowboy cabin, not bothering or caring about my trespass.

"Um, guys?" I asked, after knocking and pushing open the door.

Woods was at the stove, pushing something around a skillet. Marshall, a young, blond, and wiry cowboy from a neighbor ranch, sat at the table in front of an empty plate. "There's a rattlesnake in the hay barn."

They both looked at me for a long minute, disapproving expressions indicating I had childishly interrupted the adults, and I should really grow up.

"You wanna get that, Marshall?" Woods asked. "I've got lunch cookin'."

Marshall stood, unhurried.

I felt like I did when I used to wake Dad with tales of monsters under the bed.

Marshall picked up a shovel from beside the cabin and followed me to the hay barn, where I pointed out the dark and shiny shape.

"Oh, yeah," Marshall said, understanding smoothing his voice as a parent might the top of a child's head. "That's one of the mean ones."

"Mean ones?" I repeated, not knowing rattlesnakes came in any other variety.

"A green," Marshall said, then drove the shovel point down into the coils in one violent stroke. "Mojave green."

"Oh," I said uselessly, watching him scoop the twitching body onto the metal shovel head to carry it out to the yard.

"Do you want the rattle?" he asked, pausing before the firepit.

Why—for earrings?

I shook my head. "No thanks."

He tossed the limp loops onto the charred logs, then walked back to the cabin, as unhurried as he'd walked out.

I went back to my buckets and finished my chores, but I watched where I stepped a little more closely the rest of the day.

I wanted a ranch call today because Sage isn't our only patient.

Not being able to ride Lena yet, I've been hand-walking her at least two lengths of the park every day, just to keep her fit. Her gait still isn't even, though we've checked with the specialists, and I'm hoping that her new shoeing and more rest will give her the comfort she needs to saddle up again. In this weather, to avoid the mud in the park we've had to alter course, walking along the frontage road—a sight that gives passing freeway traffic much amusement. I've learned to just wave and keep walking.

When I enter Lena's corral today, halter in hand, I notice that, for once, Marty isn't pestering her.

Marty's harassment of Lena is an activity that both of them usually enjoy: she backs toward him, he stretches out his neck to nuzzle her hip, she feigns insult by stomping a foot, he jerks back as if startled, then they do it all again. At least once an hour, we'll hear a squeal when he actually nips at her and she complains either from the force or the affront of it.

Today, they're standing at opposite ends of the pen.

Strange.

Lena pulls away as I reach for her. Also very strange.

I talk to her, rubbing her shoulder while I get a rope around her neck, asking her to allow me closer. She holds her neck stiff and away, barely allowing me to unlatch her mask.

Once it's off, I see the raw, oozing, bloody mess that used to be her eyelid.

I remove the mask slowly, controlled movement still a challenge with just one arm. The saturated mesh has dried, becoming part of the scab. Lifting it free hurts—she jerks away, restarting the bleeding.

When the vet arrives to treat both her and Sage, Dr. Crosby suggests we trailer her into the clinic.

"You can't mess around with an eye," Dr. Crosby says. "They're too fragile. You don't want it to get infected and lose it."

No, I don't.

"You can park her with us a couple days," Dr. Crosby suggests. "A little horsey bed-and-breakfast plan for the holiday weekend. We'll stitch her up and look after her—keep her from getting messed with for a few days."

Holiday weekend, I think, slow to remember. Right—Labor Day. Until now, I've associated it with looking forward to Brent's and my anniversary—some time off together, maybe a trip. This year, labor seems the right word to describe most of my life: I am working at everything, hoping and hustling for better.

I have very low expectations for either a holiday or anniversary celebration. Brent has transitioned to a Phoenix life during the week: new job, new apartment, new future free from the ranch. I'm choreographing my chores, grouping the majority for days when he doesn't visit. Wanting to make his time visiting me and the dogs and the ranch as pleasant as possible, I've been trying to clear periods of ease into the weekend days—times when I'm not on call, times when we can hike or stroll around Flagstaff like a normal couple. I envy my mare for what will be a few days' vacation, even if her bed-and-breakfast is located at the vet clinic.

The holiday passes, observed. I feel disembodied, noting Brent's play with the dogs, joy on horseback, care to hold my hand before crossing the streets. This is the man I fell in love with: the man who jokes and jests with life, waking with a smile on his face. He's energetic and purposeful, excited by the prospects of his new position, eager to chase new transit projects in the West.

It's not that I miss his sadness, but the change from despondency to this alacrity feels like I missed a formative scene in the movie of his life, and for the rest of the plot, I'll be a step behind, not quite getting what I'm seeing.

Still, we've cleared five years together in what's felt like a narrow victory in an Olympic-scale, high-jump effort.

I don't ask probing questions.

Neither does he.

A few days later, we're all back to our normal routines. Sage has healed well enough to be running the herd with Cheyenne, Lena is home with a stitched-up eyelid under almost a quarter inch of ointment, and I'm working with Freckles now, trying to make him a competitive trail horse. He seems to like the work, pricking his ears more frequently, even swishing his tail when I approach.

To make the trail course, Mom and I drag fallen branches out from under the pine trees to form L-shapes, a box, and step-overs scaled to both walk and trot. Freckles places his feet thoughtfully and doesn't mind going backward or sideways, even with obstacles in the way.

Finding an enjoyable activity is good for both of us.

Trail is something I can do with just one arm. It's a skill-based activity, requiring negotiation rather than pace. Instead of speed or power, it's a job of foot placement, direction, and focus. I'm finding that Freckles favors subtlety: the more gently I ask, the more willingly he responds.

It's a little sultry as I finish a ride, and I hose Freckles off before returning him to his pen, which is a few down from Lena's. She knows that my order of work calls for her to be haltered next for our walk down the road. Usually, she would be standing at her gate in anticipation of the outing, but today I don't even see her. I wonder if Mom already took her out.

I don't see either of them at the hitching posts as I step into the tack room to switch halters, slug some water, and step out again, removing my hat to wipe my sweaty forehead. I've given up on cowboy hats, ball caps, and visors. I am now wearing a Spanish-style, straight-brimmed straw hat with a stampede string. It sits well, shades well, and, most importantly, ties on. But any hat is hot right now, and I'm glad for a moment to air out.

Wondering why I haven't seen Lena, I cut my break short, swing my hat back on, and walk back toward her corral, now truly confused.

She is still not visible, nor is she at the wash rack or in the round pen.

I wonder if she could have gotten out—or maybe somebody took her. Maybe that guy who drove in looking for mares the other day. I had told him I had one of the breeding he really wanted. I even walked him over to see Lena. That was stupid—I should never do that again. I always want to trust people.

I see her.

My beautiful, fastidious mare is writhing in the cinders.

Her mane and tail are matted. Her coat is grimy. She is sweaty. Filthy.

Marty stands at a distance, tender worry in his eyes.

I hurry to Lena, trying to be soft with my steps. I don't know whether I should kneel or stand beside her. I don't know anything except that she is in horrific pain. It rises from her in waves as she twists, trying to free herself from it.

I know she can't. Not on her own.

The equine digestive system's main and most important component is the small intestine, which can be up to fifty feet long. It's crammed into a space about the size of a beer keg, and, when things go wrong, it cramps, twisting up on itself, creating serious blockages. In the worst cases, it becomes impassable. Any variation of this is called "colic," and it's the leading cause of death for horses.

I register the manure matted in Lena's tail, her sweat-soaked neck, her mane—almost indistinguishable from the cinders that have been ground into it.

I have to get her up.

If I can get her up . . .

If I can get her up and get her walking . . .

If I can get her up and get her walking . . . and keep walking. Then . . .

If I can get her up, then maybe . . .

I fumble it. I don't want to scare her, but I know I have to. I have to insist. She has to be convinced it will be worse for her to stay where she is than to get on her feet. I ask, I plead, I urge, I insist, I shout.

I hate myself.

As soon as she's up, I get her haltered and walking. Stepping slowly—so slowly—so unsteadily.

Her ankles twist beneath her.

She buckles.

I urge her forward. I insist she must go forward.

I dig for my cell phone between tortured circuits of the yard. I make calls.

Time passes. Lena staggers.

People arrive: Brent, Heidi, Mom, the vet.

The vet says there's nothing medical they can do—she'll need surgery, but they don't perform that sophisticated procedure. She'll have to go to Phoenix.

Brent hooks up the truck and trailer to take her. He says he'll drive her. He says I don't have to come. He grips my shoulder and kisses my forehead.

I nod. I'd like to tell him how much I appreciate this, but I can't form the words.

Because we know—we all know, looking at her, that she's not going to survive that trip.

And yet, she can't stay here. The ground is too shallow to dig to bury her, and I won't have her picked at by scavengers.

I realize I've already made the decision.

It's a bizarre thing to call a transfer facility—a place that's seen the last of everything—and have them try to make you feel better.

"I need to bring in a horse," I stammer.

"Oh," the woman on the line says. "A horse . . . oh . . . oh, I'm so sorry."

"Yeah," I say. "Um, how does it work?"

"You're a Coconino County resident, honey?" she asks. Her voice is comforting, like the duty teacher during recess who finds you with the wind knocked out, having fallen from the monkey bars.

"Yes."

"Then just bring your ID. We'll take it from there," she says.

I don't want her to have to take anything. I am winded, beaten, broken, and I can't get up for this. But I have to. I know I have to.

I struggle.

"I understand," I say.

I've lied. I don't understand. I don't fucking understand. I will never—

"I'm sorry to ask you, honey, but if you want to do this tonight, you need to be here in another forty-five minutes. We'll have to do some digging, see, and—

"It's all right," I tell her. "We'll make it."

We have to get Lena into the trailer.

I don't want to.

I'm crying, even as I click at her.

I swear she rolls her good eye at me. Just once. It's small. But she's never been able to stand me fussing. She disapproves of fussing. Mostly I think she disapproves of me. In between loving me. Which was most of the time.

She loads perfectly, without fuss. Of course.

Then she folds in on herself, kneels, and lies down.

Dr. Crosby assesses her from the trailer door, then turns to me with a question.

There's only one answer. I nod.

The syringe is bright pink.

Ketamine.

Then it isn't. The cylinder is dull and empty.

"I love you," I choke.

I see Lena's eyelid flutter.

She knows. She always known everything.

"I love you . . . I love you . . . I love you . . ."

FARRIERS AND
OTHER HUMORISTS

The world is enamored of extreme sports. We love to watch people climb, run, drive, swim, dive, and zip along on wires, pursuing ever-increasing heights, gladiators, sharks, trucks, storms, bulls and other hazards, betting on whether or how long we can cheat death. Ranchers don't want any cheating where death is concerned: they don't want to lose cattle to it prematurely, and they don't want to lose money when it comes time to sell the herd for harvest. Words like "harvest" and "processing" make the inevitability and necessity of death more comfortable. In some ways, we know we're in the death business, but it's just as much a business of life: of feeding, growing, breeding, and sustaining populations. This is not what we think about. We think about the business: prices, weights, range conditions, genetics.

I am enough of a rancher to accept that with livestock, mortality is inevitable.

I am not enough of a rancher to think of Lena as livestock.

She was the most feminine thing about me. She was sass and flirtation, beauty and opinion. She was a mother and seductress, showgirl and best friend. She was archetypal, just by being herself.

She was love.

I am less without her.

The horses still in my care are not her, nor are they livestock to me. They are investments to the ranch, needing to be liquidated for cash, so my work goes on.

Horseshoeing is a job that requires you to be near all the dangerous parts of a horse: near his teeth, with your butt and back exposed; near his tail, with your whole self in just the right position to be kicked or, ahem, dropped on; and right under his feet, just asking to get stomped on.

Not only that, but horseshoers, properly called "farriers," carry prongs, hammers, nails, red-hot metal, and a reluctantly raised limb attached to a twelve-hundred-pound beast that really doesn't want them around.

As such, the farriers I've met have been calm, quick, and practical. Those I've grown to like are also curious, observant, decisive, and funny.

Brent and I learned some of the basics about trimming and filing from a farrier friend in Washington when he came to trim Marty.

After hearing us say that we'd like to learn a little about taking care of our horses' feet, he assumed a wry expression and handed me an old file, saying, "You're not going to get into trouble with this. It's too dull for you to really take much off with it. But if you use it every few weeks, you'll get a feel for how the hoof grows and how to shape it."

I took the file from him and picked up Marty's front foot, adopting the farrier's stance: face toward the rump, knees in, crouched over in a squat, balancing and holding the foot and leg between my two knees with the strength of my inner thighs. Within seconds, I had a head rush, backache, and dry throat, and my legs were trembling in the unfamiliar, weighted position. I managed a few quick swipes with the file before staggering out of that ungodly pose.

"Uncle," I pronounced, shocked.

The farrier just laughed.

Brent smiled, took the file from me, picked up Marty's hind foot (much heavier than the front), and gave me an "I'll show you" grin. Within a minute, he was swaying and sweat was beaded on his forehead.

He stood and steadied himself, his hand on Marty's rump. "It's not so bad," he claimed.

Uh huh.

As if there weren't enough already, farriers also confront the additional workplace hazards of the well-meaning-but-idiot owner.

Horses attract all kinds: people who love them for their mystery, people who love them for their athleticism, people who love them for their exclusivity—at some price points, and others who just love them. The first and last categories tend to be the most dangerous, because they're the owners who will work hardest and least effectively at providing horses good care. Being one of them, I understand the penchant for reading every available article on grooming, vaccinations, shoeing, and other horsemanship from journals and magazines, online, and in breeders' circulars. I know the excitement of learning a new term and the empowerment of feeling you understand just a bit more about this massive and wonderful enigma we call "horse." I also know that whatever it is I seem to learn usually doesn't stand up to an actual professional's experience.

One memorable time, at a horse show, I was grouped with some other riders at the in-gate where bridles are exchanged, horses are brushed off, chaps are rolled down, jackets are taken off—all the little finishing touches that make up the transition from warmed up to ready to show. Behind me in the warm-up area, a woman was unsuccessfully trying to get her horse to perform a flying lead change—a maneuver that sounds exciting but is actually a little like a stutter-step or skip to quickly change direction. Basketball players perform it with two legs mid-dribble. The horse does it on four mid-gallop.

This well-intentioned lady was giving all the cues, even unto painful exaggeration, trying to get the change in between a left and right circle. Her trainer was standing aside, near the rail, having given up telling her that right before her class was maybe not the best time to drill until exhaustion on any one maneuver. A friend of my trainer's, arms hooked through the fence rails, observed, in his country twang, "I think that horse has a back problem."

My trainer and I looked at the ongoing spectacle, then turned back to the man.

"What? He seems fine—what do you mean?"

The man shrugged and nodded. "Look at what's on his back."

Jim the Farrier would never challenge the Marlboro Man to an arm-wrestling contest, first because he wouldn't have the time, and second because it's not in his nature to humble a hero for something as silly as ego. If, however, Mr. Marlboro forgot to close a gate or dared smoke his cigarettes near the hay barn, Jim would take a rasp to his butt in ways that would leave him de-horsed for quite some time.

Tall, lean, and tucked-in, Jim approaches our herd the way an officer might a ragged line of new recruits, partially because he knows that life. When he's not shoeing or looking after his own cattle herd, he's flying for the Air Force. I consider him an authority on all things cattle, but whatever topic he chooses, he can always make me laugh.

"Owners," he says, while he's bent over trimming and shaping a foot, "have no idea—most of 'em—of how to run a ranch. They tell you they want to make a profit, and then they tell you to do the stupidest thing imaginable that's just going to end up costing them money." He shakes his head. "I've been hired by some real pieces of work."

I nod, trying not to smile as I stand holding the horse he's working on. "Hard to find a good owner these days."

"No kidding, it is," he says without artifice. He stands to gesture at me with his file. "At least you'll say when you don't know something, and you'll talk to people. Most owners just come in, lay down the law expecting me to say 'Yes sir,' and that's it."

"I might enjoy that sometimes," I joke.

He grins. "Cowboy troubles?"

"Oh, you know." I weigh whether or not I want to tell these stories and quickly give in, knowing I have a sympathetic and knowledgeable audience.

"OK, so the latest is that the guy that helps run things for us over the winter—Cody—told me that next time he sees Woods he's going to settle things up between the two of them the old-fashioned way. He's standing there basically telling me he's going to try to beat up on another one of my employees."

"Sure," Jim says, as though I've just observed that fish need water.

"So, I have one guy whose dog attacks me, and another guy who wants to attack the first one," I say. "And I don't know a lot, but it seems to me I just might have an HR problem."

"Nah," Jim says, standing and rustling through his shoeing box. "That's just cowboys."

"Jim," I cringe. "That can't possibly be true."

"Sure it is," he says. "All these guys get in a fight and a wreck at least once a year—more like twice—it's just part of the job."

"Why?" I ask, dumbfounded that he can be so lackadaisical about this.

"Just how they're raised—how it's done—how everybody does it," Jim says.

"But . . ." I search for an argument. "It's dangerous."

Dear God, I sound lame.

"So's everything else they do," Jim says, glancing at me from the corner of his eye. "And it's not like you're working with the cream of the crop here."

He fits a cooled shoe to the hoof to test its shape.

"I should know. I can tell you," he grins, "you have to be a little nutty to want this life. There's a story I heard once . . ."

He goes back to his forge, tosses the shoe in, closes the door, and turns it on.

"Government dude comes out and says, 'We've had some complaints about the work environment here. Maybe you can tell me who does what.' Guy says, 'Well, there's the guy that runs cows dusk to dawn; the one that drives the truck, throws the feed, fixes fence, fights with the bank, fixes pipe, brands, and breaks ice out of the troughs; and the one that rides the other pasture and then goes in and sleeps with my wife.' Government dude says, 'Sounds like I should start with him. Who's that guy?' Guy says, 'There'll all me—I own the place.'"

Jim grins even wider, picks up a pair of tongs as he opens the forge, withdraws the red-hot shoe, then places it on his anvil to beat with a metal mallet, changing its shape and angles.

I don't respond except to smile. I wish I could laugh, could feel some sense of pride in being part of the group, but I still feel like the rookie who hasn't paid her dues.

And nobody's sleeping with me these days. Even when Brent does, we don't.

Jim looks at me quickly but closely as he finishes, then drops the shoe into a bucket of water where it steams.

"You're trying to do the right thing here," he says. "I can see that. Your heart's in the right place. You'll be fine."

I take a deep breath and look away. "I don't feel so fine, Jim."

"I know you don't," he says, withdrawing the shoe from the water and shaking it as he steps back in to nail it on. "That's just all part of it. So, how's your beef business going?"

His reassurance feels like a coach's clap on the back. I pick my head up.

I tell him I'm getting calls from people interested in beef straight from the ranch. This is both safe and familiar ground, as Jim and I typically exchange news about cattle prices and herd health as part of our standard small talk.

"The Jerseys haven't gone so well," I tell him. "But our next herd will be black, and heavier, and I'm trying to sell a few ahead—taking orders in a way."

"For beef?" he asks.

"No. I can't get the inspections part worked out. All we have up here is state, and I'd need federal inspections to be able to sell cuts."

"Is that right?" he asks. "I don't know much about that end of the business, but I thought you can sell cuts. I thought I've seen 'em at farmer's markets."

I nod. "You have. You can sell cuts to a person who intends to eat them and not either resell them or take them across state lines. But you have to be federally inspected to sell to a store or a restaurant, and that's what I really want to do. I've been calling all over—I figured out I could supply Bashas' grocery chains and New Frontiers if I could turn eight head a month. Even buying some feed, I figured out how to do that—I just need a hay grinder."

"No kidding?" he says, standing up, excited. "I love my hay grinder. I got it on Craigslist, and all my friends told me I was nuts. But that thing has saved me so much more than what I bought it for—"

"Right!" I interrupt, quick to jump into the fun of anticipating success. "I figured out I can grow fodder feed—you know the wheat grass you see in juice bars? I could grow that in these oven-type things—all the nutrition they'd need—and mix it with crap hay or straw for miles less than alfalfa costs—no problem—just need the grinder—"

"I hear you, man," he says. "I used to lose so much money on feed that'd go to waste because it'd get old or dry and nothing'd eat it—now I don't waste anything—"

"That's why I want one!" I say, only peripherally aware that most women wouldn't get so excited about an appliance purchase of this kind. "I could do all that and feed up the cows and get them processed and supply these stores. And it'd be great—except the shipping costs kill me."

"Really—how so?" he asks, standing and resting an arm across the horse's rump.

He's rapt with attention. For a minute, I wonder about the last time I captivated a man to this degree.

"So, I'd be making at least two trips a month down to Tucson to work with the University of Arizona meats lab. Once to deliver the cattle, and the next with some kind of refrigerated trucks to pick up the beef, because my responsibility would be to get it to the warehouses for these stores. That kind of mileage, fuel prices, or purchased shipping—there goes my profit."

"That sucks, man," he says. "You can't get anyone up here to work with you?"

"Everyone up here's state-inspected. And the big guys in Phoenix won't do custom orders. Tucson's the only one."

"That sucks, man," he says again. "Because that would be cool."

"I thought so too," I say, disappointed. "And now, even worse, I can't justify a hay grinder."

He hears the joke in my voice, and he plays along. "That's just insult to injury, right there."

"Right?"

"But you're feeding out some beefs anyway—" he prompts.

I grin, enjoying how he refers to cattle as "beefs."

"Right," I continue. "So, this is my backup plan. I'll feed the cattle and sell them as quarters or halves or whole beefs—do a lot better than just selling them back at the auction, and maybe build up a market so we could get a meats lab up here someday."

"Cool," he says. "What are you selling them for?"

"Two dollars a pound," I say proudly. "With a friends and family discount of a dollar fifty."

"That's awesome, man," he says. "You can do well with that."

"I hope so," I say. "The people calling are funny, though. I had one lady call up and ask me if I sold grass-fed beef, and I explained that we feed brewer's grain as well because I don't have enough of just grass to keep them fed. Sounding worried, she says, 'Oh . . . but my family are all gluten free.'"

Jim laughs.

"I tell her, 'Yes ma'am, and so is the beef. The whole digestion process sort of takes care of all that.'"

"Unbelievable."

He stands and gently slaps the horse's rump. "Well, this one's done. You got one more?"

I nod. "Freckles. And he's been sore, so we need to drug him."

"I'll let you take care of that," he says.

We've had this exchange before. No farrier is going to administer a sedative—it's too big a liability.

I walk into the tack room and look at the contents of the small refrigerator. No sedative, but there is a box of something I don't recognize.

I withdraw the phone from my pocket and make the call while I go fetch Freckles.

"Woods," I ask. "Do we have any Ace?"

It's a mark of how ubiquitous this sedative is to the horse world that Woods and I both know it—perhaps the one thing we have in common.

"No," he says, the connection crackling. "But we have something else in the refrigerator. It's pretty close."

"I can inject it?" I ask. "I have a horse with sore feet I need to shoe."

"It'll work," he says.

The directions on the bottle say to use between three and six cubic centimeters for a thousand pounds of body weight. Last time we shod Freckles, he was so sore that at the first tap of a hammer, he'd gone flying backward and broken his halter doing it. Remembering that, I decide to go with the high end of the range. I really don't want any problems today.

Within minutes, his neck is dropped and he's visually swaying.

"Jesus," Jim says, walking toward him with his file. "He's drunk."

"Oh, God," I say, concerned. "Do you think he's going to fall over?"

Jim looks at him for a minute, then bends to test a hoof. Freckles sways a little more but remains standing. "If he does," Jim says, starting to file around the nails, "we'll just shoe him upside down."

ROCK STARS, BACKHOES, AND OTHER AGRICULTURAL RESOURCES

The hunt for new ranch revenue continues, and I've taken the search to places that make my calendar read like something from Hollywood.

Monday morning . . . meet with film producer.

Wednesday afternoon . . . meet with rock star's accountant.

Thursday . . . meet with wine country president.

It turns out that much of what I need to know about the northern Arizona wine industry, I can learn while munching a bag of popcorn.

According to the documentary *Blood Into Wine*, produced in 2010, not only do wine grapes grow in the Verde Valley of Arizona, but they have grown so well and contributed to such quality wines that a rock star and a local winemaker partnered to create Arizona Stronghold, the state's most widely distributed wine label. They also collaborated to produce a boutique brand of wines, distributed only from a tasting room in Jerome.

It makes sense that in meeting winemakers, I'd also be meeting the celebrity set. There's an old joke:

Question: "How do you make a million in the wine business?"

Answer: "Start with two million."

Of course, as quickly becomes apparent, there's also a very different business model being practiced in the Verde Valley: invest whatever can be scraped together into growing grapes, making wine, and loving every bit of it. Even when it's unlovable.

Wine and Arizona aren't the easiest of companions. In the Verde Valley where the McKinsey is, there are microclimates set up by unique combinations of wind, shade, and topography. As I begin interviewing members of the wine-making community, I hear the cautionary tale a few too many times about the rancher who put in a whole crop of Zinfandel, only to have it devastated by cold.

In the documentary, the lead singer from Tool, Maynard Keenan, tells the story that they couldn't figure out why their Sangiovese crop outside of Willcox (in southern Arizona) was getting eaten, so they sent someone to camp overnight to find their saboteur—which turned out to be a pack of javelina. The Verde Valley has javelina too.

Because it really is a small world, when my friend Nancy from the Oregon trip introduces me to the enology expert she wants me to meet, I figure out that I'm talking to the javelina-discoverer from the documentary. In addition to that resume item, she is a professor at Yavapai College, as well as the new mayor of Jerome. Thankfully for me, she is also smart, fun, and available for consulting.

It's late September, a few weeks before our fall migration south to the McKinsey. Northern mornings are already frosty, but the Verde Valley is still enjoying swimsuit temperatures. In our case, it's jeans and work boots as the Wine Mayor and I walk the uphill pasture of the McKinsey—quiet but for the rumble of a backhoe behind us. She explains that one of the first things I have to know about my ranch is its soil.

"We need to dig some holes," she said over the phone. "Big ones— get about five feet down or so to see what the vines will be rooting in. Can you move your livestock?"

With all horses and cows safe behind other fences, we can properly assess the landscape, an unlikely parade of women, dogs, and backhoe making our way through the juniper and prickly pear cactus.

Despite her movie mention, there is nothing Hollywood about the Wine Mayor. She's about five feet tall, if she stretches, with dark, curly hair in a pixie haircut above sparkling blue eyes. She wears what I've come to appreciate as the standard uniform of the Verde Valley working world: jeans, good cowboy or hiking boots, a seasoned, long-sleeve shirt, and a wide-brimmed hat.

"We want a south-facing slope," she says, stopping to look around. "But not too steep, and not too far away from the water so we can save on irrigation, but enough so gravity will direct the flow and we don't need a second pump. Here—let's look at this."

She signals, and the backhoe crawls over. The operator, a man long on patience if short on words, lowers the bucket to the ground. Earth scoops in a way that reminds me of when I used to order rocky road ice cream at Baskin-Robbins. In this particular place, we have about three feet of coffee-colored, dense loam, a few inches of white limestone ripple, and a base layer of red clay. I smile at myself, realizing I'm fascinated by looking at a hole in the ground.

"Is this good?" I ask.

She nods. "Vines like to work. And they'll really like that limestone layer. Do you know what you want to plant?"

Oh, yes.

"I've been talking with people, and it sounds like growers have the best luck with the Rhône varietals here," I say.

She nods as we make our way farther downslope. "That's true—and Italian varietals tend to do well too."

"I read about Nebbiolo," I tell her. "I've been curious about it. It was in a book I read that took place in Washington—something fiction I just picked up—but I'd never heard of it before, and the book made it out to be something special."

"It's a hard grape to work with," she says. "Great for blending, but, you might say, temperamental? Might be great—really thrive—or might completely shrivel and die. Maybe do a couple rows of it, just to see."

I nod. "I like Mourvèdre a lot," I say. "Which is also sort of new to me, but Rhône, at least. What's your experience there?"

"Kind of the same thing," she laughs. "It's not reliable. Might be great—might just make you work without ever really producing for you."

I've had conversations like this a few times in my life. Most recently, they were associated with horse bloodlines: these attributes versus that risk; which of a stallion's characteristics would match well with Lena's lineage, temperament, and confirmation. A heavy dullness presses at my heart.

"—maybe even Malvasia Bianca—"

"Sorry," I catch up. "Did you—um—what were you saying?"

"Oh," she says, motioning to the backhoe to close in, "just that people have also had some good luck with lesser-known varietals. Malvasia Bianca, for example, can make a beautiful wine, and it grows well here, but people are afraid to put it in because no one's heard of it."

We step aside so we can hear ourselves as we watch what the backhoe digs up. "I've thought about that too," I say. "Because no one in our family is a winemaker, and there's all kinds of press about the shortage of actual Arizona grapes. I was thinking it might be a good idea to grow what we know we can sell."

"That's true," the Wine Mayor nods. "You can find grapes, but they always sell out. Arizona grapes are getting so pricey that the bigger wineries are bringing in blending grapes from New Mexico. I actually got my commercial driver's license for that reason."

Her moxie and resourcefulness make me square my shoulders and stand a little straighter.

"I think I like the idea of doing mostly grapes we could either use ourselves or sell, and then maybe put in just a few vines we want to play with. So that would mean Barbera," I tick off my fingers, "Sangiovese, Albariño—"

"Oh, good!" The Wine Mayor says, "I'd been wondering if you like that!"

I nod. Holding up the next finger. "Grenache?"

She nods.

"Malbec," I finish.

She approves. "And we're doing how many acres?"

"I sat with Stronghold's accountant to go through the books— thanks for that contact, by the way," I tell her. Two weeks ago, the number-cruncher for Arizona Stronghold went line by line to advise me on building a budget: taxes, licensing, insurance, and marketing, all the details that make or break businesses. "I think the plan is to start with ten acres, then go in phases, adding ten more and then eight more."

I have it all charted: acres, fruit yield, selling price, wine yield, and grosses.

The backhoe has turned up a whole bucket of silt. Dry, pebbly, slick silt.

"Probably not so good here?" I ask.

"Not as good as up there, but you'd be surprised what we can make work." She kneels and scoops up some of the dirt in a vial. "Forgot to do this before."

"Should I go back and test the other one?"

"It won't change that much over such a small distance. Mostly we just need to know about acidity, macronutrients, all that good stuff." She stands to dust off her hands, but not her knees. This surprises me until I realize she just assumes she'll be kneeling again soon—a habit likely formed from vineyard work, kneeling being the standard position for planting vines, taking clippings, and adjusting bubblers. As I think of it, I don't check or dust my boots off anymore either, figuring there's no point if I'll be back out in the pasture and arena within moments. Funny what we get used to.

I think ahead. "So, we test the soil, you'll draw up a planting plan, and then—"

She raises an index finger for a pause. "I want to introduce you to a winemaker. He's over at a winery outside Cottonwood right now, and he's really talented. He's not happy because the owner is—" she gives me the unique eye roll and headshake that clearly designate "nuts."

"But he's there for now, until something better comes along."

I ask, "Are there people who just grow grapes and don't make wine? It's so much capitalization, which increases your risk. And lengthens your payback timelines." I'm a little annoyed at how much I sound like my father. And yet, my family has been in a losing business for long enough. Whatever we do next has to pay.

"Well, the capitalization part I might be able to help with," she says. "You know our college is doing the Southwest Wine Center, right?"

"Yes," I answer. This is Nancy's project at Yavapai College: a fully resourced and operating vineyard and winery where students can learn all aspects of viticulture and enology.

"Part of what the center will do is make their facilities available for community growers to make their wine too."

"Really?" This changes everything. Being able to use a crusher and press without buying them saves tens of thousands of dollars. "What about the tanks?"

"Haven't worked all of that out yet, but we're not going to use all the space there right at the opening—I'm sure you could work something out," she says, scanning the dirt again. "Or, if you'd rather, there's a start-up incubator place outside Camp Verde where you can lease the big equipment from him but put in your own tanks and store everything in your own space."

"That's amazing," I say, mind blown to think that our ranch could finally get into the value end of agriculture. "You know, I talked with a friend of mine—a winery owner in Washington—and she said she'd sell me her business in a heartbeat, but in the same breath she told me not to take it. She said you have to make wine because you love it. If what you want is to make money, then, she said, open a wine shop, because the money's reliable—you know how much you'll be making from every glass you pour."

The Wine Mayor shrugs. "She's right, but it all has to start some-where!" She gestures around us, laughing. "And I just think this is the far more exciting, rewarding end of the business."

I look around us: the reds of the Red Rock-Secret Mountain Wilderness, the deep green of the trees, the ochre of the buttes, and mountains jutting out of the dry, green grasses that fade a little more each day as autumn approaches. What would a wine with roots in this quiet and rugged country taste like? What does a cultured Italian or Spanish strain of grape have to say to a landscape that has only ever been the Wild West?

I want to know.

"I can see that," I agree.

FEED AND FLIP, BREWERY BEEF,
AND OTHER BUSINESS LINES

It's October now: harvest time for northern Arizona ranchers. Either as a caution against too-high hopes or a prayer that this season will have the Midas touch, the world has gone gold: aspen glint from hillsides, sunflowers preen from the freeway medians, and Oldham Park is once again in weedy flower that makes it appear as horizontal sunshine. People actually pull their cars off the freeway, snapping pictures from the skinny shoulder as offended truckers gun by. The more adventurous rumble down the rutted frontage road, even braving their way past the barbed-wire strands to get photos from the pasture, a behavior we do our best to discourage by posting "Private Property" and "No Trespassing" signs. To passersby, we are utopia—a living legend snug in its clearing beneath the sacred San Francisco Peaks, which are visible from our south pasture. Those of us on payroll have a more backstage view of things: the rains have gone, the pasture is dry, the tanks are diminished, nothing will eat the bloomin' weeds, and the last thing we need with elk season starting is a visible example of people disregarding our fence lines in pursuit of the picturesque.

The main herd, still out on the range, has already sold by contract to buyers we've worked with before at a pre-negotiated price per pound. Between now and the day the cattle are weighed and loaded for shipping, the cowboys will do as little as possible with them, as stress level and weight are inversely proportional.

That's been my experience as well. Somewhere in these first eight months, I've dropped twenty pounds.

I want to joke about this as a benefit of my workplace anxieties, but it's probably correctly attributed not only to my new medications, but to repatterned living habits. Brent's and my typical bottle or so of wine to wind down from the day doesn't happen as often now that he's in Phoenix, so I am consuming less and sleeping both more and better. In this, as in every part of my marriage, there are tradeoffs. When Brent and I are together, there is potential for both union and discord, both of which we tend to answer with the same kind of beverages. When Brent is away, there is more equilibrium, but distance can no more sustain relationship than drinking wine can substitute for conversation.

Still, they've gotten us this far.

If our marriage were a six-year-old, it would be surviving on the emotional equivalents of chips, soda, and the promise of a buffet coming soon.

Optimism is the other indulgence we consume together.

Part of why I'm interested in the wine business is that wine is something Brent and I enjoy together not only as consumers but as hobbyists. Back in Washington, we had purchased grapes to try making it ourselves in our basement. We ended up with far more funny stories than drinkable bottles, but the experience held as the last fun joint project we'd attempted.

Brent loves the idea that maybe we'll be wine ranchers.

"I'll be the Cabernet Cowboy!" he volunteers by phone one night.

His voice is marathon-training boyish again, primed with the excitement of a new venture.

During all those miles running, and, more recently, driving and riding together, the surest topic to strengthen our bond is that of any new project. The energy of dreams and discovery is its own euphoric, the wild fun of tossing whimsy around an easy means to laughter and optimism.

Entering the wine business with a successful venture could provide a more lasting emotional satiety than wine can fulfill for an evening. On some level, I'm aware that I am at least reinforcing a crutch, if not feeding an addiction, and maybe a few at once. I know our relational nutrition is feeble; I just don't know how to source what could feed us better.

For now, I don't have to go searching. In the hide-and-seek game I've been playing with marital happiness, I feel I've been granted a brief stay at base. Time to breathe, to recover enough to look forward to the next round with anticipation rather than winded dread.

Meanwhile, Oldham Park is no games and all work, as the ranch needs every available corner to accommodate the 250 cow-calf pairs on their way in, accompanied by the extra ranch hands needed to count, sort, and load them.

Handling is not something the cattle take kindly to, and they have excellent reasons for resisting it.

Just a few months after the calves are born humans appear as long-legged, tall, and funny-smelling creatures waving harsh loops first to scare them into motion, then, come late spring, to catch them, tie them down, and drag them through the dirt and rocks over to a fire. There the calves are castrated and vaccinated in rough and relentless strokes, then released to go find their wayward mamas, who, by this time, have deserted them, preferring the relative safety of the herd. There's a reason they call it *cow*ering. And this is just childhood.

As the calves age, ropes accompany them everywhere, threatening and slapping them through the rocks and dust to new pastures where nothing is familiar except mama's side, a place that might be peaceful but for the running from ATVs, jeeps, and dirt bikes tearing across forest roads at all times of day and night.

The squares they're forced into are worse: large and barbed, or smaller, smooth but unforgivingly hard, with more and more of the two-leggeds running around, many with long sticks that poke and zap toward the smallest box yet, where they must stand all alone. Here they get shot with vaccinations, ear tags, or, if they've been sold since they ranged, re-branded.

Every encounter with humans is associated with intentional fear and pain.

Of course, as a handler, the perspective is much different.

Cows calve and wander in the damnedest places. Rock heaps, canyon slopes, juniper stands, and prickly pear groves all look good to them, until they get caught or stuck and have to be gotten out. Which is the reason chaps and horseshoes are both necessary and short-lived.

There never was an animal that chose such meandering, curving paths of travel—as though forward can only happen in a series of figure eights, on the most punishing terrain available. There will be no ambling quietly along game trails and forest roads; no, cows unfailingly choose grades, slurries, and rockslides, and at a pace that would more than qualify them for varsity hurdling. Getting the brainless bunch of meandering morons to water might ultimately feel rewarding, except that once there, they stare in paralyzed fright rather than drink it, casting vacant expressions that truly invite thoughts of drowning even in the most even-tempered of herders.

I will never feel bad about eating them.

I do wish we could treat them differently. I've read a lot of books by Temple Grandin, a renowned animal behavior expert and proponent of humane livestock-handling. She recommends curved chutes, mono-chromatic and enclosed alleys, slow motions, and reliance on natural progression. All that would take capital; but, more daunting, it would require a wholesale shift in culture akin to religious conversion.

Most cowboys are paid $20,000 to $25,000 per year for work that can last up to twelve hours per day, seven days a week. The paycheck is the least of the reasons they do the work: it's a heritage, a culture, and, most importantly, a community. A fraternity of men who know places and conditions most of the world only dreams of—and they hold themselves apart because they don't want, or need to want, the rest of the world. They want only to know that the next day they'll spend horseback, answering to almost nobody, acknowledging no necessities except for the range that is even more isolating than they are.

This is not a culture that will be changed by husbandry ideals held by outsiders who have read books but don't know their way across the range in a storm.

So I accept that as long as we have a ranch and cowboys, "hotshots" will be used to zap the cattle along in the chutes by means of electric shock.

I accept that there will always be more hurry than husbandry.

I might not accept this if I knew generations more cattle would have to endure our ways, but this season we're not just selling the calves—we'll be selling off the herd.

For me, knowing there will be no cows, or cowboys, on the McKinsey and at Oldham Park feels like armistice, a lifesaving secret I will hold until both sides have signed on the line.

For Dad, it's the opposite. He is already mourning the departure of the cattle, understanding a solvent ranch operation as part of his ongoing duty and obligation to not just shepherd assets that have been held for decades across generations, but to grow them. He understands the math pushing the decision is to sell, but it's the end of one more piece of his father's legacy. Despite a funereal sense pervading any talk of change with him, he doesn't want Brent and me to feel any sense of either loss or failure.

"I know it's disappointing to you to have to sell," he tells us once over dinner, "but I want you to know that I think your efforts have been a tremendous success. We didn't know what to do before you arrived. We couldn't have known that selling would be the best decision for us without your help, and I'm very grateful for that."

Brent is grateful for his new job. Though based in Phoenix, it could take him—and eventually us—to Orange County or to Dallas, depending on what office he likes best. It seems to me that even as the world may be opening back up to us, we have less together to bring to it than I once thought. In the sweat and the sun and the strain of the past year, I see us diminished. I wonder if we have enough of "us" to begin anything again. For now, we are apart more than we are together, partly because Brent's not the only one traveling.

The move away from Oldham Park means getting the Jersey herd marketed, sold, and cleared off; the horses moved; the tack room broken down, moved, and set up again at McKinsey; and all the equipment moved, including tractor, Gator, and implements. I have a trip from Flagstaff to either Prescott Livestock Auction or McKinsey penciled in for almost every day.

Once again, I need some help.

"Hi there, Jules!" Nancy uses my nickname when we meet for coffee in Flagstaff. She's been at an economic development meeting and has a little time before she needs to be back at the college. "How's everything? Living life with both hands again?"

One of the wonderful things about Nancy is that she really wants to know. She also, without exception, wears great shoes. Today's have a princess heel and are laced with bright purple ribbon.

"Yeah, it's good to have both arms back. Especially because we're moving back to McKinsey in less than a month, and I have a lot to do."

"I can imagine," she says. "Anything you need help with?"

I laugh. "Funny you should ask . . ."

"Oh, good!" she says. "Say, how did it go with wine planning?"

"The Wine Mayor is awesome," I say. "Soil testing is done, she's going to do a planting plan—"

"I thought you two would hit it off," she says. "And I'm so excited that maybe you want to get into the wine business. You know, I have a couple meetings you and your mother might want to attend if you're interested. There's a group of us trying to meet with the Yavapai County appraiser's office about the definition of "farm"—specifically the small farm. Our land use code changes the status—and the taxable value—of land significantly depending on how you're classifying it, and we're trying to argue there's a difference between agricultural sales and commercial uses."

"That's huge," I say. "I've seen the same thing happen in the horse world. Barns and stables get zoned out of an area because they get designated as commercial instead of agricultural. But then the big problem is that—as commercial—they close because they can't pay the taxes."

"Exactly," Nancy says, coasting easily between social and technical topics. "As you might expect, this has huge ramifications for small growers who want to do tasting rooms."

"It does," I say, understanding. "Yes, please send me the information. Sounds like something we should track."

She nods. "Good."

I sigh and sip at my latte.

"I can see that wasn't so helpful," she laughs, "adding something to your list. What can I help with, to take something off of it?"

"I need some good handy-worker help. I need a fence and gate fixed down at McKinsey so we can enter the property without the neighbors suing or shooting at us. Again."

She chuckles.

"I have some nasty weeds I need sprayed, arenas to keep up, and now that Brent's gone, I need help getting all of it done."

She focuses her wise eyes at me. "Is it good that he got a new job?"

I shrug. "I think so. I mean, it is for him. And probably it is for the family. Things were getting pretty strained."

"Working for your in-laws is so hard," she says, shaking her head.

"Plus, we've been living with them."

"Anyone would crack under all that pressure," she says. "No matter how great your family is."

I nod. My family has been great: my mother has been the one thing propping me up for months, and for all our clashes, I've learned to sympathize with Dad. Running a ranch is mostly a thankless job in which it is simply impossible to make everyone happy. There are some things we may never intuit or even understand about each other, but we have learned to respect each other's efforts. I know this because Dad told Brent and me that he feels we should be proud of what we've accomplished in a short time. Both that Dad noticed and that he said so to us are immense.

"It would feel like endless scrutiny," Nancy observes. "No matter what it actually is, that's what it would feel like. Most people can't live inside that."

"No," I agree. "We can't."

"So, will you go down and join him?" Nancy asks, deftly turning the conversation back to the future.

"I don't know," I answer. "Eventually, yes, but I have some things to finish up."

"Finish?" Nancy asks.

"We're going to sell the herd and the grazing permit," I tell her. "We're not advertising it quite yet, but that's the plan."

"I'm sorry to hear that," she says, sitting back.

I shrug. "There's no way to make it work."

"But you're not selling the land, are you?"

Part of why I love Nancy is that she understands the metrics by which I work. Herds can be bought and sold, permits can be applied for, staff can be rehired, but no land means no ranch activity of any kind. It also means the loss of a family and community touchstone, as any land sold is less likely to go to another rancher than it is to go to a developer, and anyone can see the real-time depletion of northern Arizona ranchers and range as new cabin communities emerge in formerly open parks along Interstate 17.

"No—not yet," I explain. "We want to see if there's anything we can do on just the owned land that might make it pay. Support the care of it, at least."

She's nodding, already thinking. "So, the wine might be that for you."

"Might be," I say. "It'd be nice. I just have to get the family to decide it's a good idea."

"Oh?" she asks, smiling into her coffee. "And how do you think that will go?"

I trust Nancy. I trust people pretty easily—I want to trust them—but Nancy has also already proven herself willing to help me with introductions, contacts, and unflagging enthusiasm.

"Could be hard," I say. "The family's pretty used to real estate schedules and profitability, and, you know, the wines-and-vines business isn't known for being a moneymaker."

She laughs, choking a little. "What do they want instead?"

I sigh. "More return on investment than I could offer, probably. We'll see, I guess."

She nods. "Well, I hope it works. And in the meantime, I do have some ideas. It'll sound a little strange, but actually my son and my husband both have skills you might be able to use."

A week later, Nancy's son Gabe has pulled into Oldham Park. He's tall—well over six feet—with a broadness in his body and manner that's notably different from the wiry types I've been around. He offers a handshake as we introduce ourselves. He looks me in the eyes. He's also, unlike so many men I've been around, wearing a ball cap.

I am not at the point where I equate a cowboy hat, or even our cowboy help, with outright villainy. Mostly I think Woods and Ty are exactly how their horses have acted: damaged, mistrustful because of it, and suspicious unto frightened of the wider world. This is not a background that lends itself to gallant or even generous behavior, beyond which, as I've learned, we all do as we've learned to do. I don't assume all cowboys work the way Woods and Ty do. Jim the Farrier has cowboyed, and I have nothing but admiration for his work ethic, pragmatism, and undeniable horsemanship. In cowboying, as in any job, or in life, good or bad guys can be found.

"So, you want weeds sprayed, arena worked, fence checked and fixed, and gate balanced," he says, recounting what's on my wish list for buttoning up Oldham Park for the close of season. "What's the priority?"

That he would ask for not only my list but also my preferences catapults him in my esteem from helper to hero.

He doesn't just drag the arena, he grooms the yard as well. He finds ways to fix lights that have flickered, pipes that have leaked, and gates that have squeaked as long as I've known them. He even brings his own tools.

"I learned a long time ago not to rely on anyone but me to have what I'll need to get things done," he says.

Boy howdy.

Until today, that's exactly how I've felt.

As of now, maybe I won't have to live with the constant frustration and inept embarrassment that so many things have been beyond my doing.

Mom and I have started the move and are loading and unloading trailers with cattle, horses, and various equipment, when Gabe greets us with his usual question, "Do you two need some help?"

We've learned that this is our cue to step aside and let him lift, set, hitch, or carry whatever it is we've been struggling with, which he does good-naturedly and without comment. He's humble enough that my effort still feels valuable, and it doesn't occur to me to feel weak or incapable around him—just grateful for his help.

He's also unflappable, unphased by menial requests like weed spraying, and undaunted by major tasks like resetting and rebuilding fence, which is normally a two-man job.

Today, Mom and I have dropped off the Jerseys at Prescott Livestock Auction, and we'll be returning tomorrow with an empty trailer to buy our winter herd that will graze at McKinsey.

"How'd it go?" Gabe asks when we pull in.

"We got some pretty strange looks," Mom relates. "Not many Jerseys in these parts."

He chuckles. "I'll bet."

"I talked to the auctioneer over the phone before we got there," I say. "He's kind of growly, but he said to bring them on over and he'd get them sold. We might not like the price, but he said someone would pick them up."

"Good enough then." Noticing Mom has gone for the shovels, he steps over to get one of his own, then suggests by gesture that maybe he could take over for her.

The back of a cattle trailer is brown, slick, and stinking of its former occupants. Gabe appears not to notice. "Is it still OK for me to take the three we bought down to my place this weekend? I don't want them to be any trouble to you."

He and Nancy have decided they needed a few of their own "Jersey boys" on the farm.

"This weekend works great," I tell him. "No trouble at all. We'll drop them off, then go pick up the generator from Woods's place."

"I'll be there," he says.

"I really don't want to make that run again tomorrow," Mom says, gratefully resting outside the trailer.

"It'll be a long loop," I agree. Almost three hundred miles. We'll start at Oldham Park, drive over to Chino Valley, then go south to Prescott and cut back east on Cherry Road to I-17 and the Sedona exit, coming back up to McKinsey through Cornville. Then we'll still have to get home.

"The gate's almost ready," Gabe says. "I'll have it done tomorrow, and I'll stick around to help you unload if you let me know when you're coming."

"That was quick," Mom says.

"I got the gate put in, but I still need to restring where I took it from," Gabe says. "It was an interesting day. I met one of your neighbors."

Mom and I exchange a look.

"Oh no," I say.

Gabe laughs. "Yeah, he was pretty clear that the fence was in the wrong place and I was trespassing. I apologized and told him I was new. Said we were moving the gate to try to make things easier for *him*."

"That was well done," I say.

"I didn't know what else to say," Gabe smiles. "He's an old man, all worked up. Totally irate at me for working where I was, so I thought I'd do best to just back off."

"I'm so sorry, Gabe," I say, wishing our best employee hadn't had to encounter the worst of our working conditions.

He waves me off. "It worked out fine. He ended up talking to me quite a while, explaining everything about the gate, everything about the lawsuit, all the troubles his wife's been having with her health—"

"Good Lord," I say. "You did have quite a day!"

"I wouldn't go so far as to say we're friends now, but I think he knows we didn't mean any harm."

"My goodness," Mom says, stepping out of the trailer. "We should be paying you legal fees. That's more goodwill than the lawyers could get across."

Gabe laughs, sounding like lemonade on a hot day. "Glad I could help. So how many do you think you'll pick up tomorrow?"

"Probably not more than twelve," I say. "We've only got the one trailer. We'll be starting a kind of feed-and-flip herd. Pick up one load, let them eat on what they can graze and what we bring in from the breweries, add a couple hundred pounds apiece, and then sell them and do it again."

"Sounds good," Gabe says. "Where do you get the grain from?"

This is something else I appreciate about Gabe: curiosity is clean of any judgment. He is inquisitive purely out of interest.

"So far, I've got two places, Lumberyard and Flag Brew. The brewers are actually pretty excited about having someone to give their stuff to. They have to throw it out otherwise."

"It's a good plan," Gabe says thoughtfully. "They'll brew all winter. Be a good supplement to your range when everything goes dormant."

"That's what I'm hoping." I realize I'm talking to him like a partner. His genuine interest in the ranch, my family, and our collective well-being is beyond endearing, it's like salve to a wound. The fact that we already know, spend time around, and respect each other's mothers might be a contributor, but Gabe already feels like a new best friend. He volunteers for responsibility without feeling entitled to privilege, and he accepts direction from me without resentment. So many of my male-female relationships have been fraught with some undercurrent—either of sex or of power—but this one is delightfully free of those riptides. Even if one tried surfacing, I sense they'd have no place to land: Gabe has mentioned that he's engaged, and we both know I'm married. I sense that one of the things we appreciate about each other is that those commitments are up for neither discussion nor trade.

"Where do you want to put them?" Gabe asks.

"I think in the bottom right pasture," I say, looking at Mom. She nods. "You know how McKinsey's kind of a backwards L?"

"Yeah, I know the place," Gabe says. "I'll have the gates open and water tanks full. Give me a call when you're on your way."

"Will do. Thank you," Mom says.

"My pleasure," Gabe says.

I don't know how that could be true, but it's sure nice to hear.

AUCTIONS
AND OTHER SPORTING EVENTS

One of the first things I notice upon entering the main building at Prescott Livestock Auction is that Mom and I are the only women there to buy livestock.

Women run the front office, where we register and receive our bid number.

Women also run the actual auction, keeping track of lots and prices and recording sales.

But the owner, auctioneer, handlers, and cattle buyers are male and look at us as though we must be lost.

We are there on Jim the Farrier's advice. In college, he worked for and then managed livestock auctions, so he knows his way around. He had assured me that this auction owner is honest.

"Call him and tell him exactly what you're looking for. He'll keep an eye out for you and treat you right."

I ask the inspection agents to point the owner out to me. When they do, not without small smirks, I introduce us.

"Mr. Birch," I say, sticking out my hand. "We spoke on the phone the other day. I really appreciate your help."

"Nice to have you ladies here," he says, tipping his hat and then shaking my hand. He's about six feet tall, with a classic block to his silver belly hat, weathered face, rough hands, and a wide grin, which I suspect doesn't show itself too often.

"We're glad to be here," I say. "Jim Parker speaks very highly of you."

"Good man, that one."

"He's sure been good to us," Mom says.

Mr. Birch's eyes are busy, taking in the trailers still offloading stock just minutes before the auction begins. We exist for him somewhere well down the list of the dozens of things that need his attention, but he tips his hat again before saying, "We'll have to visit more later. Excuse me, ladies, I'm all covered up."

He hurries away to where one of his handlers has ridden up the alley between corrals to get his attention.

The cattle buyers stand around in groups of twos and threes, visiting quietly, leaning on walls or fence lines. They all wear jeans and boots and collared shirts. Some wear Western hats. None of them smile.

I'm not sure the last time someone wore pink into the auction building.

Along with her jeans and lace-ups, Mom is wearing a bright pink blouse with small white dots. I'm in a floral-patterned shirt, jeans, my butterfly belt buckle, and a dusty pair of riding boots. We may as well be in golf attire, for the looks we get.

Exchanging one between ourselves, we sit to watch as the auction begins with sheep, then goats, then works its way up through the cattle by weight.

The Jerseys we're selling come stumbling in, looking dazed at the bright lights, white walls, and more people than they've ever seen. The mounted handlers push from behind, working the small herd down the lane through sets of gates that bookend a scale, then into the auction ring.

There aren't many bids, despite the auctioneer's singsong efforts and remarks about Bambi.

"They're gentle, boys, dead gentle," he remarks to the bidding audience, watching the calves step slowly around, sniffing.

I notice the handlers in the ring shaking their heads as they lean leisurely on the fences. Our doe-eyed animals require about the same herding as a sleepy toddler.

"What'd you do, feed them from a bucket?" The question is for me, announced over the loudspeaker.

I shrug, having actually thought about it at one time.

Mr. Birch mumbles something to his auctioneer, who starts bidding at sixty cents a pound—twenty cents lower than he has with other calves. The discount might be due to the fact that there are almost two dozen calves here and, just as they would anyplace else, prices always start lower with larger quantities, but I suspect it's more to do with Mr. Birch's warning to me that Jerseys are unpopular.

A very few bids later, the Jerseys sell for seventy-five cents a pound, yielding about $7,500 in shopping money.

Years ago, long before we moved to the ranch, a fellow horse girl explained the principle of "horse math" to me.

"The trick is to only count what you spent on the original sale," she said. "You figure if you buy a horse for $10,000 and sell it five years later for $15,000, you made money, right?"

Brent had rolled his eyes at this. "With monthly board at over $500 a month, there are some pretty expensive times in between those two things happening—"

But Jackie waved him off. "Nah—you were going to spend that anyway, no matter what you bought. Whatever you buy is going to have to eat and be trained and need shoes—all that stuff. So, the only important numbers are the first and the last."

By that math, we just doubled our money, but by actual accounting, counting labor and special calf feed, we're definitely in the red.

Horse math, auction math, there's even been hospital math this year—the inscrutable reports showing the costs of my medical procedures and the statements of benefits where no numbers sum up to equal each other. The trouble is that, despite any order of operations I might apply, no version of math seems to be working my way.

When I told Mr. Birch I wanted to buy cattle to feed out over the winter, he advised me to try to buy 800-pound steers, but I see from the program that there won't be much choice in that weight class. I look up at him nervously, then back at the lot of six in the 700-pound class that just came in.

Mom has circled this and a couple other lots on her program, which she's tapping against her knee as she studies the current lot.

They make me anxious too. These cattle are wild, bolting through the gate to slam into the panel fences that surround the auction ring. They're also what's referred to as a mixed lot: all different breeds and colors, with no regularity to their appearance or weight.

Mr. Birch catches my eye to give me a little headshake.

I sit back. "He's waving us off," I mutter to Mom.

"Good," she mutters back, then looks at her program. "The BL symbol must stand for 'black.' Given the option, we may as well try for that—they're getting higher prices."

She's right. We'll pay more for them now, but we'll also get more from them when it's time to sell. Puzzling over the auction program and procedure with Mom beside me feels reassuringly familiar: one more foreign land to add to a list already populated by horse shows, college applications, and cross-country driving routes we've ventured into together.

The mixed lot finishes and exits with as much energy as it entered.

Next is a pair of red Herefords.

"I'd like to try and get more at once," Mom says.

I nod, looking at the two animals roaming around the small pen. They're sleek, with shiny coats and clear eyes. Their top lines, running from the poll of their head to the base of the spine, are flat, which would be good if they were horses. I wonder if these things translate across species.

It occurs to me that additional research before the auction might have been valuable, then sigh at what feels like my motto: "If I had only known." The simplicity of my conversation with Gabe not twenty-four hours ago feels like fantasy from once upon a time: buy cows of a certain weight, place them on pasture to graze, wait until they've eaten enough to profit, then sell.

The reds are exiting now, and six black cows enter.

"Heifer!" comes the shout from the alley.

"Heifer!" call the ground handlers.

I smirk, feeling both justified in my impression that females are an anomaly here, and grateful that Mom and I didn't get similar calls when we entered the building.

"We got six mighty purty little heifers, boys," the auctioneer starts.

"It'd be better if they were steers," Mom whispers. "Prices will be lower. Plus, I kind of hate to do this with heifers, you know?"

I do. Put another way, Mom is asking me, what is the greater worth of a female life: to perpetuate a herd or to feed a carnivorous market?

We are uncomfortably close to a conversation Jim and I had when he explained, "It sounds really harsh, but I can tell you every animal on my place has a price I won't go beyond to save it." He says this with nails in his mouth as he's tacking on a shoe, but somehow, he's mastered being able to speak clearly while muzzled in this way. "Usually, that price is less than five hundred dollars. If it's sick and I can save it with some B-12 and penicillin, I'll do it. But if it needs a specialist or surgery, it's getting a bullet, because I can't bankrupt the rest of my place to save it."

The hardest aspect of the ranch is this constant valuation of life: how much I can rationalize investing for the possible market return versus the quality of that animal's life while under my care.

In ancient Egyptian mythology, once a person died, his heart would be measured, balanced against a feather of justice to assess whether its goodness merited a happy afterlife or if it should be fed to Ammit, the devourer of souls.

I feel as though it's been my lot to be measured against conflicting standards of markets and husbandry, and none of what I have faced have been featherweight questions. If I buy these heifers, I sentence them to a shorter, albeit high-quality, life span than they could get as breeding stock. If I don't buy them, they'll likely be acquired by another ranch seeking replacement heifers for those that have aged out or succumbed to other harsh conditions that ranchers account for as "death loss."

At the same time, as aware as I've been of gender roles on the human side of the fence, I am even more cognizant that heifers have a choice that steers don't, and, as murderous as I feel toward cattle on roundups,

I haven't made such a peace with these animals as protein that I think a chance at longer life doesn't merit opportunity.

We let the heifers go.

Four black steers and a red one enter the pen now. Docile, good coats, flat toplines, right weight—

"Here's a good pick for you, Boot Track," Mr. Birch growls over the mic.

Mom laughs, shocked but delighted that Mr. Birch actually called us by the name of our ranch, not so subtly intimating to the other buyers that he'd like us to get this sale.

For a minute, I forget about all the labels and measures of the day. "Think we might have made a friend?"

"It seems so," she says, laughing some more.

Mr. Birch can't actually control who bids, but I'm touched knowing that he made the effort to guide us. I wonder how many signals he's passed to more seasoned buyers using less obvious means, and I begin to suspect that for all of its taciturn suspicion, the auction hall might also be a kind of community touchstone. Perhaps it's even a kind of hallowed ground, where livelihoods are made and markets are active, supporting families of growers and feeders for hundreds of miles.

A few minutes later, we own the five steers, and within the hour a few other small lots of two and three steers each have joined them in the stock trailer.

October at McKinsey is the perfect summer prolonged. Days are warm, nights are crisp, crowds crawl along Oak Creek Canyon, and jeeps bump and twist along every mile of forest road made available to tourist enjoyment. Getting to our front gate is like living a video game, with things that want to delay, crush, or detour us popping up on every road. Arrival feels like exhausted victory to be savored every time.

That's life outside our fences. Within them, of course, is its own story.

Brent visits. He says he's missed us all. The dogs wag, Marty nickers, and I hug him in welcome, but the distance is still there between us, even in proximity. I appreciate that he made the trip, though, and he and Heidi and I decide that we need to ride out and check on our newly purchased mini-herd.

I make the suggestion with a mostly straight face, but Heidi grins widely.

"You want to chase them, don't you?" she asks.

"I want to check on them," I correct, with a telling smile.

"I want to chase them!" Brent says.

There's a game that's pretty fun to play if you have a fence line, some open ground, and enough riders to keep a herd together.

The riders approach the cattle, backing them toward the fence, and—once mostly bunched up—one of the riders walks his horse toward the herd, which naturally moves out of the way, separating into two smaller groups. This is called a "cut," and the object is to isolate one animal from the small group just cut off from the main herd, to try to stop it from getting back to its friends. It's a little like a game of one-on-one: you and your horse don't want the cow to score by getting past you.

Slick has been my new project since getting reshod. Jim worked on him a few weeks ago, tipping his hat and shaking his head at the angles people do when they don't want to tell you something.

Jim stared down at Slick's feet. "I don't like to throw stones at anybody—"

"I know," I finished for him, "his feet are a mess."

"They're horrible," he said. "Just horrible. And the thing is—" he walked around to look from different angles, then picked up Slick's foot to see the frog and feel the hoof wall, "—there's not a whole lot I can do right now except even him out. Do you see how high his heels are?"

He adjusted his hat again in frustration.

Slick's heels have been allowed to grow so high, and his toe has been so closely cropped, that he stands almost straight up and down between his ankle and his hoof. Most horse hooves are at about a 45-degree angle.

"How'd you like to go running around on them rocks in a pair of stilettos?" he asked, reaching for some tools. Within an hour, he had Slick shod in the equivalent of a serviceable pair of loafers. "Now don't ride him for a few days," he warned me. "He's gonna need some time to relax them tendons."

I obeyed orders. After his week off, Slick now seems happy to be called on when I approach him. He nudges at my chest as I reach up to buckle the halter on.

Brent is riding Blue, his new horse crush, and Heidi's riding Freckles, who takes the day's assignment with his usual calm. Marty watches from his stall, pacing in protest, hurt not to have been chosen for the team. But the truth is that Marty hates cows.

"We'll go out later," I promise him, thinking of the flats just south of the hill beyond the ranch's southern fence line. There's no better horse for loping over a clear landscape than Marty. "Maybe we'll even see some antelope." He ignores this promise and keeps pacing. Like any of us, Marty wants to be picked first, or barring that, just not left for last. He makes it clear I'll owe him.

Once mounted, we walk and trot up the hill through the brush to the gate, which Heidi gets Freckles to open with just minimal direction. Freckles is smart about gates, as we worked many of them at Oldham Park. He knows to sidle up and to wait while his rider unfastens the latch, then back up, making space to swing it open, then walk through and turn tightly around, before backing so the gate can be refastened. I'm encouraged at his future job prospects as we ride into the pasture to find our herd.

Slick is smooth and agile, his stride covering the ground easily despite the hills. He chews at the snaffle in his mouth—a bit that's considered mild for being broken at the center rather than solid all the way across. A snaffle is preferred with young horses learning to yield to pressure, as it can be applied just one side at a time. Eventually, most Western horses will be bitted with some version of a cylindrical bar, perhaps arched or even pointed in such a way as to contact the roof of the horse's mouth as well as the sides and tongue. Slick has likely had that experience, every communication with the rider's hand feeling like the metal equivalent of a shouted demand. As we get to know each other, I prefer a bit that invites more conversation, and enjoy that the snaffle is creating a banter between my cues and his responses.

"Found 'em!" Brent calls from up ahead.

Brent and Blue streak toward the large black shapes now dodging toward the far pasture fence.

"Slow down!" I call ahead to Brent. "We don't want them stampeding through the fence!"

Reluctantly, Brent reins Blue back. Blue tosses his head, gaping at the mouth, equally unhappy at the request.

"Probably best to just trot," I say, as Heidi closes with Slick and me and we follow the bouncing cow butts ahead of us.

"I count twelve," Brent says when we join up.

"There should be fifteen, but it's OK," I say. "We can sweep the pasture later. Want to be first, and Heidi and I will hold herd for you?"

Heidi reins Freckles toward the far side of the congregated cows, who pace and shift, turning in on each other—a swirling mass of stomping hooves and swinging tails.

"Uh-oh!" Brent calls as two of them bolt to the right.

Heidi nudges Freckles, who jumps after them, churning his short legs through the loose dirt to try and cut them off.

"Lost 'em!" I call to Heidi, laughing. "Come on back and we'll try again!"

Slick questions at my hands, flexing his neck against one rein then the other like a kid shifting his feet, asking if it can be his turn yet. I lean forward to stroke his neck, crooning, "Easy, big guy." He swivels his ears and settles a bit.

We walk toward the herd again, letting Brent try once more, but he cuts half the herd and they all bolt out—eight cows headed for open ground.

"Let's get 'em!" Brent calls, wheeling Blue to give chase.

"Slower!" I call, already knowing Brent will claim he couldn't hear me.

Heidi laughs and kicks out toward the opposite direction from Brent, leaving Slick and me the middle. I hold Slick to a trot at first, then allow a canter, which stretches Thoroughbred-style, rather than pedaling in a cow-horse churn, to a ground-swallowing gallop. A moment later, abandoning better judgment to visions of steeplechase, I'm as bad as Brent, no caution and all chase.

It's not cutting, or ranching, or smart, and it's not helping anything . . . but it is SO. MUCH. FUN!

APPLICATIONS AND OTHER
EXTRACURRICULARS

It's time to pursue additional sources of income. Horse and cattle sales are not enough to sustain ranching operations. Similarly, my ranch salary, though generous for the industry, does not come with benefits I've become accustomed to, such as employer contributions to a retirement account. Both the ranch and my own household can go on for as long as our savings last, but that's too short a future for comfort. While the remaining horses and cattle winter over at the McKinsey under Cody and Heidi's supervision, I move to Phoenix with Brent and fill up my desk with applications.

I've identified some grant funds for communities wanting to start a food hub—a local processing center where farm owners can process their crop harvest into more value-added products. I know from conversations with other ranchers that we'd all like to be able to sell beef cuts instead of whole cows, so I make a list and start some calls to see if I can find a grant-required partner to study the feasibility of a food hub between Sedona and Cottonwood.

"Hi, Sue," I say when she answers the phone. Sue's family of origin contributed their ranch to a conservation easement, and she married into a different legacy ranching family that manages operations for a ranch with a school and a farmer's market. I've heard that a Flagstaff burger place contracts with one of her ranches specifically to buy their beef, but I haven't asked her about it straight out. It can be perceived as rude to ask another rancher either about herd size or purchasing contracts, and I need friends even more than I need revenue. "It's Julie Wilson calling from Boot Track Ranch."

"Hi there," she says. "So nice to hear from you—how are you?"

I've learned to dodge that question. I'm still tender from losing Lena, and I can't help feeling like I failed by not being able to make the ranch pay. Brent and I are living together in what appears, to outsiders and even my family, to be a more normal and healthy marriage, but it's not how it looks to me. The ranch has changed us—shown us all the ways we differ—one of the most profound being how we deal with stress and loss. Brent loses himself further—in work, in house projects, in time alone with Blue who we now own, and, in the evenings, in stories streamed in from TV rather than explored between the two of us. Shut out from his emotional landscape, and not wanting to fit in any of his physical ones, I'm lost as well—adrift in my own sense of loss and loneliness, with little idea of how to improve either. I've made it a practice to mentally translate any "how are you" questions to "what are you up to?"

"I'm working on an idea," I tell Sue. "Do you know about the Verde Valley Agriculture Coalition?"

"I think so," she says. "Seems like we've tried to do some work with them before, when we were doing the branded beef."

"Right. Well, I'm trying to get that started again. They want to do a food hub with a meat processor and all kinds of other things, and I'm helping them put together a study to figure out what they'd need to run it."

"That'd be great," she says. "We could really use the help out here."

"I think so too," I say. "I'm really excited they're interested. I haven't found anyone working together on food projects in Flagstaff."

"It's so hard," she says. "Last year we shipped all our beef to Fort Collins, Colorado, to have it processed."

"I had heard that," I say. "I was sorry to hear you had to go all that way."

"There was no one close by to work with us, so we had to go out of state, but we can't do that every year—it's too expensive. We haven't done it since."

"Exactly," I say. "So, this is going to be a kind of needs-assessment and market study of how much beef we're capable of producing here in northern Arizona. I wondered if you'd be a study partner and help me figure it out."

"Anything I can do, I surely will," she says. "What do you need?"

"Right now, you being a study partner is enough. I'm working on a grant application from a division of USDA, and if we're selected—"

"Wait," she interjects. "This is a government study?" Her voice has changed. I recognize the suspicious slide in tone that usually accompanies discussions of government with those in agriculture.

"Our Verde Valley group will run the study," I say. "But the USDA would help pay for it."

"Oh . . . well . . . you'll have to do it without us then," she says. "We don't take government money."

Surprised, I take a moment to recover. "You won't be. Not directly. All you're doing as a participating ranch is saying you want to be able to process and market your beef, and you'll be part of discussions and focus groups to figure out how to do it."

"You know, we tried that," she tells me. "A northern Arizona beef brand a few years ago. It just didn't go anywhere."

A little like now.

Trying to ignore my growing frustration, I ask about her experience. "I don't know enough about that. What happened?"

"We couldn't make it work," she says. "We're too small and the market's too big, and trying to get into it was too hard and so expensive—"

"Were you going to sell to grocery stores?" I ask. "Because I've been talking to a couple, and they're interested if we can get the beef to them."

"Oh, it's so nice to have someone with all your energy interested in this," she says.

"Well, thanks," I say, feeling thoroughly confused that she'd like my effort but maybe not want to be associated with it. "So, can I name you as a partner? That's all it takes—I'll sign. You don't have to sign anything. You would only need to attend a few meetings."

"I guess so," she says, nervous again. "As long as I'm not signing up for anything."

In the professional world I come from, grant applications are a way of life. New transportation projects do not get built without them, unless it is specific to a private company or community, such as the Disneyland monorail. Everyone else needing to supplement their apportioned funds for highways or byways for planes, trains, or automobiles applies to the big federal pot of money filled by the gas tax. To be fair, there are programs within worlds within still-larger worlds that make up the interface between industry and federal funding, and what I know is largely informed by the mini-sphere of public transit, but it's clear that the "we helped pay into it, so let's get something out of it!" philosophy among transit operators is not shared by the agriculturists I've met.

I'm also struggling with heightened unto manic levels of impatience. Unless some kind of miracle occurs, there's not going to be enough ranch left for me to work on. An outfit from Idaho has purchased our breeding stock and grazing leases. All we have left are our owned parcels and a lingering question about whether we can make wine, solar energy, branded beef, tourism, or some other value-added type of agriculture pay enough to keep them. I have my doubts, but until we can check all the boxes, I'm not giving up—not on assessing their feasibility, anyway. I've already given up on the idea that any new venture will make enough to pay me, especially in its early years, which is why I am also filling out applications for planning positions, with a deserter's sense of guilt.

For her part, Mom applied for Bayley to join the teaching staff at an equine-oriented charter school. On one of the few rides we didn't do together, Mom said Bayley was startled and began crow-hopping. The good news was that Bayley felt good enough to buck. The bad news was that she bucked Mom right off her back and very nearly into a stand of prickly pear. A cracked pelvis later, Mom determined that she'd do better to rely on the more seasoned mustangs for her rides, and Bayley should find a younger crowd. Thankfully, the school's barn manager in Prescott Valley could not be more thrilled to have Bayley joining their team. Strong, spirited, and now sound, Bayley has a lot to teach, and the initial reports we've been getting back say that she's become everyone's favorite.

Heidi is in her last year at Northern Arizona University in Flagstaff and has been keeping Freckles, Marty, Blue, and the mustangs ridden for us at McKinsey on the days she doesn't have class, reporting that our across-the-street neighbor seems to be more and more interested in

Freckles as a trail horse. Not to show, as I had originally intended, but as a sweet and reliable trail pony for his wife. They've already decided on a new name, so I imagine I'll soon be filling out an ownership transfer form to complete that new relationship.

Of the original string I had to sell, only Vegas is left. Before we left Oldham, Marvin, Twolena, Dozer, Freckles, and Slick were all repurposed and happily rehomed from ranch ownership. Cali, too, though I flinch as I count her, knowing that I'll likely never see her again. She went with Ty to work with the ranch that bought our herd and grazing permit. Cisco eventually did get sold out of Nell's barn to a vet who wanted a trail horse. As for Vegas, Cody has the idea that he can make her into a barrel horse or breed her when she gets sound, and until then, he's content to turn her out and let her graze, which is a better life than she'd have back on the cowboy string.

Cody has also taken a shine to the ancient and recalcitrant Buster, who has such a phobia about his ears getting touched that he has broken halters, hitching posts, and trailer doors flying backward from the offending contact. He's also crafty and nearly impossible to catch—traits that he shares with Cody, which may be why they like each other.

As horse math goes, mine hasn't been bad, finding good homes for eight out of nine horses. An eighty-eight percent success rate would look good on most applications.

HOW TO START A BUSINESS
IN THREE MONTHS

Dear Applicant, the letter began. *The Coconino District of the United States Forest Service is pleased to accept your application for . . .*

My fingers find my phone and start dialing almost before I'm done reading.

"Mom!" I squeak. "We can do rides!"

"What?" she asks—requiring additional information being a natural response, though the incidents when I'm reminded that she is not actually omniscient still surprise me.

"I just got a letter from the Forest Service. They're letting us do rides. For the whole year! It's good for the whole year. They just want some final paperwork," I crow into the phone.

"Unbelievable," Mom says.

It is, as we were told they never do this. We were told we could apply but shouldn't hope for any permissions ever. We were told that last year. It's now mid-January, and summer begins Memorial Day weekend. We need to be open before that. We need to be ready by May 1. We need too much. Fast.

"Sorry," I apologize, mind outpacing our exchange. "Did I say something last or did you?"

"What are we going to do for horses?" Mom chuckles. "Due to your many efforts, the ranch is now fresh out of any extras."

I brainstorm. "I've met the outfitter who does rides close to where we board Marty and Blue. I'll contact them today."

Mom calls me out of my land of mental lists long enough to start writing things down. Within days, I am in almost perpetual motion, coordinating with the outfitter, working with a Flagstaff marketing guru and good friend, working on the Coconino County permitting application and requirements, and finalizing a projected budget for the ranch.

Things are rolling along pretty well for about three weeks—until it's clear we can't come to terms with the outfitter to lease a string of riding horses.

They want a flat fee, plus a percentage of sales. We can pick our own horses but have to go to Colorado to do it, and any horses we choose won't be available to us until May 1. There's no way we can select the horses, get them checked by vets with completed health certificates, and get them trailered down and acclimated before opening day.

In addition to the usual daily calls and emails, I have added the search for trail horses, saddlery, and staff to my list.

A good trail horse is mostly bored, gentle, unflappable, and slow. While that doesn't sound like anyone's idea of a fun ride, it is absolutely what makes for a safe one, and given that children are the primary audience, being able to guarantee safety is key. It doesn't help that our preferred means of acquisition is a lease. We're willing to pay the owner for the use of the horse for about six months—May through October—assuming all care of the horse plus a monthly fee. Most people are accustomed to this when talking about an apartment, but not so much with an animal. From the renter's perspective, we pay for the use of the animal and take over its care, and we are responsible for any damages (vet calls). But from the owner's perspective, we are assuming complete control of their asset, possibly even their pet, and a deposit against damages doesn't inspire comfort.

For these reasons, and others less clear to me, I'm not getting many calls returned.

We're only days from March when I get the idea that maybe I could just contract as an extension of someone else's rides in the area. I call around to Flagstaff horseback-ride providers, eventually connecting with Wade.

"Trail rides," he answers his phone.

"Hi, I'm calling from Boot Track Ranch in Flagstaff. I understand you offer horseback rides in the area?"

"You're who now?" he asks.

I try again.

"Yeah—well we're up there, but not until May," he says.

"Oh. You have a winter operation too?" I ask, my heart sinking.

"We're doing rides out here by San Tan Mountain," he says. "My wife gives lessons."

A winter operation and ongoing lessons sound ominous for me. "I'm calling because I just got permitting to do horseback rides off my ranch this summer, and I wondered if you might have any extra horses available that I could lease from you?"

"Now, where are you?" he asks.

I take a deep breath, wondering if he's distracted or really this diffi-cult to talk to. "The ranch is just south of Kachina—between there and Munds Park. You know the area?"

"Yeah—oh yeah," he says. "So, you haven't done rides before?"

"I haven't been able to get the permitting from the Forest Service until this season."

"I tell you," he says, "this might be perfect, because we've been trying to find a new location. Been working out of that stable right around Kachina for the past few summers, but the owner never got permitting either, and last summer the Forest Service came in and shut us down. So how long have you done rides?"

My whole consciousness cringes at his lack of attention both to the conversation and, it seems, to legalities. Still, I persevere, figuring that I'm interviewing him and his horses for rides, not information recall.

By the end of the call, Wade has agreed to meet Mom and me at Oldham Park.

A week later, Mom and I are standing by my truck in the cinders when a yellow VW Bug comes rolling in.

A graying, middle-height man with a small paunch, dressed in a T-shirt, shorts, and straw fedora, hops out of the driver's side and greets us over his shoulder as he beelines toward the corrals, "Hi, I'm Wade! Let me take a look at a few things—"

Mom and I exchange a look at the already opposite-of-usual interview protocol, but gesture for him to go ahead.

Wade paces up to the round pen, then down along the corral fence. He paces back to his car, then out toward the cabin like a supercharged action figure before joining us in the tack room.

"Yep, it'll work," he says. "Where do you want the rides to go?"

I gesture to the north. "We'll go up the forest road there and up and over the hill to another park like this one called East Oldham. Then we come back."

"An out-and-back?" he says, doubtfully.

"Yep. I'd rather have a loop, but we got permitting because we said we would stay on the road only."

He nods. "I wonder if there's a way to make it a loop."

Did he not hear me just say loops are out?

I blink. "Even if there were, we can't do it—it's not permitted."

"Well," he shrugs with a conspiratorial smile.

Very much hoping Wade's string of horses is worth what I anticipate to be many future headaches, I ask, "So, you have horses available?"

He nods. "My ex-wife does. We'll have to ask her for them. We own them together."

I pause, unsure whether he has both a wife and an ex-wife, or just one he gets confused about.

"It's no big deal," he assures me. "She's been wanting to find a way to get them out of the heat this summer anyway. Plus, we still live together. We talk all the time."

"Oh," I say, careful not to look at Mom because her eye roll is palpable. "How would this work?"

Thankfully he understands that my question refers to his horse arrangement rather than his domestic situation.

"I would come to work for you as a guide. I've been doing it all my life. And you'd lease the horses from Chrissy. Two separate deals."

"I see," I say, very much an overrepresentation. I don't know, and am a little afraid to ask, who Chrissy is. "And the horses are available now? Could we come look at them?"

"That'll be up to her, but I don't see why not."

"I'll give her a call," I say. "So, what happened to your rides? You said the Forest shut you down?"

"Yeah, well," he says, adjusting his hat in the way I've seen cowboys do when they don't like what they have to say. At least in the cowboys I've known, it's a harbinger of truth, however uncomfortable. Wade, in his shorts and fedora, doesn't have nearly the same effect. "We applied for the permit, but it was taking forever, and we didn't have time to wait, so we just started doing rides. Figured the permit would catch up with us. But it never did, and the Forest came in and asked the stable what was going on, and the owner just kind of shrugged and said, 'I don't know—it's not my business.' We shut things down pretty quick after that."

Mom has been noticeably silent while listening to all this, attacking cobwebs in the tack room with not just alacrity but aggression, as though trying to drive off the stories Wade is more than capable of spinning. Now, as I struggle to know what to say or ask next, she steps over to rescue me with a pleasant smile on her face. One of the things I love about her is her default to flawless manners in the event of an awkward encounter: meeting boyfriends she senses won't last long; sitting through my insistence to the college admissions representative that I'm not worried about Minnesota cold ("It can't be that different from the Arizona mountains"); and, lately, my telling her that Brent and I are doing fine. As uncomfortable as I can see she is about Wade's casual attitude toward authority as well as his sense of entitlement to employment with us, she chooses diplomacy over dismissal of Wade because she knows I also really, really want the chance at any business that might pay enough to keep the ranch open.

"What a shame," Mom says. This is something else I love about my mother; her artful responses can sound sympathetic to a passionately wrongheaded speaker and yet concede nothing of his point. "How was business before that?"

"I have something like 200 people that always come ride with me every year. My phone's going nonstop come May," he says. "We always have a good season up here."

Two hundred people sounds like revenue from the gods, even if working with Wade might be its own brand of hell. Relentlessly plunging toward both, I offer, "Maybe we can find a way to get you riding from here instead."

"That'd be great!" he says. All enthusiasm. None of which I trust.

"Do you also have tack, by any chance?" I ask, indebting myself further to the Devil. "We have some saddles and bridles, but—"

He waves me off. "We have all that stuff. Well, Chrissy does. She owns all of it. We'll just talk to her about it."

Mom speaks as neutrally as she can as the VW rolls away. "What do you think?"

"I think we're desperate or we'd never do this," I admit. "But we need at least ten more horses, plus tack, and I think we at least have to check this out."

We're both silent for a minute as she nods.

"We really wouldn't do this unless we were desperate," Mom says.

"We actually don't have to do it at all. I mean, we have the permit, but—"

"But that's just it!" Mom interrupts. "We finally have it! It seems like we should at least try this for a season. Or how are we ever going to know?"

Relieved to hear that she, too, feels the urgency I do to put some experience next to what I've only been able to estimate, I say, "We'll take a look at the horses, then we'll decide. But I also want Cody to come with us. He's done this before, and he might be good to have along."

One of the many components to our touchy and intrepid ranch hand's past is that he used to have a contract with the cruise ships in Cabo San Lucas, running horseback rides as passenger shore excursions. He's described guiding people along who are too drunk to sit up, holding a saddle horn with one hand and a Corona with the other. Why he wants to work with my family, which does nothing without a contract and considers an untucked shirt a slight to professionalism, I don't understand. Why he loves my principled and perfectly mannered mother, I *really* don't understand. But both must yet be true as he joins us to go assess Wade's horses, who, a phone call confirms, are all owned specifically and individually by his ex-wife, Chrissy.

The San Tan Valley sits at the developed edge of metropolitan Phoenix, with a hopscotch pattern of signed dirt being churned by earthmovers interspersed with rural lots still fenced by barbed wire. Many faded T-posts down a dirt road, we come upon an empty lot still more desert than dirt, with a fenced enclosure less than even half an acre confining what look to be two dozen head. One bale of hay is on the ground outside the reach of the herd, and the horses in the pen stomp and shove for the few flakes that have been thrown on the ground. There's no shelter or shade, which is illegal in Arizona, but it's not like there are a lot of passersby who are going to report things.

"Turn around," Cody says after getting a look at the stock. "Don't even get out of the truck."

"Now, Cody," Mom says. "They—"

"I'm serious," he cuts her off. "Turn around. They look horrible."

He's right. Every horse we can see is skinny, mangy, ragged, and dull. I don't even want to contemplate the state of their hooves or teeth.

I shift the truck into park, remembering. About a year before Brent and I left Washington, a former barn-mate "came upon hard times" that were much harder on her herd. Several horsemen in the area, my trainer included, repossessed horses from her rather than allowing them to continue to starve. I remember being present when my trainer brought one of them home: the sickening shock of seeing this formerly Santa-shaped horse shake on his skeletal frame just trying to stand upright once he backed out of the trailer.

That was real desperation.

So is this.

I exchange a look with Mom. "Our ranch is turning into a rescue mission."

"If they can even be ridden," Mom says.

Wade is eager to show us all the trails, suggesting we ride as long as we like.

Chrissy tells us the horses we don't take will summer in a pasture in the White Mountains.

Cody announces to anyone listening that the whole herd could use some weight put on.

"They have to work to eat," Chrissy answers.

Out of a desire that they get fed more, I agree to a short trail ride each rather than just a few circles around the enclosure.

Seven meet my standards as being safe for the public: Gracie, Spot, Lola, Jack, Logan, Mae, and Annakin. I don't want to leave the others in Chrissy's "care," but I also don't feel right about calling Animal Control. My experience tells me that cases take a long time to prosecute, which would be better spent helping the horses we can and leaving the remainder to be shipped elsewhere.

I don't want any of them to have to return to this, but one emergency at a time.

Along with the seven we select from Chrissy, Cody has three that he's contributing to the ride string and is considering two others that he could ride as guide. Brent's contributing Blue as a guide horse, and, in a pinch, we can use Marty. Sage and Cheyenne are on loan from Mom and Dad as either public or guide horses, and Heidi is letting us use one of her sweet older barrel horses for any purpose we'd like. That brings the tally to thirteen public horses and three guide horses. If we cap rides at eight riders, which is "recommended" by our insurance provider, we can rotate at least half the string every other ride.

Over the next two days, Cody hauls the new herd up to the McKinsey.

I'm hauling as well: horses to McKinsey and dogs and me to Flagstaff. I've done as much as I can for the ranch while still living in Phoenix. Maybe for my marriage too. Even in the months we've been in our new Phoenix home, we've been living around more than with each other. Brent is happy with his new job, for which he's been traveling, making my time alone with the dogs feel very familiar: the same kinds of days spent caretaking animals and worrying about the ranch, just in a new place. When I mention staging out of Flagstaff when ranch operations move back to Oldham, Brent makes no objection.

Never has there been more pressure placed on a few summer months: if the horseback rides work, they could be enough to save Oldham. If I can get family approval to spend the ranch's capital on a vineyard, it could be enough to save McKinsey. The beef business won't save us, but it will sink us if it fails. If anything fails, I will have to cut either Cody's job or Gabe's. If they all fail, I'll have to fire them both.

As I drive north, I'm very aware the next few months may be the last for everything I've been trying to save.

We have less than a month to get the new horses acclimated before they'll go to work at Oldham Park. They must be wormed, vaccinated, bathed, groomed, and ridden for increasing time and distance, in between farrier visits from a friend of Jim's who fills in for him when he's doing his military tours.

It's as though Jim's talking when his friend eyes the new herd and states, "You've got your work cut out for you, huh?"

On the bright side, the horses are eating regularly, and we carefully introduce additional supplements for some of the hardest cases to help get their weight up.

In the meantime, I thought I was going into the horseback-riding business, but I seem to be in the business of making things up. I need answers to all kinds of questions:

"Julie, what are your business hours?"

"How much will your rides cost? Will you do group discounts?"

"Can people reserve their rides online or by phone only?"

"Have your guides been CPR certified?"

"How much parking capacity do you have?"

"Do you accept credit cards?"

I'm also trying to make up for the attention I've never paid to technology. First, because the ranch has no Internet, I have to choose among wireless electronic tablets, deciding that none of us would want to hamstring ourselves or the ranch by trying to run payments from only one of our phones. Then there's the matter of website functionality and its interface with an online reservation software. I feel very much in need of the First Aid and CPR that Cody and Wade are getting certified in via online programming, once I get to deciding among credit card payment systems. I wish I had the tablet's facility at processing new information: I am so easily overwhelmed by jargon and fee structures, knowing this is all for a business that may only run for one summer. The more investment I make, the harder it will be to turn a profit. Judging from our initial conversation, it's as though my anxieties have also telegraphed themselves to the bank, which calls to express concerns.

"May I speak with the manager of Wilson Brothers Boot Track Ranch? My name is Carrie from Wells Fargo and I'm calling to verify the activity on the ranch's account. We've been getting warnings of suspicious transactions."

"I'm the manager," I say, wondering what she could be referring to. So far, all we've done is test the software by booking and selling rides to ourselves. "How can I help you?"

"Can you confirm that (she names several of our pilot transactions) happened on this date?"

"Yes," I say. "We've been testing out sales using our new tablet and payment software. We're about to run horseback rides."

"We're going to need to see receipts for these accounts and a utility bill that goes to the business. We just need to make sure that you are who you say you are."

I already have a headache from another palm-to-forehead minute that seems to come with ranching in the modern world. "Well," I clear my throat, trying to keep my tone neutral and noncombative. "You are our bank and should have access to all our accounts. If you need me to come in and talk to a branch manager, I will happily do that. The power bill won't help you because the billing address is different from the business, which is a cattle ranch split between two properties."

"Oh," she says, taken aback. "Wait—what is your business again?"

"We are a cattle ranch," I explain more slowly. "We are offering horseback rides for the first time this summer. That's why you see us making and then deleting sales. We're testing our card reader."

Her tone shifts from workday to weekend. "Oh, that sounds fun! OK, all that makes sense then. I just had to call because of all the activity on the account, you understand. It just looks like what we've seen before with drug trafficking."

It's my turn to be flummoxed. "Drug dealers are using card-reader software?"

"I don't know," she says. "I just make the calls. I guess so. Sorry to have bothered you."

"No problem," I say, figuring if the rides venture doesn't work out, we're now equipped for a wholly different kind of trade.

EQUINE CAREER COUNSELING
AND OTHER RESUME BUILDERS

It shouldn't be surprising that a horse acts differently when he's fed than when he's hungry.

Our new expansion herd has taken on a few quirks since they've started getting regular meals, and I've had occasion to remember the saying about "biting the hand that feeds you" more than I'd like.

With three weeks of three meals a day, regular grooming, and minimal demands, the herd is looking pretty good. It may also be showing its true colors.

Gracie crow-hops. When taken in a direction she doesn't like, or asked to go a little faster or slower, she protests by popping straight off the ground, all four feet in the air. This is the very move from Bayley that left my mother with a broken pelvis, and I don't want to send Flagstaff Medical Center any new business.

Spot spooks. Solid-looking, he's in much better shape than most of the herd, but he can be walking pleasantly along and then dodge to the side for no reason I can see coming. This too often has the effect of separating horse from rider, as it did to me when Cisco spooked at the birds flying up from the hay bales, so our "benched" list now contains two names.

Lola is simply a bitch. Her ears are perpetually flattened against her neck in a pissy expression that sports teeth anytime anything moves past her. So far, she hasn't dumped anyone, but her snaky neck and evil eyes could scare off any new rider. I hope her attitude improves, but I won't count on it, increasing our bench to three.

Jack will work hard to keep from working. On a day when I invited Mom and Dad to visit and see how we've been progressing, I chose Jack, expecting a ride as lazy as his nature. My first problem was his balking as we left the stable yard. I wasn't alarmed so much as a little annoyed—the equivalent of a mother saying to her toddler, "Come on! Let's go to the store!" while toddler sits, crosses his arms, and whines, "I don't wanna go." No big problem: I jiggled my reins a little and petted him before encouraging him with my legs. He obediently moved on, but steps later, balked again. It took a few of these exchanges before we finally reached the arena, where I asked Jack to trot to limber up. Reluctantly, he jogged a bit. I nudged at him with my heels to give me a little more pace, and he stopped—all four feet planted. Reaching back, I swatted him on the butt with the palm of my hand to reinforce my authority, and the next thing I knew, his head was in my face and his front feet were at altitude, pawing in air. The unsolicited Trigger act didn't unseat me but did inspire my parents to suggest that maybe my ride was over for the day. I agreed, and Jack joined the bench.

Thankfully, Mae is pretty and athletic and sweet, steering and stopping without a fuss. She's a little stiff to the left, but most riders won't ask for any kind of special agility. The truth is, most riders won't ask for much at all, being content for their horse to simply follow the others in the procession. This she can do.

Logan is older than we thought, his hips, spine, and shoulders protruding due to age rather than hunger, but saddling can hide or camouflage much of that. He's tall and lanky but unfailingly gentle, with a slooooooooow stride that gives the impression of riding a giraffe.

Annakin is small and cute, stands still to be mounted and petted, and will steer and stop. Homebound, he's speedier than I'd like, but that can be managed with a bigger bit and a savvy guide, who can help advise the riders as to how to keep him in line behind horses who don't mind being crowded.

Sage and Cheyenne are dependably wonderful.

Cody's two, Samson and Joa, are enormous draft horses with small aspirations beyond going where they're steered. Their size makes them great to have on hand for adults, as most of the weekend recreating public is far from fit. There is a catch in that both horses were first trained to hitch by someone who didn't handle so much as manhandle their reins, making them more difficult to navigate for those afraid to kick or pull, but they'll work.

Buster is testy but thinks little enough of most of humanity and enough of his own pride in work to simply ignore his riders and do his job.

Freckles, I know and trust implicitly with anyone.

Cutter, Heidi's barrel horse, is swaybacked and not much to look at, but he is patient and kind and happy to walk along behind other horses doing the same thing. He's also the kind of old and slow-moving model that comforts parents in the same way a Buick would comfort parents of a newly driving teenager.

Marty is being held in reserve. As matchless as he is in an arena, he's a terrible trail horse, tripping over every rock and reacting to every cue, which new riders with little control over their body and limbs can't help but give.

The final string is much less numerous than I'd like, as my intention was to have a ready reserve for each working horse in case of sickness or injury.

Wade has asked that we keep the four of his that I want to bench, saying he could ride them when he guides, but I don't trust them not to misbehave and hurt another horse, if not Wade. I call Chrissy to let her know that, per the lease agreement, she has two weeks to tell me where to send these horses to return them.

Trust is foundational to safety for me. Well beyond talent or ability, what I want most is a willingness to work with me that I trust as unconditional. Marty, for example, does not like water. No mater its depth or shape, he does not want to be asked to step to or through it.

However, if he sees it before him, he will not spook or try to flee. He will not rear or buck or try to unseat me. He will simply prick his ears as though they are magnetically drawn to the water's edge and slow, sniffing. These are behaviors that accommodate both his fear and my need to keep going down the trail. Husbandry of any kind requires a practicality and patience with shortcomings: I may not love that Marty, who is fearless about so many other things, comes with a water phobia, but neither do I have to insist that he get fully past it just for my own convenience when it costs me nothing but time and a little extra effort. By contrast, Blue, like Spot, spooks at shadows of his own making. There is never any relaxing for me around that horse because at any moment, he can lose his mind to nothing that I sense or can see or hear coming. There is no way for me to prepare for his antics; no way to keep myself safe by steering him away or gripping the saddle horn. The only thing between me and another broken wrist or worse is his perception of danger, known only to him. He gives me nothing to work with to get past his fears, and, as a result, I do not trust him.

I don't like that the penalty for lost trust is so often separation. Mom had to face it with Bayley, when her young and excitable nature couldn't guarantee that she'd never spook again. I had to face it with the filly I left in Oregon. Income limitations aside, she was willful, wanting to push her boundaries, and I was not horseman enough to hold them. It's not that trust is always lost willingly. In Bayley's and my filly's case, with the four horses I am sending back, and even with Blue, there is nothing personal about the horse's behavior toward me. A horse's behavior is only ever a mix of its own nature and experience. I do not fault horses for having either too little experience or too much of the wrong kind that has taught them to be angry or fearful, but I also know I cannot trust where we cannot work together.

I also don't like how much reflecting on trust reminds me of Brent. Every time I look at Blue, I see Brent and the many parallels between them. Strong and athletic and handsome. Friendly. Curious to get better acquainted. Then ten feet away and wary when I've done something that reminds them of a bad time that I know nothing about and never will because they're not talking about it.

If it were all up to me, I would know what comes next; with both horse and husband, acknowledge that trust is gone and find them a new home.

But it's not just up to me. Blue is Brent's horse, and while I can limit who rides him, I cannot remove him from the ranch. Similarly, Brent is my husband, signed and sworn before God and family. We've already tried rehoming, and removal is not an option. The trouble is that, without it, I can't make my own thinking work. It's like an equation where a sum is not allowed—where the correct answer is already deemed not only incorrect but impossible—forcing focus always back on the problem rather than the solution.

A problem that may be one among many more, if my permits don't come through.

Despite the fact that I've jumped through all of the County's hoops to secure permission to operate, and delivered proof of it along with other documentation requests to the Forest Service, we still don't have our actual use permit.

It's the week before Memorial Day. We are open and advertising, and I'm getting calls for bookings, but I still can't legally take people into the forest.

If we use a page from Wade's playbook and just run the rides until the permitting catches up, we expose ourselves to fines and worse. This is a nonstarter, given my father's career as an attorney.

Instead, Mom suggests creating a forest-inspired obstacle course on the ranch itself. "Look—we have all this debris. We have some nice trees, some gullies, we can build a bridge here and there. We have more than enough to ride through."

As usual, she's right.

We build a walk-through maze.

We build a walkover "tentpole" track that looks a lot harder than it actually is.

We fill in some hollowed-out logs with leftover cinder sand to build a "bridge."

We nail flags up to create steer-through-the-trees obstacles.

Then there are the cows.

It occurs to me that if we move the beef herd from East Oldham to Oldham Park, we could offer people "roundup" rides where they move the cattle from inside the arena to outside and vice versa.

Of course, getting the cattle from East Oldham to Oldham Park is the usual circus of pushing, chasing, stopping, cutting, and turning, well-peppered with some spicy swearwords, but with cattle and obstacles staged, we can do business.

Memorial Day crams it in.

Grandparents bring in grandchildren visiting from Phoenix. They all want to ride Annakin.

A bachelorette party visits, all wanting to ride Mae.

Families drop in on their way up to Flagstaff for the weekend.

Then a local bank branch calls for an office retreat. They want to bring eighteen people out for the afternoon.

I want that revenue, but I tell them they're going to have to take shifts.

"We can only send nine out at a time," I say.

"That isn't a problem—I'm sure there are other things to do around the ranch while we wait," the woman says.

"Sure, there are!" I assure her, having no idea what those things may be. I doubt any waiting rider would get excited about cleaning pens.

Again, Mom comes through, ordering cornhole games and setting them out by the picnic table we're using as a check-in point. We arrange some hay bales with dummy steer heads for people to try their hand at roping. The fact that none of us currently working on the ranch can actually demonstrate this successfully, we do not mention.

Unfortunately, a bunch of adults without beer are harder to entertain than these games can handle, so I decide to do a participatory grooming and groundwork demonstration.

I lead Cheyenne to the waiting group.

"Now you can tell everyone you've met a real-live mustang," I say, making up my schtick as I go along. "This is Cheyenne, and she came off of the BLM lands in eastern Oregon. She's been trained and she's safe, so she's OK to touch. But she's awfully dusty, isn't she?"

A few smiles.

"Who wants to learn how to brush her off?" I ask.

A few less smiles.

"I'm serious!" I say, smiling wider. "Part of good horsemanship is knowing how to take care of your horse, so I'll demonstrate, but I want to see some volunteers."

I start with a curry comb, and then the dandy brush and the hoof pick.

As I explain how the hoof is constructed, I see a few people checking email on their phones.

"So that's one side done," I say. "Who wants the other side?"

"I'll do it, I guess," a man says, raising a hand.

"Yeah, you're the manager, you should show us," someone jokes, to a few pity laughs.

Rough crowd.

"The first thing you want to know is how to walk up to a horse," I say. "They'll talk to you as you're doing it. You just have to be able to listen to what they're saying. What you want to focus on is their ears, their teeth, and their feet."

Cheyenne takes that opportunity to stomp a front foot.

The man takes a step back.

"So—I know that was surprising, but if you look at this mare's body, you can see what was going on," I explain. "Her ears are forward, her mouth is relaxed, and all four feet are even on the ground. Chances are that was just a fly."

The chance to see the branch manager get kicked in the head now has the full group's attention.

"As you walk up closer to her, you want to come in at about her shoulder, where she can get a good look at you and you can keep an eye on her whole body. Remember that a horse's eyes are on the side of his head, so the worst place you can be is either directly in front or directly in back—those are the two places they can't see you," I go on.

"And one of them's shitty," somebody snickers.

As the jokes and jeers get worse, I smile and silently pray the first ride will come back early or that we'll have a freak thunderstorm that forces us to close down.

I take the manager through the grooming. He's a dusty, hairy mess by the time we finish, but he's also smiling. So is everyone else. Not gloating, just smiling.

I relax a little.

Next, we go to the round pen, where I demonstrate lunging: getting a horse to walk, trot, or lope a circle around you. This is far more action-packed than picking crud out of a foot, so I have a few more willing volunteers.

We don't even notice that the first ride is back. It's the sound of cars starting that draws my attention.

I'm not really surprised that the first round of riders doesn't want to stay for a horsemanship demonstration. I don't think Cheyenne is disappointed either.

"How'd it go?" I ask Cody later.

"Good," he says. "Nice groups of people. Real friendly. All the horses were good. Annakin sure likes to come home fast, though. I had to grab his halter to keep him from running off, but that was all right 'cause the girl riding him was cute."

I manage not to roll my eyes.

"The only thing is that they're stingy for a bunch of bankers," he adds. "Nobody tipped."

"They did," I correct him. "They did when they paid. It was by credit card."

"Really?" Cody brightens. "How are you going to pass that around? 'Cause I did a whole lot more work with those groups than Wade—"

I sigh. Tipping math. Just one more arithmetic I have to learn.

HOW TO STIMULATE
HOME APPLIANCE SALES

The good news is that the roundup rides have been very popular. The bad news is that we might be running the weight off our herd.

A strong monsoon has made the park grasses lush, doubly valuable to the ranch both as a spacious green invitation to stop and as added nutrition for the cattle. To supplement their grazing, Gabe and I have been playing "brewery bingo," regularly picking up spent grain to feed to our herd and conducting weigh-ins to monitor our progress.

Cody will enthusiastically substitute when either of us can't make the drive, as picking up the full grain bins gives him an excuse to talk to the brewers—maybe even stay awhile and have a burger or some other of their fare. Both he and Gabe are now on growler terms with all the brewery managers.

I like that our staff and stock are happy, but I worry that the herd isn't getting much heavier.

"I'm not surprised," Gabe says as we watch the scale balance at a lighter weight than I'd like. "You've been working 'em pretty hard."

"The question is whether they're worth more to me running or standing," I say, interested in his view of things. Talking to Gabe feels like opening a window after the rain has passed. There's comfort and expansiveness in his thoughtful deliberation, but also a calm that's unique to him. With others, I feel pressured to know things right away, to both be and appear to be decisive—the stoplight on all ranch traffic and commerce. Gabe acts for me a little like a school crossing guard, offering safe, unhurried time for me to step through my thoughts.

Today's weight check on the scale is intended to be both progress report and forecast; if we can figure out how much weight the cattle have gained, we can estimate how much they may still grow, using that latter figure to better estimate how much revenue the ranch can expect at their harvest.

However, the scale, like every other part of the ranch, has its quirks. We bang open the metal door that protects the weight beam and balances, freeing both from occupation by a field mouse that had taken up residence in a lower corner. We know there's a problem today when our two red cows weigh in together at nineteen hundred pounds. Two weeks ago, their weight was sixteen hundred, and neither their size nor shape has visibly changed.

"I like the nineteen hundred number better," I say to Gabe.

"I'm sure you do," he chuckles, examining the weights and wires.

We offload the cattle to let them munch some grass in the adjacent alleys while Gabe cleans, oils, and tests. Cody and I resume the daily horse chores.

An hour later, Gabe calls me back, gesturing at the apparatus.

"It all has to do with how the weights are laying on each other," he shows me, beckoning to Cody to move the cattle from the alley to the scale. Cody whistles and stomps the steers forward, and a moment later he bangs the gate closed after them.

Gabe manipulates the balances.

"Sixteen hundred," I read.

"Get 'em out, Cody," Gabe calls.

The gate opens for the cattle to charge back out. Of the two activities they've been offered, free-range grazing is much more to their liking than standing in a box.

Gabe lets the scale settle. "See how it doesn't quite reach zero?" he asks, pointing.

He's right. Even empty, the scale isn't balanced.

Gabe bends down, picks up a pebble, and places it on the upper weight.

It balances.

"You're kidding!" I laugh.

"Nope," Gabe grins. "Bring 'em back on, Cody!"

Hooves clatter and the gate clangs again.

"Eighteen fifty," I read happily. "So the sixteen hundred was too low and the nineteen hundred too high."

Gabe nods.

"I feel like I should get this scale rebalanced, though, you know? I don't feel quite right about customers having to rely on whether or not we have just the right rock in place."

"Yeah," Gabe agrees. "This does look a little ad hoc."

"Ad rock?" I ask. I can't resist.

He laughs kindly.

I wish I could find some way to tell Gabe how grateful I am to get to feel confident, genuine, and appreciated in a man's company.

Since off-loading the larger cattle operation, I no longer feel like something scraped off the bottom of the cowboys' boots, nor do I have to feel either inadequate or defensive around my father.

Now Dad's interest feels more professorial, as though he is monitoring me as a favorite graduated student, and while I still feel the obligation to deliver something that will rate high marks, familial fondness and forgiveness are present.

With Cody I feel like something of a sitcom boss, well-meaning but a little hapless, and comically idealistic.

With Wade I feel less like a boss and more like a Tom and Jerry cartoon, with me at least a step behind his schemes.

With Brent I feel somewhere between apprentice trying to earn promotion and reality show contestant trying not to get voted off. What I never feel is admirable.

As ironic as it is given his handiness and my relative ineptitude, I feel better than admirable around Gabe: I feel capable. He listens to me as though I say things worth hearing. He speaks to me as though I can both handle the information and master it.

If I tried to thank him for any of this, I would only embarrass us both, to say nothing of freighting one of the only healthy working relationships I have with an unwieldy dynamic. I'm married. Gabe's engaged. We speak of neither fact from day to day, nor do either of us want to change them. Introducing a heartfelt conversation without implying any change of heart is the rockiest of emotional ground. And yet, "thank you" seems so little to say. As it is the best available, I say it frequently, and Gabe is gracious enough to simply return it with "you're welcome."

Wade doesn't take part in the cattle part of the operation. As it turns out, Wade has his own use for the chutes.

I realize I have a much bigger problem with him than any I'd anticipated when I start finding a new broken halter each day.

I'm just entering the tack room one morning when I see yet another canvas strip and broken buckle hanging from the hitching post.

"Again?" I ask Cody as I gesture toward it.

"Wade scares 'em," Cody says. "He moves too fast. Buster has always set back, but now Wade's got 'em all setting back. I tell him, but he don't stop."

I nod my sympathies. My talking to Wade about a still-growing list of client and staff complaints has also been ineffective.

"I'll keep an eye out today," I say, feeling I've already seen more than enough.

I'm remembering a mother who'd come in with two children, an older boy and smaller girl. The Forest Service finally (finally!) came through with our permit, allowing us to guide rides along the dirt road over the ridge, and it was Wade's turn to lead the ride. I helped him saddle and the riders get mounted. Typically, I act as an extra hand during mounting—the most dangerous part of the ride, because horses are the most annoyed to be going out and riders are most unsure of themselves. Combine that with having a rider's weight in approximately three places at once—one foot in a stirrup, one foot on the ground or on a hay bale, and both hands on the saddle—and there's a lot that can go wrong. To compensate, I've implemented a full-coverage policy: whenever we have riders getting mounted, anyone working is to be in the yard, making themselves helpful to the process.

In this case, we got everyone mounted, giving the little girl a perch on old Logan—by far our most reliable horse—but the minute he started to move, she began to scream.

Wade tried shouting over her, telling her, "No problem. It's a little different at first, but just kick him! Kick him. Kick him!"

The little girl looked like she wanted to kick Wade. I would have helped, but I was too busy telling Wade to stop.

He threw me a disgusted look as I took hold of Logan's reins. "What's wrong, sweetheart?"

"I don't want to ride!" she cried.

"Just leave her then," her annoyed mother said to me before turning toward her daughter. "If you're going to be a big baby, you can stay here!"

The little girl slumped but didn't relax her choke hold on the saddle horn. Tears streamed down her face.

"I can get her going," Wade said, riding over to grab Logan's halter, pulling him from my hands. "Come on, sweetie, we'll just go this way . . ."

The girl whimpered again, and I hustled to take back control of Logan. "Wade, stop!"

Though I had used my best boss voice, Wade kicked back in his saddle, overdramatizing his frustration by throwing his hands into the air.

I was an unimpressed audience, directing my attention instead to our young, crying rider. "Do you want a few minutes to get used to being up there, or are you done?"

"I'm done," she said, and put out her arms for me to help her down.

"Take the other two, Wade," I said. "We'll stay here."

He wheeled as though insulted, spurring his horse to gallop to the head of the small line of waiting riders to emphasize how much of a delay I had caused.

"Just let her sit there," the mother dismissed us both, turning her back.

Shocked and hurt on our rider's behalf, I walked the little girl and Logan to a nearby straw bale doubling as both parking barricade and bench, where I asked her to sit while I tied Logan back to the hitching post.

Gabe, ever watchful, came striding up from where he'd been fixing the latest breaks and leaks.

"I've got this—you go see to her," he said, nodding at the little girl.

My heart could neither contract nor expand quickly enough, being simultaneously lonely for this kind of empathetic assistance from my husband and tremendously relieved to have it at all.

I don't know how to reconcile that when I am at the ranch, so far from my marriage, I feel not only purposeful, but hopeful, thrilling in setting even the smallest foundations for the future. Whereas when I am in our marital house with Brent, I am not at home. I feel empty, as though what's around me is a hologram with no future, just a run time. The irony could be crippling if I let myself dwell on it: the ranch has no future unless one of these ventures pays. My marriage should have only future, except that it already feels like a failed venture.

Logan's former rider and I had both been relieved to play some cornhole. Within a few minutes, she had beat me at every variety anyone had ever seen, plus a few of her own versions:

"Run around the tree, kneel down, and throw backward!"

"Hop on one foot, sing 'I'm a Little Teapot,' and throw left-handed!"

We were winded, laughing, and completely engrossed when the riders returned.

I might not have noticed at all except that my playmate's mood suddenly darkened, her smile shrinking back inside of her as her mother's laughter sounded across the park.

I don't know if I will ever master letting things alone that aren't mine to fix. As I looked at the dismissive mom coming back for my cornhole victor, I felt like I was looking at Ty leading Cali, a tyrant claiming an innocent.

I stood waving for a long time as they pulled away, trying to believe as I eventually had to with Cali, and perhaps as I must with myself, that goodness can still find its way to us, even if we can't, at the moment, give it directions.

"You know," Wade said, busting up my reverie by plopping down on a hay bale. "I've been doing this a long time. I know what I'm doing. You need to let me lead my own rides."

I let my hand drop as I looked at him in disbelief. I didn't dispute that he had a point, but I was shocked that after the attitude he'd already displayed horseback, he thought he could open a discussion of it by complaining of *my* behavior. I flashed to the naked moments when I stood in front of my boss in an early consulting job, diminished to inches by her words: "Your only job is to make my job easier." I sensed from Wade that he has perhaps never been humbled or directed in a similar way, and I felt I was entitled to an unapologetic employer moment.

"Wade," I said. "No one is going to be forced to ride on my place. Not ever."

"But I know how to handle it!" he said. "You've just gotta get 'em past the first turn, and then they forget they're scared. You've just gotta—"

"No," I said. "They don't ever *have* to do anything. If they're scared and don't want to go, they're not going. Period."

Very few things have been clear to me since moving to Arizona. Most days, I've wobbled between not knowing what to do and knowing what must be done but not knowing how to justify it. This was one of the rare times I felt sure both of my actions and my reasons, and I wouldn't be talked down, despite that what I uttered as a directive with a period, Wade treated more like a comma.

Cody and I are saddling when inexplicably, Cutter pulls back. We manage to calm him, retying him to a different hitching post. Later, when I tie Cheyenne where Cutter had been, she pulls back too.

Now I'm really concerned.

The only time Cheyenne has ever pulled back was when I tried to bridle her and, unknown to me, she was sore. A chiropractic session later, I learned her whole jaw was out of alignment: her head must have been throbbing like Saturday night speakers.

Neither Cutter nor Cheyenne has any reason that I can think of to be sore or frightened now.

"What's going on?" I ask Cody.

"They don't like it there," Cody says. "None of 'em like that hitching spot anymore. It's where Wade saddles."

Deciding I will get to the bottom of this, I stroke Cheyenne's shoulder as I examine every detail of ground. I don't see anything out of the ordinary.

Cheyenne's hitching post is located a foot from the cattle chutes. Thinking there might be something bothering her from inside the chute, I walk over to investigate.

Cheyenne tenses, ears and feet moving back.

"It's OK, girl," I croon at her.

She swivels her ears.

I walk back to her, telling her what a good girl she is, what a pretty girl she is, as I loosen her tie rope. She backs up a few steps, ears still swiveling. I stroke her awhile. She relaxes but won't step forward.

Weird.

I retie her loosely before walking into the cattle chute again.

Cheyenne's ears swivel as I approach from across the chute wall, and she steps farther back.

I stop, looking around, listening, smelling—ugh.

"Cody?" I call. "Have you had horses in here? It smells like urine."

"Nah," he calls back, saddling from a different rack. "The only one going in there is Wade."

"Going in there," he said. Did he mean going, like, to the bathroom?

I sniff a little more. Definitely urine.

"You mean to tell me that Wade's been peeing in that chute?" I ask.

"Yeah," he laughs. "You didn't know? He must do it three times a day."

I think back. I've seen him walk into the chute to that spot, facing away from the horses. How had I not put this together?

"That's what he's been doing in there?" I ask, scandalized.

"For weeks now!" Cody says.

"Oh my God." I walk over to the straw bales, my makeshift office, fingers already dialing Wade's number.

When he picks up, I skip the greeting. "Wade, I see you've been missing the porta-potty."

"What?" he asks. "What do you mean?"

"I mean you've been peeing in my cattle chute," I say. There's a joke to be made about being pissed off, but I'm too angry to bother.

"No, I—" he clears his throat. "What? I haven't done anything like that."

"I think you heard me," I say. "You've been walking into the cattle chute to pee when the porta-potty is five yards away. You've been doing this in front of my staff and in front of clients. Now it smells, and it's spooking the horses."

"Well, I—" He stops himself again. "I didn't think anyone would notice."

I wish I could say that this man's relationship with the truth is unbelievable, but it's exactly what he's shown me ever since our first conversation. I can believe it, and I'm sickened, both at him and at myself for putting myself and the ranch in a position to be lied to. Still, there's something to be said for the flagrantly bad behavior because I am, at least, clear on what I need to do.

"We did notice," I say, summoning my authority. "It stops now. We'll pay you for what you worked last week, and you're welcome to come collect your stuff, but that's all the work you're going to do for us. No more."

"Really?" he asks, sounding more shocked than wounded. "You're serious?"

I guess I can understand why he'd ask. In his world, a crying child isn't to be taken seriously, so what's a little potty break in a cattle chute?

"I'm very serious," I say. "We will mail you your last check."

"All right," he says.

I suddenly have no idea what to say. "Thank you" isn't true. "Good" isn't genuine. "That'll be all" isn't me.

He hangs up, saving me the trouble.

After that, hitching post incidents drop to almost none, but I still have the cattle herd weight to manage.

It's Gabe's idea that maybe we split the herd. "Once they're sold, you probably don't want to risk them getting hurt on one of your guest drives," he suggests.

Which is why, as they sell, Cody helps me cut the chosen steer from the herd and sequester it where it can eat safely and in peace, simply being beef without having to endure the multitasking of also being rider entertainment.

What I don't foresee is feeling like people's personal shopper.

"Hi," a typical call starts out. "You're selling beef?"

"I'm selling cattle," I correct. "You can buy a whole one yourself, or you can split it with friends, and I can recommend a processor who will butcher it for you just the way you like it."

"Oh," comes the surprised response. "Well, how much beef is in a cow?"

"We sell at about a thousand pounds," I say. "Of that, you'll probably get between four and five hundred pounds of meat."

"That's a lot," the caller reflects. "How much do people usually eat in a year?"

"If you figure you're going to make a pound of burgers or a casserole for your family once a week," I say, "you and three other families could probably split a cow. If you eat beef more frequently than that, or you have a larger family, maybe you want a half."

"A half sounds good," a lot of people respond. "Yeah, sign me up for a half. Oh, wait—"

Here it comes.

"Will all that fit in my freezer?" is the question that absolutely every buyer has asked me.

"Probably not," I say. "You might want to buy an extra freezer to store everything. Or see if you can use a neighbor's. Maybe he'll even go in on the beef with you."

Then I usually hear a story about how someone the caller knows has done just this, and it was so great, and they really loved it, and the beef was so good—"and how much is it again?"

"We charge two dollars a pound for our beef," I answer. "On the hoof."

"What's—?"

"We charge you two dollars per pound for whatever their weight is when we load the steer on the scale before delivering it to the processor of your choice," I clarify.

"And then what's that charge?" the caller starts to add things up.

"Count on about $250 for processing," I say.

The caller works out the math: "That, plus the freezer . . . oh, wow." Enthusiasm drains from the voice by the word.

"Is about five fifty a pound of ready-to-eat beef," I say. "All in. Not too bad when you consider what even grocery stores sell their steaks for. At natural food stores you might pay—"

"Oh, yeah," the caller cuts in. I have a perfect record of never having to offer another price comparison. "It's ridiculous. OK, put me down for a half then."

I don't check, but I'm fairly certain that freezer sales around here are up this season.

HOW TO CONDUCT A
ROUNDUP IN FRENCH

The best and worst thing about being open for business to the public is the public.

Cody tells the story of a couple who showed up wanting a real Western experience. "I was just having them ride down the park, getting them used to the horses, you know, like you say to do, and the next thing I know, this guy has whipped off his shirt and whipped up Samson, and off they go galloping past me!"

"'What the—?' I ask his wife," Cody goes on, loving the retelling, "and she says, 'Oh, it's all right. He's an Indian.'"

I can only shake my head—both at what passes for explanation and at the image of a half-dressed man careening toward the freeway on a draft horse who steers progressively less as his speed increases.

As the stories compound, I wonder if we're putting a little too much "wild" back into the West.

"It was weird, Julie, I'm telling you," Cody recounts a different ride. "We had this whole group going up the hill, and out comes this rabbit. This thing was the size of a German shepherd, I swear. And it didn't move the whole time we walked past it. Didn't move until my horse was right on top of it, and then she spooked right into Buster, so of course he hopped a little and his rider came off." (I wince.) "But that's all right, because she was a doctor and she knew there was nothing really hurt. That rabbit was weird, though. I think I need to go shoot it."

I think differently and am thankful that the rabbit never re-emerges to test Cody's and my variance of opinions on the matter.

I didn't grow up around guns. The few times I was in the company of a starter's pistol as a kid, its sound sent me into hysterics—any of my races had to start with a whistle. I'm not opposed to guns in the hands of trained and practiced marksmen; my grandfather hunted duck for my mother's family to eat during the winter. Brent enjoys hunting pheasant and speaks fondly of his grandfather's teaching him to shoot by giving him one bullet at a time to shoot the snapping turtles who'd attack the cattle trying to water on their farm pond. I accept that guns have a place in this world. For example, sometimes under Brent's front seat. He manages his permits and his practice and doesn't ask me to participate. I don't know if he talked with Cody about doing the same, but I suspect there is more circumspect carrying going on than I know about. Most days, the suspicion is just part of the daily ether—I trust Cody to use weapons the way he does his cigarettes—on his own time, out of public view, without involving minors, and away from me.

All of which is ancillary to the issues that are far from ethereal and threaten to choke me every day: I'm having big troubles accepting the casualty count as it is, without adding anything to it.

Doc is gone. Last time Brent visited, it was to say goodbye to our beloved friend. Together we drove him to the vet; together we stroked his soft, golden fur. Together we watched the pink fluid fill and then leave the syringe. The next day, we went to the animal shelter and found Lucy a playmate—a coyote-looking puppy with sharp, pointy ears and a wise expression. They've been inseparable. Brent and I . . . haven't.

I both feel responsible and know I shouldn't. The care I've given is far more than many would offer and excruciatingly less than I wish I could. Doc's death is different than Lena's, in that he had some time left. Our choice had been made out of a sense of his diminishing quality of life, rather than an immediate mercy to inarguable suffering. As such, we'd come as close as people do to playing God, and I am very clear that I don't want the job.

I dare not dig into those feelings too deeply, as I don't know how to reconcile that I have only ever done my best and that it has guaranteed so little: my mare died, the ranch is hemorrhaging, my marriage is fraying. I am uncomfortably aware that they all have my efforts in common, and that, so far, the only response I've been able to find is to put in more effort, albeit on different tasks. I wonder if all of life is a series of trials and errors—if all we ever have is our effort and what we learn from it so we can better direct it next time. What I can and can't do on my own has been made all too evident, and with Doc's death there is an odd sense of both pardon and penance. We're designed to be human, and only that; thus, we all have our limits. I've just met quite a few of mine on the ranch, and it's been uneasy company to keep.

Thankfully, I don't have to be alone with these realizations because the ranch rides attract both the extraordinary and the endearing.

A family visits whose father struggles to fit his foot in his stirrup without dislodging or setting off his electronic ankle bracelet. I can see their smiles from across the stock tank as they ride into the woods together.

Another family comes to celebrate their five-year-old's birthday, and I'm out of horses. I get Marty out, saddling him with the smallest tack I can find. It's still miles too big: the stirrups fall at least six inches beneath her feet.

"Come on, Dad!" I call to the girl's father. "We're gonna need a spotter here!"

Good naturedly, he jogs over, walking with us through an impromptu obstacle course and mounted "Simon Says" game.

Marty trips, repeatedly. Like me, ever willing, despite the stumbles.

The little girl is clutched back into position by her father, both of them laughing as though all of this is an adventure. Maybe that's the difference between an adventure and actual risk: the former turns to the latter only when there's no leaving it.

Or the difference might be about fun.

A mother and daughter come out for a roundup ride while they're touring Sedona, and the daughter likes it so much she comes back for her own ride the next day.

"She wanted an advance on her allowance," her mom tells us. "She said she'd spend her own money just to get to ride with you again."

I think it was probably the novelty of chasing the cows and not me, but I'm touched, nonetheless.

The best and most memorable rides I sell are to a family who piles out of their rental car speaking French. I beckon Mom over, grinning widely. Mom taught high school French and has kept it up.

Both my mother and the visiting mother are beaming as they converse, then introduce me to the visiting father, a horseman, with his daughter, who has been taking riding lessons, and son who has no interest in horses at all. Just father and daughter will be riding, and they want the full cow-chase experience. This I give to Cody, offering to take the mother and son out in the Gator so they can take pictures.

I saddle Sage and Cheyenne while Mom explains that Dad and Daughter will be riding real American mustangs.

Dad looks impressed. Daughter does not.

That could be the sight of the Western saddles, Dad explains, as they have never ridden Western.

"In Belgium, we ride only English," he says. "And very—eh—tense."

"These horses are a little different," I explain. "They like slack in the reins . . ." (blank looks) ". . . longer reins. They also turn away from pressure," (I move my hands as though reining in the one-handed Western style), "rather than toward it" (I move my hands as though reining in the two-handed English style).

Dad translates all this for Daughter, who nods understanding.

"Your body will be different too," I go on. "In the English saddle, we sit a little bent forward," (I tip from my waist), "but in the Western saddle, we sit back." (I lean back now.) "We think about sitting back on the pockets of our jeans."

Dad smiles. Daughter doesn't. She's wearing pocketless breeches.

Cody is thrilled at what will be another great story to tell, and within moments has charmed both riders, having them laughing even before they reach the arena.

Mom is eager to follow lest she miss more photo opps. Son likes the look of the Gator, shrieking with laughter as we bounce over the ruts and rocks en route to the park.

Moments later, Dad and Daughter grin back at us as they trot into the open park. I wave, enjoying the sense that we're filming a home-grown version of a scene from *Hatari*, the cattle unwitting prizes to our family-scale safari adventure.

As Dad and Daughter break into a gallop, I wheel the Gator, trying to stay close to Sage and Cheyenne for the benefit of the pictures, but far enough away not to spook the cattle. Cody's attention is on keeping the cattle grouped up on the open end of the park rather than stampeding toward the corrals, so I feel it's my responsibility to try and assist Daughter with Cheyenne, whose reins are tight enough to have the mare's nose drawn almost to her chest. Sage is fighting Dad's hold as well, though less gracefully, gaping and gagging his mouth rather than bending his neck.

Grateful to Magic Mom for yet another unanticipated reason, I wave, shouting, turning off the Gator so my mother-coached French can be heard. "*Doucement! Doucement avec les mains!*" (Softly! Softly with the hands!) I motion a release of my hands and extend my arms.

Dad sees, flashing me a thumbs-up before slackening Sage's reins.

Sage immediately stops fighting.

Daughter gives about an inch. Cheyenne's ears swivel, a clear warning sign that she's considering a more physical protest.

"*Comment s'appelle t'elle?*" I ask Photo Mom.

"Chloe!" she says proudly.

"Chloe!" I call. "*Doucement! Beaucoup doucement avec les mains!*"

I slaughter what little I know of the language, as Chloe gives another inch.

Cheyenne's posture indicates she's still far from comfortable.

"*Beaucoup! Beaucoup!*" I insist. I motion again, releasing my hands as though slackening rein.

Chloe gives Cheyenne about six inches more rein.

Cheyenne's ears go back to normal.

"*Bien!*" I call with a thumbs up.

Photo Mom asks, "Eh—*parlez*—?"

"No," I interrupt.

We both laugh.

The sky is a brilliant blue, and Son cheers with the whipping wind as I bounce the Gator around in our mad chase to shadow the riders. Dad flashes more thumbs, and even reluctant Chloe is glowing, her grin visible from across the park as she and Cheyenne race after maverick cattle.

Nothing about the joy of the day is lost in translation.

STRAW BALES
AND OTHER HUMAN RESOURCES

We've been rained out.

After barely being able to open in May, we have a blazing June and July before the rains start in August, going on and on without end.

I can count on two hands the number of rides we guide in August. I can count September's rides on one.

Revenue has fallen to barely a trickle, and it's clear we have to close, first the rides, then the rest of the ranch.

Even though it's the only view to take of things, I find myself searching for a window. I know we had only one year's permitting; I know the rides were only ever going to be temporary—a few months at most. I know that the goal of the whole undertaking was to see how it would work; I just don't want to see that, financially, it hasn't.

Earlier in the summer, I figured out that we needed about twenty rides a day to break even. A handful of times, that actually happened, but our average is four. Interestingly, there's not much difference between weekdays and weekends, and it's not tourists who are our best customers, it's grandparents from Munds Park—families wanting something to do with the kids when they come up visiting.

We've had repeat visitors, for which Cody and the horses deserve the credit. Cody has a following among some of our adult riders; he'd also like to say he keeps the women coming back, but that fan club belongs to Mae. Annakin and Logan are favorites among the kids. I've kept us safe, and Gabe's kept everything working, but even without Wade, this is a prohibitively expensive, labor-intensive business if we run it up to my standards.

Cody looks at me sadly. "You do too much," he counsels. "Insurance and workers' comp. You do it all by the book. You do it right. But it costs."

It does.

Lawsuits and accidents would cost more, which has justified the expense, but the accounts simply can't sustain the continued spending.

I feel good about what we've accomplished: so many people have horrible trail-ride stories from when they were children. No one will have that story who's been here. We've had only one person come off, thankfully unhurt, in over three hundred rides, and that was because of the rogue rabbit.

It amazes me how few people even ask about whether we're insured, how much experience we have, or how long we've been in business. I'd like to say our matching shirts and general atmosphere of care speak volumes for us, but I'm afraid it's also that people are gullible. They see an open business and assume it must be legitimate. I cringe at how many corners I could be cutting.

It's the best and worst about being human. We want to trust each other.

I have been privileged to get to confide in my team for rider safety and ranch operations. For me, having a team was the high point of the summer, which makes the now-inevitable descent to the low of having to end their jobs all the more painful.

The rides haven't paid well enough, and the family doesn't want the vineyard.

I have waited to mention anything about employment terms until I had the final tally from both ventures, but now the financials have been and gone—shared with and disapproved by the family landowning partners, who don't want the vineyard's risks or long-term timelines. They offered that if I wanted to invest the capital to start wine operations, they would allow me the use of the land, but I've already seen what trying to run a business on land I don't control is like, and I don't have the personal capital both for the land and for the vines' installation. I know because I checked, rerunning the numbers every way I could think of, which is when I discovered I also don't have the water.

When dealing with a well, there are two numbers to know: the rate of water delivery and the rate of recharge into the tank. Gravity flow makes water delivery no problem, but our pump can only call on the water available from the aquifer, and the aquifer recharges at less than the rate of a garden hose—nowhere near the amount it would need to water the vines through the heat of summer.

I haven't told Gabe yet because I can't stand the thought that I'll have to lay him off. Selfishly, I also really don't want to have to tell him I couldn't make something work. It's been good to feel capable, and I don't want that to end.

I draw out what tasks there are for as long as I can, until a call with Dad clinches it: it's time to close things down as quickly and inexpensively as we can. Even though it's a reasonable, even anticipated, pronouncement, I feel my pride pucker from the constant rub against unattainable metrics. I know Dad's right, but I want to feel that he doesn't understand—that trying to earn his approval has rubbed me raw—that what's happened up here has been about hope and courage and guts and grit and a kind of nostalgic faith in what should be possible just because of hard work. And that's just the horses. The human element has been infinitely more, both in cost and value. I want to think that Dad has just disregarded the overall worth I've been working for, seeing only that the bottom line has bottomed out. If I could feel that way, then I could also feel that my team and I had made a noble effort that was only ever doomed to fail, that I had no real part in its demise. If I could feel that Dad never really got it, never really backed it, then I could let myself off at least one emotional hook.

But that escape is not available to me. I have to acknowledge all the expenditures Dad has approved: for horse care, for marketing, for staffing up, for spiffing up. Oldham Park is clean and signed, flowered and furnished for the riding public, and our staff is clothed and covered as befits professionals. Dad has happily partnered in all of that, giving me what I needed to run a rides business we could both be proud of. I suspect that I feel the way Dad felt for season after season with the cowboys. He hoped that employing people could grow the business to prosper for not only us but for them and their futures. I also suspect that

I'm now feeling the same failure Dad did when he had to sell the grazing herd and rights to the range months ago. He had to close that part of the ranch; now it's time for me to close down the rest.

Gabe has been fixing yet another water pipe when I walk up to have the conversation I've been dreading.

"So, I figure for next season we do something just a little different with this," he says.

"No," I say.

I rarely flatly disagree with him, so he's visibly surprised at my response. "We don't have to, of course, I just thought maybe you'd want to consider—"

"There's not going to be a next season," I say. "I have to close everything. In two weeks."

He looks at me, shocked.

I can't stand myself. I just dropped a bomb—a complete bomb—on a person I would never want to hurt.

"I didn't know," he says. He isn't quite looking at me.

"I didn't want to tell you—" I cut myself off. I'm going to cry and I don't want to, because it's not my pain that's important now. "It's not because of you."

"I didn't think it was," Gabe says, confused.

Oh, brilliant. As though the shock of finality isn't enough, I have now tossed in culpability. I am an oaf. A stumblebum monster stomping a confidant's visions with one foot while sticking the other in my mouth.

He looks at me a little sideways, crossing his arms. He's never taken that posture before. I feel a stab in my heart, hurting for hurting him, which I force myself to accept may be inevitable but could at least be done with more professionalism.

"You have done everything I, or any of us, have ever asked of you," I struggle. "And so much more besides. I am beyond grateful."

He shifts his feet, watching his boots.

"I don't have enough water to make the vineyard go," I say. "I checked everything again, and I realized I can deliver the water just fine. But I can't pump it fast enough. I looked into buying more tanks to try to beat the recharge rate, but it just doesn't work."

He works his jaw once.

"I can't do the vineyard, the rides haven't worked, and those were my last two ideas. I can't make the ranch pay, so I have to close it."

It's the first time I've said the words out loud. It's like calling a time of death; the words simple, the meaning shattering.

"I wish it weren't that way, but I can't make it work. I don't know if you'll want to work for us anymore, but we've got two full weeks left, plus the breakdown and probably some hours each month, checking on things after we're gone. There's never been help better than you, but I'd understand if you didn't want to help us anymore."

Gabe removes his ball cap and steps over to his omnipresent red truck. He tosses the cap on the hood to scratch at his hair, then nods and retrieves the cap to shove it on again. He places both hands on the truck hood and looks at them, then looks at me.

"I want to work for you as long as you'll have me. You guys just let me work, you know?" he looks at me earnestly. "I have ideas, and you take them and you don't try to manage me—"

I start to laugh. "God, Gabe. We'd be utterly lost without you. Nothing would work! You know that, right?"

"Yeah," he admits, chuckling. "But I've never worked for people like you before. I've felt . . . part of something."

I nod in agreement. I've been trying to make the ranch, and myself, into new and better versions of ourselves: build horses and business and marriage and family, and all of their futures, into not just something but something more than they were. Yes, trying for all of that has been not only something, but something else.

"God—I mean—it's just so disappointing that it didn't work out," he says, thumping the hood of his truck.

"It's why I didn't tell you earlier. I'm sorry."

"Yeah," he looks up at me. "I mean it's your business—"

"No!" I say, hearing my outsize tone, then pulling on every bit of steady I can find to control my words and voice. "It was exciting to think of doing the projects we'd talked about. I was really going to like working with you because you are so capable and so dedicated, and they were going to be really cool projects we could both get excited about."

He nods acknowledgment.

"I am so sorry. I can't make them happen," I pronounce each word very deliberately, stacking them on the scale of effort I can't get to balance.

He looks at me, then back down at his truck hood. He nods.

"Thank you," he says, reversing our roles just for a moment, showing me that the ranch and I provided him with feelings and experience he hadn't had before, either.

There is no better example for me to follow than the one he has set, time and again, so I answer with his very familiar words, "You're welcome."

"I'll have this done in another few minutes," he says, gesturing to the dismantled pipes, our normal roles and congeniality immediately restored with his characteristic skill.

After the shock of our impending closure has passed, there's a kind of fraternal playfulness about the place.

"Hey!" Cody says. "You guys gonna take this shop vac? Because if not—"

"Cody, when have you ever vacuumed anything in your entire life?" Gabe asks, grinning. "Now, the power washer—if you're not gonna use that—"

"Not the power washer!" Cody argues. "I want that. I could use that."

I laugh. "What do you want me to do, pick a number?"

The welcome banter goes back and forth. I take it as a sign that I'm forgiven. That they know sometimes businesses fail, and they don't hold me responsible for the loss of their jobs, which I am, of course. We all know it. But I feel they're also letting me know that they know I tried. And that maybe now I've joined them in the hard knowledge that sometimes trying isn't enough.

It also helps that we have one last project to accomplish together. Sending the sour horses back to Chrissy had been fine with Mom and me, but we both agree that Logan, Annakin, and Mae can't go back.

"Why don't I just buy them?" Mom asks. "How much could—"

Cody shakes his head violently. "You can't offer to buy them yourself."

Mom gives him a questioning look.

"If she knows it's you offering, she'll jack up the price to $10,000 a horse. And they ain't worth that in solid gold," Cody says. "You let me do this. I'll say Gabe wants to buy 'em."

"But Wade knows Gabe," I remind him. "How about I call Heidi and see if we can use her name instead?"

"Whatever," Cody says. "We'll make up a name—I don't care. We'll just say I have a buyer who wants 'em and will pay forty-five hundred for all three. How's that?"

Mom nods at the math. "I think we could get that back, don't you?"

I do. "It's about what we averaged on most of the others."

Plus, as it turns out, Heidi really does want them. Since graduating from college, she's opened her own burgeoning business, especially popular with children and amateur riders, and she's always looking for sweet, affordable, affable mounts. I send her pictures and video of all three, and she calls me back the next day.

"I can sell Annakin and Mae tomorrow," she says. "No problem. But Logan's going to take some time."

"I'll pay the board for him," I say. "Take all the time you need. He deserves a really good home."

She understands—of course she does. Heidi always did.

Chrissy takes the deal. We pay Cody, he pays Chrissy, the horses go to Heidi, and all of us enjoy our little intrigue.

I also enjoy that it puts my "saved and repurposed" count up past a dozen animals. It's good to see that tally alongside the ones of the things I haven't accomplished. The latter is longer and will weigh heavy for some time, as repurposing my own life requires additional reconstruction, but knowing the horses got new lives shows that it's possible—proves that we don't have to end where we begin.

Post-ranch destinations sort out in the next few weeks, with Cody and Gabe sharing their plans as we sit out one evening on the straw bales we'd used as parking markers.

It's the time of day between afternoon and evening when everything seems to take a breath and be still. Except for Cody, who is fidgeting as he faces Gabe and the sun setting behind him.

"So, you're gonna try to take the riding business south?" Gabe asks Cody.

Cody nods. "I want to see what I can get going on that land near McKinsey, maybe build a track there if we can work something out."

He looks at me, and I shrug. "You know how Dad is," I say. "Work up a lease."

He grins. "Everything by the book," he agrees. "But I think people would like it, you know? Come out and race their horses for time? Maybe have some obstacles."

His voice drifts off and he's far away now, envisioning his next big venture. Last week it was driving large equipment. Cody doesn't have small ideas.

"You're going back to work?" Gabe asks me.

I nod. "I have more applications started. Maybe a planner job at the airport. Maybe something else."

"Airport would be cool," Gabe says.

"I think so too," I say. "We'll see. Depends on who picks me up."

"Yeah," he agrees. "I've got a couple jobs I've been asking about. But I also wanted to ask you—are you moving those feed bins?"

I look over at our stack of grain bins. "No. You're welcome to them."

"Really?" Gabe says. "That'd be great. I've been talking to the brewers, and if you're all right with it, they've said they'll keep calling me to pick up like we've been doing. I can get a few head from my neighbor and maybe start a beef business."

"Really?" I crow. "That's so great!"

"Yeah!" he laughs, adjusting his hat. "I'm pretty excited about it. So's my neighbor, 'cause now he thinks I'll owe him more favors."

We all laugh.

"The processor's real excited about it," Gabe says. "He says he's been wanting to advertise beef."

Gabe, ever helpful to any in need, quickly endeared himself to both processors who had visited the ranch for our beef-buying clients. He had bravely moved slop buckets, gathered up offal, and kept me from getting too close lest I get disgusted or physically ill at the mess.

I look at Gabe now, starting this new business, and think maybe we rescued each other.

Each of us may have been the first nonfamilial person who never once doubted the other's abilities.

Heidi, true to her word, had Annakin and Mae sold within a week— both to ladies who arrived with halters still shiny from the store, bags of carrots, big smiles, and all the appreciation in the world for their new horse friends.

Logan took a little longer but eventually went to a family with two little girls.

"He has a special stall, and special feed, everyone knows his name, he has his own turnout," Heidi listed for me. "I think he'll be happy."

Years later, she will still be getting calls from the family, thanking her for finding him for them.

After closing down the rides, I moved Marty and Blue down to Phoenix, where Blue acclimated as Brent's trail horse while Marty quickly let me know that he'd had enough of that life. After Jim the Farrier tacked on some sliding plates, I hauled Marty to lessons with a trusted reining trainer and old friend. In less than a month, Marty had sold back into the horse-show world where he'd always excelled.

"You've taken good care of me," I told him as I stroked him goodbye. "Across three states and six years. You kept me riding, wouldn't let me quit, and made so many people happy in the process. Even me, sometimes. And I know that was hard work."

He glanced at me, maintaining his perfect record for understanding much more than a horse should have to.

"I'm going to miss you. Every day I will miss you," I said, tearing up. "But you need to go have your kind of fun again. And I can't do it with you. I have other work to do."

He leaned into me a little. Marty always did like his hugs.

His new owner walked over, and I handed her his lead rope.

Marty pricked his ears when he saw the trailer. The trailer means a ride. It means an arena. It means shows.

He hopped right in.

I walked away.

As it turned out, a few months later, so did Brent.

From our home, from our marriage, but most of all, from me.

I have a lot of building and rebuilding to do before I understand the new emotional and spiritual scaffolding I will construct for myself, but the base is that no future can be built on either a past promise, love, work, or hope alone. Even combined, they may not be enough to overcome what might be termed "the limitations of design." My marriage had been built to be a home for some long-held hopes and a haven from our personal demons. Much like Oldham Park, it could only do that temporarily, for a few choice seasons. The limitations were built in from the beginning—the architects convinced their plans would be enough for the work they could foresee there. At the ranch and at home, no one could see how much more might be asked of that space, and how little it would be able to meet the requests.

Having learned that neither the ranch nor I could go any further as the current version of ourselves, for the next few years we both retreated into individual cocoons as time and life spun around us. The ranch was used intermittently, moving from hand to hand along an increasingly careless stream of tenants. I moved around Arizona. In those exploratory years, neither the ranch nor I found permanent employment as something else with different partners, perhaps because our work together hadn't finished and required the perspective that only more time and experience can bring.

BEGATS

There have been several transformations in the life I lived ranching and the one I'm living now, a timeline sometimes maddeningly reminiscent of a bumblebee flight pattern. The sting is always in the wait: the aching hope that today's barb will contribute to tomorrow's blessing. More often than not, I find it does. Perhaps I seek that kind of utility naturally: I am the granddaughter of a survivor of the Great Depression, who turned newspaper into dolls and learned to make any recipe with only half, as opposed to a full, can of condensed soup. Perhaps it's an exercise in faith: my religious background celebrates the miracle of life after death, and while I never aspire to personally experience quite that level of grace, each time I find a way to make some prior loss or pain instructive to myself or others, I feel I'm receiving a part of it. Regardless of where any of us finds spiritual truth, there is sublime peace in seeing lost hope recycled, revised by subsequent events and experience to be resurrected as joy.

HOW TO GET
BACK IN THE SADDLE

When Brent and I first became engaged, I turned to him one afternoon, intent that he understand something fundamental to my very being.

"I need to tell you something."

He was driving at the time; his hands clenched on the wheel as he glanced at me, his expression stricken. "OK," he agreed.

"I am always going to need horses in my life."

He exhaled, laughing. "God, I thought you were going to say something awful. That's it?"

"That's everything," I assured him. "Always. I mean it—always. Maybe I won't have to own them, but I have to be with them somehow. My whole life."

Still chuckling, he asked, "Isn't there some kind of twelve-step program for that?"

"Yes," I said without taking a beat. "We have one already, so that'd be eleven more horses."

Such was the exchange when we were preparing to marry.

By the time we were preparing to divorce, I was not only horseless but not riding, not volunteering, not grooming, bereft of all things equine—the best indicator I can identify of how far afield I was of myself.

The ranch had deconstructed many of my most foundational mythologies, but it took Brent's leaving for me to release the one that had perpetuated our marriage: that our union was salvageable either by something I took on or by something I gave up.

We all hit walls in life. I have no doubt that far before the day he wouldn't come home, Brent felt concussed by the number of times he'd tried finding some new way to make me happy, only to crash into the obstacles of my self-doubt or depression.

The ranch had both exposed and cracked these and other chinks in our marital armor until the gaps prevented us from shielding ourselves from our demons.

I still hadn't put my own medical nightmares to bed. Depression is an especially nasty affliction in that the wrong cure, even the wrong healer, can be debilitating enough to make the depressed abstain from "care," but I started the long process of auditioning therapy, medication, and herbs for my helping roles. It would be years before I found the combination that was right for me, which is another of depression's wicked tricks: we can be "doing everything right" to address it, but until the combination is right *for us*, everything may still feel wrong. This is the worst and most selfish of depression's afflictions: that we, the afflicted, would love to feel grateful, hopeful, adjusted to the fact that life is not as bad as it seems, except that depression is always, always there to remind us that because we are depressed, life will never be for us the way it seems to be for others. We are defeated before we begin, with little sympathy and even less understanding available as we try to work our way out from depression's influence.

While still married, I viewed depression as a condition Brent had never signed up for and didn't deserve to live with. It might lead me astray into wrong thinking or feeling, but by damn, I would find my way back.

Whether he knew it or not, Brent's leaving was the one thing I couldn't come back from.

Daily life had tried us, moving had strained us, ranching had distanced us, drinking was dulling us, family had wedged us apart, and I had resolved to each new tension that there must be something I could do to change it. If Brent hadn't left, I might have tried even more ways to pretzel myself into posturing to both of us that our problems were circumstantial. Because he left, I was finally clear that our union was no longer serving either of us.

We separated for a few months, then I filed for divorce.

I used to joke about how I was freighted with the super-jumbo collection of emotional crayons, whereas Brent seemed to thrive with a typical eight-count box. Lots of my marital discomfort was attributable to my trying to sort through my mosaic of emotional colors, but the divorce process was numbing for being so very black and white, legal and not legal, joint and individual, agreement or disagreement: binary choices pounding what had been a union into unrecognizable disarray.

I didn't know Brent by the end of it. I barely knew myself.

Such was our estrangement that getting to a decree took eleven months. Getting the decree's orders settled took another nine.

Impatient to get on with my life, I moved, changed jobs, started writing, started riding, tried out new groups, and traveled. I was the picture of perpetual motion, trying to find a new version of myself, which makes it fitting that I met a man while I was literally up in the air.

Asked by my parents to come meet a potential agribusiness partner in the Hawaiian Islands, I found myself seated beside a golfer and his buddy en route to Maui. Gregarious and charming, he wanted to talk more than read, and I liked laughing with him more than pounding attempts at a fiction manuscript into my laptop. Time flew by in every way, and when we disembarked, we politely said goodbye.

Only to say hello again that night at my hotel's bar.

We had not discussed where anyone was staying. We had not exchanged numbers. We simply found ourselves at the very same evening's end and decided we were fated to laugh some more together.

He seemed delighted by my company, describing me as "stunning."

I was stunned at how delightful I was finding his company.

Still, things stayed very proper: both of us were separated but not divorced, traveling, and unwilling to be a tropical cliché, so we exchanged numbers for the expedient of a drink the next night only and said goodnight.

Our numbers got more exercise than the following evening's call, but nowhere near enough to have me in shape for his phoning the following spring to tell me he was bound for Malaga and Madrid that summer, and did I want to go to Spain?

By then, I was three months officially divorced, doing laps in the dating pool, breathless and sputtering at how hard it was to start over. I had also resumed Hunter/Jumper lessons with my favorite former horse trainer, where, I was relieved to find, I hadn't lost much but time. My seat was still good, hands were good, legs were weaker than I'd like but still knew their job. Compared to my dating skills, my riding was on an Olympic level, but I was participating just casually in both worlds, not wanting to get into partnership with a horse or a man too quickly.

The idea of joining a man I barely knew in a foreign land for a week was the relational equivalent of stepping me up from walk-trot to a Grand Prix jump course. It was ill-advised. Preposterous.

"When?" I asked.

It shocked both of us that I'd consider it. Shocked us again when I bought a ticket to Madrid, but not before checking out what horse adventures I might have in the area.

I built myself an itinerary that would put me outside Seville at a horse farm learning dressage for a week before joining my golfer in Malaga. I would be on my own in Spain for ten days before joining him for five. More than anything else, I wanted to know if the world was still open to me as a single traveler. I wanted to know how far I could go, how much challenge I could withstand, how much discovery I could handle. I wanted to know if I should expect my world to be bigger or smaller, now that I was on my own without a marriage.

To say that the trip was an awakening would be an understatement akin to saying that Las Vegas kind of likes lights.

Revelation found me at least once a day: the glory of a great city, the exhale of miles of olive trees, the ease of train travel, a fascination with flamenco, the buoyancy of soccer songs, and the accordion push-pull of learning choreography I'd only ever seen, but never attempted, with a horse—and then a man. Many times I flubbed it, blistering with the awkward effort of trying to keep up; a few times I got it, thrilling that there could be such feelings in the world.

Despite those similarities, my expectations of events were exactly opposite to actual outcomes. I traveled to Spain expecting to excel but shrug at dressage before jet-setting into the thrill of a new relationship. Instead, I struggled with but loved the riding and received another major relational setback, both of which were likely surprising to no one but me.

Part of what makes divorce so difficult is the reassembly of oneself into a single entity. The heart's pieces look like they should still come together, but the connective tissue does not adhere in the same way. What once pulls now pushes away; what strained once flows easily. The same puzzle forms a new image. In my case, a week's fling led to a lasting romance with Spanish horses and dressage and not with the guy, which might have been predictable, given that I seem to have a horse in my head.

This poor golfer had invited a high-strung mare to stable with him, having no idea how sensitive and temperamental she was. I was a flighty, quivering, suspicious prancer sensationally reactive to anything that could be a cue. He was a guy on vacation. Despite the unlikely matchup, we had some fun. We even became, and remain, friends. And I did come back from Spain in love: just not the way I thought I would be.

HOW TO DANCE
WITH NEXT STEPS

Over the next two years, I went back to Spain to ride dressage at the farm twice more. In between times, I sought out a dressage trainer in Arizona and began taking lessons, coming to understand why dressage has been described as "dancing horses." A horse that knows how to move, hold, and balance its individual parts makes a ride feel musical, or like a joining rather than a meetup. When my riding parts move as fluidly, there is harmony rather than dissonance. As with most dances, there is a beginner's aping and a master's art, but the joy is that it's dancing, no matter the level.

Not only did I love the steps, I loved the lessons. Dressage instruction felt like learning parts of a language that had always eluded me before, as though I had only ever used subjects and verbs and was now being introduced to the wonder of adjectives, articles, and, best of all, conjunctions—new connections I had sensed but never made.

Even more exciting, with this new language I suddenly had something meaningful to say to Bayley, Mom's Babbitt-bred mare who had been handicapped by, and yet had mostly overcome, early injuries.

As a filly, Bayley was the horse I had never been able to help. I was no expert to teach her and sorely resented the humbling lessons she taught me. Now, she and I suddenly had much in common: we had both moved back to northern Arizona still limping from a long-acquired, just-treated injury.

Mine was the divorce.

Bayley's had been tendon adhesions that developed due to some disproportional use to care that's understandable for a school with budget constraints. Mom had rehomed Bayley to the school when she stopped riding due to a bad back, troublesome foot, and our no longer living within the same geographies. To its credit, when Bayley repeatedly came up lame, the school called Mom, who accepted Bayley back and purchased the surgical procedure for her when it was clear that neither pasture nor time would heal what was wrong.

In the months that followed, Bayley recovered slowly, going from hand-walking to being led alongside another horse on rides out, which she allowed but did not accept.

Neither Bayley nor I were built to be led.

When I started riding Bayley regularly, I thought it was to get her back into school condition so she could go back to a job as a teacher.

My idea was to start her with some of the very basic dressage exercises I had learned, hoping the incremental progression would suit her need to relearn how to use her newly improved body.

My beloved Spanish horse farm family would shudder to hear me say that beginning dressage work is a little bit like the hokeypokey: right hip in, right hip out, right shoulder in, right shoulder out, then the same on the left side. (There is no choreographed shaking, for which both horse and rider are grateful.)

Despite the physical difficulty for her in performing the isolations, Bayley thrived on the work, going from an uneven walk and trot, and a canter resembling a bunny hop, to three true and even gaits in both directions within just three months.

I thrived too. Bayley became a real-life example of healing and transformation: the ability to create new possibilities for the future just through a willingness to learn. I was proud of our progress and increasingly protective of our partnership, deciding within a few weeks that Bayley deserved more time than just the few months left before the school term would begin to fully recover.

I told myself that delaying sending her to the school was for her benefit.

Except that when Bayley and I went out together, my heart found home: I breathed more deeply and fretted less, appreciating the peace we eventually found together. I felt more settled, as well as more open and receptive, which, fittingly, were exactly what I had been teaching her to be through the course of our dressage work.

That I could learn what I thought I should teach was her first lesson for me.

The next was about speaking up. Bayley is never shy about letting me know when she does not understand or dislikes a suggestion. She is never unsafe, but she can be willful when communicating her limits; sometimes she simply stops. Other times, she shambles. When she's desperate, she limps, eyeing me as a professor might when disappointed with a student's dull mediocrity.

As confident as she is with me, however, she is not that way with other horses. Because either she is not or thinks she is not as strong as other mares, Bayley immediately relegates herself to lower status in a herd and does not fight back when her food is stolen or a male gets physical about expressing his affections.

As with so many of us in a bad situation, it took a courageous third party to point out what we couldn't see. Heidi had become a successful horse trainer with her own thriving business, but she never got too busy to welcome our horses. After trying a few other stabling options, Mom and I agreed that we couldn't do better than Heidi's care, especially since she had found a way to come back to northern Arizona. We had enjoyed a reunited season, feeling like we'd gotten the band back together: Bayley and me, Sage and Cheyenne the mustangs, and Heidi, all at Oldham Park. Except that living with the mustangs didn't seem to be a solely happy reunion for Bayley, which I didn't notice at first. Playing the role of "dutiful girl" to perfection, Bayley never fought off the other horses while I was around to witness it, leaving me to wonder what could be the cause of her underweight and scarred frame.

"Bayley's getting mounted," Heidi told me one day at the hitching post. "She's not fighting it off or anything—but that's why she has these nicks and scars."

I could feel my stomach contract, twisting at the animalistic expedient of reinforcing dominant and submissive roles through the use of sex.

"And then they steal her food," Heidi concluded.

Such are herd dynamics. We speak of an animal kingdom—a hierarchy, not a democracy. Individuals are utilized, not valued. I wanted to ask how another horse would dare assert himself over this intrepid mare, who is tougher than any other in the herd for all she has overcome, but I know that's nonsense. To me, Bayley is teacher and guide, mirror and mentor, but in a herd, she is a horse, and a damaged one, prone to being preyed on.

I was terribly and uncomfortably aware that both Heidi and I have had to sort through similar relationships: those that transform us versus those that keep us down. If our sorority has anything in common, it is the voluntary move from victim to hero of our own lives, and in so doing, from student to teacher. We'd earned tenure from the University of Hard Knocks, the diploma being taking ownership of ourselves.

I went a step further.

I talked to Mom, took over Bayley's stabling, and registered myself as her owner, becoming officially partnered for the first time since my separations from horses and husband began.

Bayley was moved to new, individual, quarters.

I keep moving, myself.

I like to think of both of us not as damaged, but able. Back in the saddle and riding into not sunset but the sunrise of beginning again and again, together, day by day.

HOW TO MAKE
A PLAYGROUND MIX

In March of 2020, with the onset of COVID-19, most people's lives went indoors. They stopped going out for anything but suddenly impossible-to-find essentials, stopped seeing all but the select few people they couldn't live without. Many began living through an agonizingly slow atrophy of both equilibrium and outlook.

For a few weeks, and through the staggered closures of public spaces and entities, we had the impression these changes were temporary; that after we'd paid the necessary time and distance, the virus that was shutting down everything we'd come to think of as normal would move on, and we would be released back to daily life.

Back to daily life, back to normal, back to how things were—everywhere in conversation, and maybe expectation, we voiced the hope that though our worlds had gone careening off course into zany dystopian sci-fi hell, we would find our way back.

Back.

Why back?

It was not a direction I wanted for myself. Though I had returned to northern Arizona the year before, my move had nothing to do with the ranch. I had been forging ahead with learning to be a writer. A few of my manuscripts had won prizes. I had been selected for a competitive workshop. A short story and a poem had been published. I had been invited to read my poetry publicly. By any metric, I had become not only a writer, but an author and poet, and I had found a new purpose in serving the stories that came to be written.

One of the stories was my friend's in Spain. He owned the horse farm where I had been introduced to dressage. He had moved not only countries, but continents. He'd started and sold not only horses, but businesses, and he was not only content but happy. I was overjoyed to help him write his memoir, gleefully flying myself to Spain one winter, where I spent my mornings by a fire and his armchair recording his memories, then afternoons in the arena learning more dressage from his daughter. Evenings I spent cramming everything I could process into my laptop. As such, I was lining out the elements I most wanted in my life, and it was a compelling sketch. I was drawing the life of a writer and a rider beyond any of my divorce-era imaginings, and I dearly wanted to keep adding to that picture.

Over the winter months before COVID's first spring, Heidi and Dad chatted about the possibility of her coming up to Oldham Park with a string of horses for the summer, and by spring they'd worked out an arrangement and a start date. When Dad shared the news with me, he asked if I might be available to help get the ranch ready for Heidi's summer business.

I like Heidi. We've stayed in touch since the ranch days, as she understands not only riding horses, but caring for them within the context created by their owners, and she's diligent about keeping up relationships on both the horse and human sides. She's also had a daughter, the most charming combination of budding cowgirl, rock star, and princess on two legs, besides other future ambitions proclaimed by her T-shirts. Like her mother, she can sit any horse she climbs on. The two have not only my respect and my love as kindred spirits and horsewomen, but also my empathy as ladies rebuilding their lives after a divorce.

When I first moved to Flagstaff in April 2019, I had no ambitions of returning to Oldham Park for any reasons. Driving past it, I had made my peace that it was from another time, another life—one I had moved on from, grown out of, and knew better than to try again.

It was no longer the place of my dreams.

But Heidi had kept dreaming about it. A summer there, for her, would be a dream come true.

It also meant I would be able to ride Bayley and the mustangs in the cool pines instead of the Phoenix heat, because if Heidi came north with her business, our horses would come too.

I told Dad, sure, I would help.

Spring rains have been frequent, and I slosh around in muck boots making note of needed repairs. Little remains up to my standard of horse-ready shape.

Multiple tenants have used Oldham's facilities for varying durations since I was last here. Most recently, an outfitter from out of state said he would use the park for the summer, but he occupied it with far too many animals year-round. After ignoring Dad's insistence that he relocate part of his herd, he managed the inevitable, literal, watershed of problems associated with snows and spring thaws by scraping off the top layer of filth from the corrals—cinders and all. When Dad finally succeeded in getting the outfitter gone, Oldham lay sad and sodden, needing a thorough mucking-out. Cody came back for a summer season to do just that, but for the past six months, Oldham has lain dormant except for the degradation of time going by.

Besides the scraped and scrapped footing, fences are in disrepair or have been supplemented with long-rusted wire, standpipes are missing hoses, shelters are missing panels, welds have popped, and trash is everywhere.

The last is the worst infraction in my mind, because it's not routine wear and tear or mistaken equipment ownership—it's just carelessness.

Over the next few weeks, I pick up bags full of trash, meet the plumbers to repair water tanks, meet them again to repair water lines, buy and attach hoses, and make dozens of trips to the hardware store for, among other things, paint, lumber, and plumbing fixtures.

In all the back-and-forths, I decide that Oldham has a predictability: things are always more broken than they appear; the first fix won't be enough; I'll get to the point of regretting any and all effort I ever put in; then I will meet someone who will make all the trouble seem worthwhile.

For a while, it's Oscar at the local hardware store, who recognizes me on-site and accompanies me to fixtures.

Then, it's Deb of the woodchips.

Of all the places I'd go to find someone with whom I'd like to share brunch, a landscape supply company would be among my last guesses, but Deb is so sunny, so warm and heartfelt and kind on the phone, that our discussion of log grind feels like an emotional mani-pedi.

"Log grind?" I ask.

"You can go see it, if you like," she offers, providing directions. "What we're talking about is in the lightest pile on the far right. You know, it's what a lot of people use for playgrounds."

Which is why I step over the cement-and-cable fence and photograph the inert mound with as much enthusiasm as if I were walking into a carnival.

I contact Deb to let her know she's right, log grind is exactly what we need. She messages with a quote, offering us the material not only at the time we wanted but at a discounted price.

"I just so enjoyed talking to you. I have so much heart for you, Julie, I want this to be successful," she says when I call to check on the adjusted price.

I tear up.

"Well, I have to tell you that this offer is not only perfectly timed because we've had more expenses than I counted on—"

She chuckles her understanding.

"—but because just yesterday I went walking through the woods down a path that someone's designated as 'the fairy trail' where people have placed toys charms over the years—"

"So Flagstaff," she quips.

"I know—classic—except that I put a blingy dog-paw earring there last fall after my dog died, and yesterday as I was walking through I came upon the fallen log where I'd left it, completely barren— everything gone—except a note saying that 'fairies like homemade offerings best.'"

Deb gasps.

"Right?!" I glory in our shared indignance. "And I will just tell you that I was pretty ready to give up on people, and now here you are making me think people aren't so bad—"

"I love this, Julie," Deb says. "Because that's exactly how I feel when we talk!"

Faith restored and delivery date booked, we sign off.

Deb calls again on delivery day to let me know they're running a bit late. This is not only thoughtful but fortuitous, as so are we. Cody has met me at Oldham Park with a new work colleague from his barnwood reclamation business. They're fueling and firing up not only our tractor but his, and Oldham is about to look like the heavy equipment test-drive farm he'd proposed years ago as a business venture.

"And it's dry enough there—you're sure?" Deb asks. "Brent wanted me to check."

I hiccup mentally at the name as she adds, "He's been our driver for over twenty-seven years."

I only made it with my Brent for eight. Most days I don't think too much about my "was-band," but standing in Oldham's isolation with too much to do that I can't accomplish on my own, Brent's name seems like an apt echo to add to the others already swirling around.

"I walked it," I tell Deb. "I think it's fine. I know I could pull my truck and horse trailer through here with no problems. We haven't had rain out here for at least three days."

"If there's any trouble, he'll make it work," Deb assures me. "Brent's amazing."

When the semi comes down the dirt frontage road, it's clear that I have never paid enough attention to how much, in tonnage, an 18-wheeler is definitely not like a truck and horse trailer.

Brent-of-the-Twenty-Seven-Years folds the rig through our gate, across the cattle guard, and up our driveway, where I run out to meet him, indicating the corrals where I want the material unloaded.

Brent eyes the gates the way I would a Shetland pony that's been hyped as a horse. "Are those ten feet?"

"One's eleven, one's twelve, and one's fourteen," I point. "But I wonder if you should just put all the material in the one, because I think the approach to the others with this thing—"

"Yeah," he agrees before I can finish.

Not only is the semi far longer and heavier than a horse trailer, it is also taller—taller even than the power line strung between the tack room and the corrals, under which the semi would have to fit to back through one of the gates.

"I could put half of it over there," he says of the corral with the largest gate. "Then pull back out and drop the other half there in front of your building closer to the other two pens."

"I'd hate to waste any," I say. "Let's just drop this whole load in the largest corral there and we'll see where we are."

Which is a nice sentiment, except that I was (also) wrong about things being dry enough for the delivery.

"Is he gonna be able to get that out?" Cody mutters, taking a break from dueling tractors to sidle up to me with obvious concern.

The semi has sunk such that only half the tires are visible.

"He says so," I report brightly.

Cody now gives me the Shetland pony look. "I s'pose we could pull from the front—with both tractors, we could maybe move him a little once the back is empty."

The tractors have been scurrying around the corral like worker ants to a queen, trying to spread the wood chips faster than the truck's machinery can push them out its back end.

"The horses are gonna drown in all those chips," Cody warns.

I smack at his shoulder. "They are not."

"OK," he laughs as though I'd insisted that, yes, a draft horse will fit in a Christmas stocking.

Thankfully, what I had grossly underestimated in weight I had calculated just right in area. Not only would the horses in that particular corral not drown, they wouldn't even be wading to the ankles, and we would, indeed, need a second load of material for the other two corrals.

Assuming we can get the truck out.

Having lived in Colorado and the state of Washington where weather tends to cause traffic to slide off of roads, I turn for the hay barn and the two shovels I have thankfully thought to bring out. Never mind that their heads are smaller than half the size of the truck's formerly shiny hubcaps, I hold one out to Brent. "I'll take this side, if you want to try that one."

He stands with his shovel, leaning against the handle for a few minutes, probably trying to decide if he's being punked. When my shoving, stomping, pounding, and thumping of the unfortunate tool against the newly packed ground make it clear the suggestion is for real, he starts on his side.

Half an hour later, I have dug a quarter of the tire's height loose.

Most of Arizona doesn't have basements because of the "caliche" layer in its surface geology—a calcium carbonate stripe that's shrugged at as being "impossible" to dig through.

This is not that, and yet, I have never admired backhoes more.

A driver of merely twenty-six years would have had to ditch the truck and catch a ride back into town, but Brent does the nearly impossible, rocking the beast like a recalcitrant dragon up the shallowed holes and eventually out of the corral.

"That second load could absolutely go right in front of the tack room building," I wave toward Brent's suggested spot after congratulating his driving.

"Sounds good," he says, God-love-him, straight-faced.

Oldman Park does it again—from mayhem through misgiving to miracle by the help of an unsung hero.

A few weeks later, anxious to get out of the crucible that is a quarantined Phoenix metro area with summer coming on, Heidi unloads horses at Oldham Park two weeks before Memorial Day. It is a photo finish between me and the trailers, but the plumbers and I fix the cabin pump and water heater, and the corral troughs' last leak, just as the trailers cross the cattle guard.

Restoring Oldham to working order might feel like victory except for the humiliation of the race to get here: it had never occurred to me to check that the corral troughs would have stoppers in the drains before attempting to fill them. Then again, our former tenants took hoses, panels, and saddle racks. Why would they not also take tank plugs?

The oddest part is feeling a sympathy for both sides.

To a landowner, taking what doesn't belong to you is not only a breach of trust and stewardship of an asset given to another's care, it's theft, pure and simple.

To the rancher, or tenant charged with use and work on the land, there is simply too little compensation for the hardships experienced and never anticipated. The cold snaps and heat waves that can cause horses to colic and grass to stop growing; the public, fonts of tossed trash and culprits behind cut fences; immediate and physical problems ranging from trespassers who break and enter to lameness-prone horses losing shoes more than a mile from home. In such problematic situations, no solution comes without risk, and most are faced alone, with support by phone or a good thirty minutes of travel time away, assuming you're still near the actual ranch. Which is to say nothing of the other types of problems that surface in modern-day business, from which ranching is no exception—client whims and gossip, price fluctuation, market shifts, the constant rub between work and home life—all in a world with too little time or patience or trust to consider your reasons, most of which, being attributable to living, breathing, thousand-pound beings, are less flexible than the urban mainstream world's expectations.

The hardships lend themselves to some bragging rights, which, in truth, I find I still enjoy while talking to sympathetic Oscar at the hardware store. Knowing I've faced up to wind and weather and the uncertain world makes me walk a little taller through my log grind because, even with the little the urban world's people get about ranching, they know instinctively it's no playground.

Life at the ranch is always taking. The returns are minimal, hard-earned, and, depending on your outlook, meagerly disproportionate to the effort required to make them.

Those ground down far enough might feel that ranching has stolen from them so they're justified in taking reparations.

There are plenty of opportunities to play victim.

The ranch is an outsize stage. Desires, reactions, even daily events seem amplified by the ranch setting. Perhaps it's that the volumes involved are so much greater: the tonnage of livestock, acreage of land, miles from town, gallons of water in the tanks—all on a grandiose scale compared to spilling a mug of coffee, or other comparatively miniscule accidents that could sour a morning at the office. Moreover, the stage changes people, inviting shows of kindness, pathos, generosity, rage, sympathy—shows revealing of parts of our character. Some shows I'll never forget for their beauty and selflessness. Some I wish I could forget for their cruelty. None are likely to happen in a living room or even a grocery store parking lot.

Now, it's five o'clock, and I'm driving to Oldham Park with a happy-hour assortment like none other: brownies, padlocks, horse feed, and wine.

Like many times going to Oldham Park, I am far more worried than happy.

Unlike many other times, I'm doing a drop-off and won't be staying.

I rumble across the cattle guard into deceptively peaceful scenery: a groomed yard standing quiet and empty before corrals swishing with windblown hay and horse tails. A few hours ago, I witnessed one more in the ranch's string of cinder-yard dramas. Heidi had told me an unhappy client was coming in to pick up his horse. He was, absurdly, convinced she hadn't been riding it, and hadn't been so nice about saying as much on the phone, so just for safety's sake, would I be there when he came to pick up his horse?

Of course.

Neither of us anticipated that his groundless dissatisfaction would turn to outrage. He raced in, a spray of grit and dust, shouting accusations and nasty names, then promising retribution for being cheated before rushing his poor animal into the trailer, where he must have bounced every joint loose racing out again.

Oldham Park is surrounded by forest and barbed-wire fence. A few snips of the pliers, and we're vulnerable to losing anything this man might want to take should he return. We can, of course, call the sheriff, and have, but there is too much damage that can be done, too much that can be stolen, possibly lost, in the meantime, starting with our own peace of mind.

Live by the sword, die by the sword, goes the saying.

This same piney space visited most days by sun and ravens is the only silent witness we have should a bad actor decide to return and cause a scene.

Neither of us can control what might choose to visit us. Heidi has the lingering threat of a venomous now-former client. I have flashbacks to every cowboy confrontation, every failed effort, every outsize fear of harm or loss. The range of responses to threats, be they real, imagined, or remembered, does not change: do our best to diagnose our own blame, learn what lessons there are, and protect what we can from further damage.

Which is why I have driven back out with supplies.

As I climb from my truck, the space echoes with threats, ugliness hanging like a gallows in the open air.

We unwrap the padlocks, aware that they are mostly a deterrent, not a guarantee.

Heidi laughs at the rest of what's in the bags. I suspect that the rainbow-sprinkled brownie will be her dinner and the wine will wait.

Neither of us will sleep well.

She, because she knows the ranch will simply demand another day's performance at sunrise, regardless of the toll it took the day prior.

I, because I have handed Heidi not only goodies but the torch of whatever the ranch will become. Whether it stays, sits, is sold, or relocates will be her story, in which I will be, at most, a drop-in character. Some of the stories calling me to the keyboard are set in Arizona, but their resemblance to Heidi's life ends with the fact that they often leave me sleepless. My current manuscript likes nothing better than to keep me awake. Heidi's world at Oldham Park is no longer my world. We will both dream, discover, and ride, but she will do so at the ranch, whereas I will be in worlds, and a life, I'm still creating.

Glossary of Ranch Terms

Glossary: A list compiled by the Author to provide additional information about the words she uses. As such, it is simultaneously as inexpert and well-intentioned as she.

ARENA: A fenced enclosure ranging from a bit larger than a basketball court to almost twice that size, for horse-related activities in which the object is for the rider to simultaneously stay atop and in control of a horse, sometimes but not always in pursuit or avoidance of other objects in the arena such as cows, cones, or jumps.

BIT: An interchangeable part of the bridle assembly inserted into the horse's mouth, composed of material ranging from rubber to several forms of metal. It's available in linked, straight, or formed shapes only slightly less numerous than Legos. Generally, the less and softer the material used, the gentler its effect on the animal.

BOOTS: Can refer to human footwear or horse gear intended to temporarily protect feet, legs, and/or ankles from strain or bruising.

BRIDLE: The combined assembly of headstall, bit, and reins, worn on a horse's head to allow a rider theoretical control while horseback.

BULL: A male bovine capable of reproduction, but too often incapable of taking any friendly attempt at handling or direction.

CINCH: The assembly of braided yarn or leather worn under the horse's belly, joined by leather strapping to the saddle to hold the saddle, and rider, in one place. Can also be used as a verb to describe the tightening of the strapping, which horses may find, at least, uncomfortable, and at worst, offensively objectionable.

CINDERS: Harvested remains of a volcanic explosion, used as landscape material where geology has made it comparatively more available and less expensive than sand or gravel; like sand and gravel, it's available in varying sizes and weights.

COLT: A male horse of less than three years.

CORRAL: An interchangeable term with "pen" for an outdoor, fenced enclosure for horses or cattle.

COWBOY: As a noun, the male person charged to complete all the horse-, cattle-, and range-associated tasks assigned by the foreman. As a verb, the doing of said tasks. As a pseudonym, a derogatory term for one whose half-hearted, coarse, or outlawed attempts fail to meet expectations; e.g., "Bob's a cowboy for Smith Ranch." Or "Bob cowboyed for Smith Ranch for five years." Or "Bob was such a cowboy, the Smith's fired him after a season." (See "Hand")

COWS: Female bovines, aged out of their heifer days, capable of reproduction. Also the collective or general term for bovines of any age or sex in a herd, most often uttered after a pejorative or profane descriptor.

DRINKERS: Troughs intended to hold water, and the second thing cursed, after the pipes, in the daily event of a leak.

FILLY: A female horse three years or less in age; at adulthood (usually four years or more), she's referred to as a "mare."

FLANKS: The ticklish area between a horse's belly and its haunch, recognizable for its upward-running hair in a feather pattern, or by the raised and threatening hoof aimed at s/he who makes contact with it.

FOREMAN: Top of the cowboy chain of command, with job responsibilities including but not limited to grazing and herding cattle, fixing fence, maintaining stock tanks, feeding and caring for horses associated with cattle and range work, caring for vehicles associated with cattle and range work, and managing up, lest ranch owners and/or managers create more responsibilities than there's time for.

FROG: The V-shaped underside of a horse hoof, composed of pliable tissue that expands and contracts as the horse walks, making it both a miracle of natural design and a constant worry for bruising.

GELDING: A neutered male horse, often preferred by amateurs and parents of young riders for relative steadiness attributable to freedom from hormonal swings.

GUIDE: In trail-ride operations, the employed rider charged with wayfinding and the safety of the mounted clientele.

HALTER: The headgear worn by a horse over its nose and ears which, when attached to a lead rope, has the same effect on equines as a collar and leash on canines. Does not necessarily guarantee control.

HAND: The job title for one under the supervision of a ranch foreman; can be synonymous with "cowboy" or refer to those who do non-cow-related work. Also a complimentary term for one who can complete a ranch-related job with obvious skill; e.g., "Bob had the full string saddled and loaded in twenty minutes. That guy's a hand."

HAUL: Used as a verb to describe a distance traveled with a usually heavily and expensively loaded trailer affixed to a towing vehicle. Used as a noun to describe an unpleasantly long trip; e.g., "We hauled from Vegas to Sedona in a day." Or "We went from Vegas to Sedona in a day over Mingus Mountain. That was a haul."

HAUNCHES: The aft or nether region of an animal, used interchangeably with hindquarters, rump, behind, buttocks, or similar.

HEIFER: A female bovine not yet aged to sexual maturity. Also a derogatory term for a human female—use with care.

HOOF: The collective frog, wall, heel, and sole that comprise a horse's foot. Effectively, the hardest part of a horse to care for, aside from the teeth, without expert help.

LEAD: Similar to a leash, even in pronunciation, this is the rope part of a halter that a handler grips while stopping or moving, hoping the horse at the other end will remain in proximity.

MARE: A female equine four or more years old.

MCKINSEY: The one hundred twenty-acre property named for a former owner, nine miles on three forest roads north of Highway 89A between Cottonwood and Sedona, used as a winter headquarters by Boot Track Ranch.

MUSTANG: An equine of crossbred heritage and wild upbringing in herds still ranging on public lands in the American West. More locally to Boot Track Ranch, the collective term for Sage and Cheyenne, who were adopted out of Oregon herds, much to the betterment and delight of the Wilson family.

OLDHAM: Short for the southernmost sixty acres of Oldham Park, located along I-17 about 10 minutes south of Flagstaff.

QUARTER HORSE: An American equine breed celebrated and named for its speed racing a quarter mile; also capable of infinitely more distances and skill types.

PAINT: A horse color named for the markings that make the animal appear as though it's been splashed or splotched with paint. Old joke demonstrating the wordplay: "Every barn needs a little paint."

PALOMINO: A horse color referring to an equine with some shade of gold or yellow body hair and a white mane and tail.

PARCEL: Refers to a piece of land or property, not necessarily to the legal assessor's description.

PARK: A (blessedly) open, grassy piece of ground in a forest teeming with trees and rocks. In more bucolic settings, it might be called a "meadow."

PASTURE: A lot assigned by the U.S. Forest Service to annual grazing permit-holders. Does not necessarily guarantee grass or edible forage from year to year.

PEN: A fenced enclosure for housing horses or cattle, functionally synonymous with "corral," though perhaps used to describe smaller spaces.

POLL: The point on a horse between the ears, forming the first and topmost portion of the equine spinal column.

RANGE: As a noun, used interchangeably with "pasture" or "grazing" to describe the area where cattle roam seeking grass and water. As a verb, used to describe what the cattle do as they wander about on said pursuits.

REINS: The lengths of cord or leather that attach to a horse's bit.

ROPE: A verb describing the quick pursuit, then catch of a moving cow by a horseback rider by throwing a loop over the bovine's head or under and around its hind feet. A noun describing the coated, coiled, fiber spiral carried by a cowboy to chase, scare, or catch cows.

SADDLE: Unless otherwise described, assumes a Western-style seat that is strapped onto a horse's back with the intent of providing both horse and rider with a more comfortable and balanced ride. Western saddles are recognizable for a front horn that provides an anchor for a flung and/or tied rope, a rear cantle that holds the rider well forward of the horse's haunches, and skirting between the two that provides space for tooled leather, silver, or a simple connection for a second back strap designed to keep the saddle from sliding forward should the horse and rider be trekking downhill.

SEASON: Collection of some months resembling the summer or winter weather pattern of the same name, used to refer to the length of time spent grazing; e.g., "We'll finish the season at Oldham before moving to McKinsey."

STEER: A castrated male cow.

STOCK: A collective term, interchangeable with "herd," usually referring to domestic animals.

STRING: Horses under the care of a single person or used for a single purpose; e.g., "Each cowboy feeds his own string."

TACK: The collective term for saddles, bridles, halters, grooming supplies, and other horse-related equipment.

TANKS: The short form of the phrase "stock tanks," which are cabin- or house-size depressions in the earth with shallow-angled sides suited for walk-in water access for grazing stock.

YARD: The open area at Oldham Park between the cabin, tack room, and hay barns, used for parking trailers. Any resemblance to recreation or prison is purely metaphoric and likely temporary.

ABOUT THE AUTHOR

Julie Morrison is an Arizonan, horsewoman, dog person, and writer of both poetry and prose to celebrate all the aforementioned. Two of her short stories were selected by the Desert Sleuths for their 2019 and 2021 mystery anthologies; another short story was awarded in 2020 by *Writer's Digest* as top ten in literary fiction. Her poem "Western Girl" was named an honorable mention by the 2020 *Arizona Literary Magazine*. As a manuscript, *Barbed* was the 2018 runner-up in nonfiction in the San Francisco Writers Conference contest and was shortlisted in Chanticleer's 2019 Journey Nonfiction Awards. Ms. Morrison is pursuing a master of fine arts in creative writing from Seattle Pacific University (2023). This is her first book.

ABOUT THE PUBLISHER

Soulstice Publishing brings to life "books with soul" that inspire readers with stories of human potential realized and celebrate our unique position in the Southwest.

Soulstice took root in our mountain town of Flagstaff, Arizona, which sits at the base of the San Francisco Peaks, on homelands sacred to Native Americans throughout the region. We honor their past, present, and future generations, as well as their original and ongoing care for the lands we also hold dear.

Surrounded by ponderosa pines, enriched by diverse cultures, and inspired by the optimistic Western spirit, Flagstaff abounds with scientists, artists, athletes, and many other people who love the outdoors. It is quite an inspiring place to live. Considering the dearth of oxygen at our 7,000-foot elevation, you might say it leaves us breathless.

Learn more at **soulsticepublishing.com**.

Soulstice Publishing, LLC

PO Box 791

Flagstaff, AZ 86002

(928) 814-8943

connect@soulsticepublishing.com